# PERSUASIVE ENCOUNTERS

# Persuasive Encounters

## Case Studies in Constructive Confrontation

Gary C. Woodward

PRAEGER

New York
Westport, Connecticut
London

**Copyright Acknowledgments**

The author and publisher gratefully acknowledge permission to reprint excerpts from the following: "Tolerance for Truth in America," Remarks of Senator Edward M. Kennedy at Liberty Baptist College, October 3, 1983, by permission of Edward M. Kennedy; Edward R. Murrow's 1952 Address before the Radio and Television News Directors Association, by permission of the Edward R. Murrow Center of Public Diplomacy, Tufts University, and by permission of Mrs. Janet B. Murrow; Transcript of "Donahue" program #02107 © 1987 by permission of Multimedia Entertainment, Inc.; "Back Wards to Back Streets," by permission of *TV Guide* Magazine, copyright © 1980 by Triangle Publications, Inc, Radnor, Pennsylvania, and by permission of Thomas S. Szasz; and "The Freedom Abusers," by permission of Thomas S. Szasz.

**Library of Congress Cataloging-in-Publication Data**

Woodward, Gary C.
    Persuasive encounters : case studies in constructive confrontation
/ Gary C. Woodward.
      p.    cm.
    Includes bibliographical references (p.  ).
    ISBN 0–275–93091–2  (alk. paper).—ISBN 0–275–93092–0  (pbk. :
alk. paper)
    1. Persuasion (Psychology)  2. Interpersonal confrontation.
3. Persuasion (Psychology)—Case studies.  4. Interpersonal
confrontation—Case studies.  I. Title.
BF637.P4W66  1990
303.2'42—dc20        90–32132

British Library Cataloguing in Publication Data is available.

Library of Congress Catalog Card Number: 90-32132
ISBN: 0-275-93091-2 (hb.)
      0-275-93092-0 (pbk.)

First published in 1990

Praeger Publishers, One Madison Avenue, New York, NY 10010
An imprint of Greenwood Publishing Group, Inc.

Printed in the United States of America

∞

The paper used in this book complies with the
Permanent Paper Standard issued by the National
Information Standards Organization (Z39.48-1984).

10 9 8 7 6 5 4 3 2 1

To
Phillips Biddle
and
Trevor Melia

In my world . . . people each day make money and lose money, find community and lose community, discover information and forget information, embrace ideology and forsake ideology, appropriate ideas and misappropriate ideas, find hope and lose hope solely because rhetoric has had its way with them.

*Rod P. Hart*

# Contents

# Preface

The idea for this study emerged while I was collaborating with Robert E. Denton, Jr., on a persuasion textbook entitled *Persuasion and Influence in American Life*. Our work on that project had the effect of triggering two conclusions that are reflected in these pages. One was the realization that there is a particular kind of persuasive setting—persuasion directed to a hostile audience—that is irresistibly fascinating. Most forms of everyday communication take place in an environment of at least implicit concurrence. We usually engage each other in conversation because we expect that our ideas and our egos are relatively secure. By contrast, the communicator faced with the need to unravel opposing beliefs functions in quite a different environment, one that is far riskier and much more unpredictable. I became intrigued with such persuasive encounters. They provide a kind of Technicolor vividness to elements of the persuasive process that are often lost in the monochrome routines of everyday communication.

In addition, in our earlier book we attempted to lay out as clearly as possible some of the theories, approaches, and practical recommendations that define the broad discipline of persuasion. Such an emphasis on theory has obvious validity, but it necessarily limits the time that is available to pursue the details of specific cases. The prospect of reversing this emphasis seemed to hold promise. The ultimate measure of any theory of human behavior does not lie in its abstract purity but in its quality as a window into real human events. The result of this approach is not a study of the "golden ideas" of persuasion but a more open-ended exploration of how some of these ideas work—or fail to work—as ways to explain the illusive process of effecting attitudes. The six short case studies and their five chapter-length counterparts offered here are intended to anchor the discussion of persuasive options in specific instances bound by the very real constraints of context and talent.

Two basic assumptions are implied throughout the book. One is that an understanding of communication processes can never be very far from the analysis of communication events. A nearly infinite range of variables can color how messages are understood by their audiences. The public personas of advocates, the recent histories of groups, the ebb and flow of public attitudes on contemporary issues, and the variegated approaches taken by persuaders all combine to make every event different. In the final analysis, the study of communication is both limited and informed by the defining features of specific moments.

A related philosophical assumption affirms that confrontations can be positive forces for change. This hardly needs to be said; it is a fundamental axiom of any democratic system that dissent can yield productive growth. Even so, the case that is made about the futility of conflict (and the need to reduce it by "resolution") is now so pervasive in American life that we may be in danger of ignoring how enlightening communication that defines differences can actually be. This book is not a plea for more abusive talk show hosts, or for the mindless name-calling sometimes employed by advocates who want to infect others with their toxic prejudices. Rather, the instances discussed here are meant to suggest that there are limitations to the inclusionary ethic that now governs our judgments of so much public communication. Collectively, these cases are meant to show that the interests of candor, courage, and truth may sometimes require an abandonment of the usual amenities of conciliation.

Finally, a word about the episodes chosen for this study. The range of confrontations here is deliberately eclectic. Any book that manages to cite on adjacent pages the words of singer John Lennon and Civil War abolitionist Wendell Phillips is probably safe from the charge of being too narrowly focused. And yet I plead guilty to several biases. In most cases the advocates studied here come from high visibility places in the mass media or national politics. I have generally emphasized public figures from our *recent* history, not just yesterday's headlines. One reason is practical: Time has a way of providing a clearer perspective. More important, some of the cases cited in this book reflect my belief that there is still more to be said about what almost amounted to a second "civil war" fought in the United States throughout the last half of the 1960s. Edward R. Murrow's 1958 address cited in Chapter 4 in some ways predicted the crush of events that would begin to reshape American life at the end of the Kennedy presidency. The battles that Americans waged at home and abroad over government actions in Southeast Asia and the struggle for civil rights beg for the same attention that has long been given to the American Civil War.

The case study approach taken in these pages provides some flexibility as to how readers may use this book. The opening two chapters are meant as a unit. The first offers a number of introductory cases; and the second follows with an overview of some of the theoretical issues raised about the nature of rhetorical conflict. The remainder of the case studies can be profitably read in any order.

I have made no attempt to link artificially these very different events into a single, continuous theme. Each offers its own contextual and analytical points, while still providing room for readers to render their own rhetorical and historical judgments.

A number of people provided help in the preparation of this study. Special thanks are due to Paul Frye, Dan Hahn, Harold Hogstrom, and Richard Vatz for their constructive comments on some of the ideas raised. Help was also provided by the Trenton State College Faculty and Institutional Research and Sabbatical Committee, Karl Gottesman, the Roscoe West Library, the Museum of Broadcasting, and the Community Assistance Unit of the Mayor's Office of the City of New York. I owe a large debt to Professor Robert E. Denton, Jr., whose enthusiasm for examining the practical applications of persuasion helped me clarify why I wanted to pursue this study. I am especially grateful to some of the subjects of this book who freely gave permission to quote and comment on their public rhetoric, especially Phil Donahue, Senator Edward Kennedy, and Dr. Thomas Szasz.

# PERSUASIVE ENCOUNTERS

# 1

# The Politics of Confrontation: From John Lennon to Wendell Phillips

One of my greatest pleasures in writing has come from the thought that perhaps my works might annoy someone of comfortably pretentious position.[1]

John Kenneth Galbraith

Among the many varied forms of human communication, one of the most important but least studied is public persuasion directed to a hostile audience. Persuaders usually take what theorist Herbert Simons calls the "co-active" approach, using appeals that minimize conflict and maximize shared themes.[2] Unlike John Kenneth Galbraith, whose observation opens this chapter, most communicators do not set out to upset or "annoy" anyone. But Galbraith has described an important and valid rhetorical motive: It is intrinsically interesting and often socially useful to confront an audience with ideas its members do not uphold.

A persuasive encounter occurs when an individual attempts to confront and challenge a hostile audience within a public setting. An audience is considered "hostile" if many of its members disagree with the general conclusions advocated by the communicator they have gathered together to hear. Persuasion is "public" when arguments offered to a group are widely reported in the mass media. Representative examples examined in this book include a widely admired 1958 speech given to the Radio and Television News Directors Association by Edward R. Murrow and a more recent "Donahue" program taped in the Soviet Union. In both instances, these broadcasters became advocates for viewpoints significantly at odds with their immediate audiences. Murrow, for example, challenged the nation's news broadcasters to face the reality that they were "currently wealthy, fat, comfortable and complacent." Donahue urged his audience of Soviet teens to be more critical of their government's foreign policies.

Encounters like these provide opportunities to observe specific communication patterns and strategies not easily seen in more casual transactions. We are never more interesting than when challenges are made to the legitimacy of our beliefs. In addition, the publicity that results from encounters makes all the participants part of a public drama. Because both the advocate's and the audience's cherished attitudes are put at risk, a confrontation may itself assume importance as a representation of a larger dispute in which thousands have feelings at stake. For these reasons and more, persuasive encounters not only are moments of intense communication but are frequently important cultural barometers as well. We sometimes look at them as moments that define the tensions of an era.

## LENNON MEETS CAPP

By any standard it was an unusual and strange confrontation. John Lennon and Yoko Ono were about to meet Al Capp in their Montreal hotel room, hopeful that an unusual publicity event could be used to make yet another political statement against the Vietnam War and in favor of "peace" in general. A conviction for possession of marijuana momentarily kept the pair out of the United States, requiring a plan for generating antiwar publicity from a close outpost. Their strategy was as simple as it was bizarre: to stay in bed for more or less a week and to invite other celebrities and the news media to participate in the 1969 "bed-in" by dropping in for well-publicized chats. "Is there not a more positive way of demonstrating in favor of peace?" asked one journalist. It is a matter of "gimmicks and salesmanship," the white-pajamaed Lennon noted, "and if that's what will put it across, then that's the way to do it."[3] What emerged was the bedroom equivalent of Lennon's popular anthem "Give Peace a Chance." In addition to members of the press and a television film crew, the room was often filled with various friends and hangers-on hoping to stay within the orbit of the musical icon. Over the course of several days, visitors ranging from poet Allen Ginsberg to black activist Dick Gregory dropped in. But the most unlikely person to appear at the foot of the Lennons' bed was Al Capp, creator of the comic strip "Li'l Abner" and known in 1969 for his lecture tours to college campuses.

Capp had made virtually a new career for himself as a polemicist against much of the student and black activism that came in the aftermath of escalations in the Vietnam War and the assassinations of Martin Luther King, Jr., and Robert Kennedy. The hillbilly Abner Yokum, who lived in Capp's "Dogpatch, U.S.A.," occupied a place far removed from the counterculture that the Lennons represented. If Capp's political views were more complex than those of his menagerie of characters, he seemed to share with them a simple patriotism and a distrust of anything hinting of youthful rebellion. Capp's distrust of the 1960s dissent was reflected in the "silent majority's" puzzlement and anger at the United States' educated and increasingly disenchanted youth. In many ways, he was the perfect surrogate for members of the generation who had lived through the deprivations of the Great Depression and World War II, many of whom had little tolerance for the tide of youthful nihilism that coexisted with American prosperity. Always dressed in a perfect suit or blazer, Capp had the booming voice and aggressive presence of a military leader or corporate CEO. His lectures on the college circuit mixed praise for American values with stinging barbs about "protesters" and "thugs." William F. Buckley, Jr., fittingly described Capp's major rhetorical weapon as the "surrealistic put-down," a style the cartoonist described on Buckley's television program "Firing Line."

Oh, every now and then some student arises, quivering with rage, and says: "Mr. Capp, you detest us, so why are you speaking here at Chapel Hill?" And I say, "For three thousand bucks, and I wouldn't spend an hour with a bunch like you for a nickel less."[4]

The gulf separating Capp and the Lennons was equal to the yawning chasm between the music of the recently disbanded Beatles and the patriotic songs of Kate Smith, whom Capp admired. It was an unlikely meeting, made all the more interesting by Capp's barely concealed contempt for nearly everything Lennon stood for. As he came into the room, the cartoonist jokingly introduced himself as "that dreadful, Neanderthal fascist," applying labels that his detractors might have easily used. The conversation quickly turned to the subject of a record album—"Two Virgins"—picturing Yoko and John completely nude. Capp noted that Lennon had once said he was "shy." He relished the irony of holding up the album in full view of the press and spectators. "If that is a picture of two shy people, I'd like to know what shyness is. Hah! What filth."

"Do you think that's filth?" Lennon asked.

"Certainly not," Capp replied in mock seriousness. "I'm denouncing people who think it is. . . . And I tell you that's one of the greatest contributions to the enlightenment and culture of our times."

"I'm glad you noticed."

"I want to tell you that it's hard *not* to notice. Now, you have a song, and one of the lines—and correct me if [I'm wrong]—is 'Christ, it ain't easy; everywhere I go, they're going to crucify me.' "

"Lennon interrupted. "Rubbish. I didn't say it. The lyrics go, 'Christ, you know it ain't easy; you know how hard it can be; the way things are going, they're going to crucify me.' "

"Well, now, that is a very unkind thought to plant in my mind," Capp rejoined. "I want to tell you that this may stay with me and I may wake up screaming. This is not true. What did you want it to mean?"

"They're going to crucify me, and you and everyone else."

"Well, I didn't permit you to speak for me."

In growing frustration, Lennon tried to explain the obvious. "I was speaking in behalf of people in general, you know, in a poetic sense."

"You're speaking for yourselves," Capp said.

"As a representative of the human race I'm speaking for us all, whether you like it or not."

"Well, whatever race you're the representative of, I ain't part of it . . . I'll let Kate Smith sing my songs."

"Who do you write cartoons for?" Lennon asked.

"I write my cartoons for money, just as you sing your songs: exactly the same reason."

"You think I couldn't have money by some other way but sitting in bed for seven days taking shit from people like you? I could . . . I could write a song in an hour and earn more money."

"Now look here," Capp angrily replied. "You got into bed so people like me would come and see you."

"Not for money."

"It won't do you any real harm."

"But I can earn money in plenty other ways than doing this."

"I could make a lot more drawing people like you and then confronting you, and I must say it's more appetizing drawing them, 'cause then I can leave."

Throughout this exchange Yoko tried to repeat her view that the bed-in was their way of focusing attention on the need for peace in the world. Capp laughed at her naïveté and, without hearing her out, interrupted with a pointed question to Lennon. The query was a marvel of perverse economy, combining an ad hominem attack with a reference to the acid-tongued wife of a deposed Vietnamese leader. "Good God, you've got to live with that? I can see why you want peace; God knows you can't have much. I'm delighted to have met you, 'Madame Nhu.' You are a tower of answers."

Then, a final dig. As he got up to go, he said, "I'm sure the other three guys, the other three fellas, are Englishmen."

"What does that mean?" Lennon inquired.

"Think about it."

In a few short minutes the meeting was over, and the John Wayne of cartoonists exited to Lennon's half-spoken, half-sung line: "You know it ain't easy; you know how hard it can be; the way things are going, they're going to crucify . . . Capp."

## HARRISON MEETS EMERSON

One of the most successful plays in London's West End in 1972 was Brian Clark's *Whose Life Is It Anyway?*[5] Its commercial success on Broadway several years later was perhaps even more unlikely, given its unusual and potentially gloomy subject. Clark's play focuses on the plight of Ken Harrison, a bright young sculptor who falls victim to a traffic accident that has left him paralyzed from the neck down. The surprisingly funny and touching drama deals with the limited options left to him and his physician by his catastrophic accident. The British playwright shamelessly loaded the deck to give the play potency. A creative and energetic artist in the prime of his career and on the verge of marriage is suddenly confined to a bed and the constant care of others. His survival is at once a medical marvel and technological debacle. The play unfolds by forcing us to witness Harrison's moments of rage and self-pity and the sometimes funny absurdities with which he must now cope.

It does not take long for Harrison to realize that the person he was can no longer be. He has a fully functioning mind in a withered body. Played in the 1981 film version by Richard Dreyfuss, Harrison wants to be released by the hospital and allowed to die. He meets his match in the senior physician responsible for stabilizing his condition. The film's Dr. Michael Emerson, played by John Cassavetes, has no medical doubts about the case. He lives in a world of professional certainty that declares that doctors are in the business of saving patients, now allowing them to die. He rejects any discussion of the possibility of releasing Harrison, knowing that his patient would last only days without the positive intervention of the staff for treatments such as kidney dialysis. In the quiet battle of wills that develops between Harrison and Emerson, the seeds for an unusual confrontation are sown.

Emerson is a symbol of modern medicine. He is not a callous or indifferent man, but his compassion seems to have been sublimated into the clinical procedures he can manipulate. He is a cripple of a different sort. He perhaps knows, but will not acknowledge, the unsettling truth that modern medicine's technologies are often better at keeping the body than the soul intact. His professional optimism communicates a certainty about Ken Harrison's medical needs that does not allow him to hear what Harrison feels. His technical skill functions as a kind of "trained incapacity" that saves him from even considering the sad ironies created by his patient's crushed spinal cord.[6] His heroic efforts have unintentionally imprisoned a healthy mind in a ruined body. The medical judgments that have been made for Harrison in the name of the Hippocratic oath seem to carry a heavy sentence. Harrison is forced to become a helpless spectator to the full lives of the nurses, doctors, and others whose orbits include his sterile room. Their independence, mobility, and sexuality weigh increasingly on him as reminders of what he has lost.

The showdown that is to come in the third act over Harrison's legal right to reject treatment is predicted in the opening moments of the play. Emerson decides that his patient's agitation over what he has lost requires more sedation. But Harrison's razor-sharp mind ceaselessly calculates and recalculates the terrible costs he will pay for his survival. With the inability to move anything but his head, he has only his vocal rage to resist a syringe of Valium intended to calm him. He pleads to a sympathetic doctor for no more sedatives: "My consciousness is the only thing I have, and I must claim the right to use it." A tranquilizing drug used on someone like him is really for the helpless physician rather than the patient. "I'm paralyzed and you're impotent. This disturbs you because you're a sympathetic person . . . So I get the tablet and you get the tranquility."[7]

In the ordinary world, people who have become quadriplegics usually muster the extraordinary resources needed in order to reconstruct their lives. But Harrison will have nothing to do with the attempts of social workers to make the best of what is left of him. With the help of an attorney, he establishes the right to a legal hearing in the hospital for a writ of habeas corpus. The legal question behind this kind of appeal is whether a person can be deprived of their liberty without good cause. Emerson's testimony to the judge is predictably that his patient is depressed, hence not capable of making decisions regarding his treatment. Harrison's response—supported by a psychiatrist—is that whatever depression he has is logically justified. "I'm almost totally paralyzed," he says. "I'd be insane if I *weren't* depressed."[8] "I choose to acknowledge the fact that I am in fact dead, and I find the hospital's persistent effort to maintain this shadow of a life an indignity and it's inhumane."

"But wouldn't you agree that many people with appalling physical handicaps have overcome them and lived essentially creative, dignified lives?" asks the judge.

"Yes, I would, but the dignity starts with their choice. If I choose to live, it would be appalling if society killed me. If I choose to die, it's equally appalling if society keeps me alive."[9]

As it concludes, the play provides a resolution of the civil dispute between the patient and the doctor, but not before the idea of conflict is turned on its head. This dispute carries no malevolence between the parties. Indeed, the calculated agony of the play lies in an inverted pattern of interests. Life itself is what Harrison seeks to end and what his physician argues to preserve. In the end, as critic Richard Eder notes, the audience is left to consider a tragic irony:

Ken Harrison wins his fight—that old ass, the Law, has routed those new asses, the experts—but those he has won over with his lucid, funny and valiant fight for his dignity smile proudly at him and leave. He is a dying man and his dignity is appallingly lonely.[10]

## KENNEDY MEETS THE STUDENTS

There was always something different about the way Americans reacted to Robert Kennedy, even after his assassination in a hotel corridor during the 1968 California presidential primary. R. F. K.'s political career was like the American public's response to it: a bundle of contradictory images. It began in controversy when Kennedy worked as a staff attorney for the red-baiting Senator Joseph McCarthy. McCarthy's notorious penchant for convincing others to share his fantasies about communist subversion is now a permanent blight on the political history of the 1950s. The "red menace" he fabricated usually came only after the truth had been ignored and the reputations of innocent people had been sullied. Kennedy's career as a single-minded prosecutor continued in his work with John McClellan's Senate Rackets Committee, which conducted a crusade against union bosses and labor corruption that he documented in his book *The Enemy Within*. In both McCarthy and McClellan, Kennedy found temperaments similar to his own. He shared with them a hatred of social demons bordering on paranoia. The failures of society were not to be found in its economic and political structures but in the malfeasance of crooks or ideologues in high places. Such a view not only played well to the public's taste for simple scapegoats but also matched each man's desire to redefine social problems as the work of agents with corrupt motives.

As most politicians grow older, they usually replace their impulse to seek out villains with a more tolerant and benign conservatism. But for Robert Kennedy this normal flow of impulses was noticeably reversed. He became more liberal on social issues and more convinced that public villainy had its roots in the failures of the social system, not those who managed it. But the transition was not easy. In 1960 he was selected as attorney general in his brother's presidency, a position that would leave him open to charges of nepotism for the remaining eight years of his life. The experience turned him into a different kind of leader—in biographer Jack Newfield's words, part Puritan, part fundamentalist, but also more cautious in assessing the motives of others.

In his youth he was simplistic, conservative, and authoritarian. But he became a new kind of liberal, leaping over the old liberalism he thought was obsolete. . . . He was more interested in the nonworking poor than in the satisfied union members; more drawn to decentralized decision-making than more Federal bureaucracy; more oriented toward the nonwhite underdeveloped world than Europe; more in tune with the new generation of urban blacks who wanted power and pride, rather than integration and sympathy. But he never lost his Puritan strain of moral conservatism that led him to urge a year's moratorium on all cigarette advertising, and refused to permit *Playboy* to interview him "because one of my children might see the magazine."[11]

After President John Kennedy's death in 1963, R.F.K. showed the strains of a man worn down by the compromises of everyday life. More than ever, he was impatient with the complacent incrementalism that usually marks the thought and action of the political mainstream. In his fatal attempt to gain the Democratic nomination for the presidency, he became a crusader for the disenfranchised on a platform of broad social reform.

Kennedy could be a loyal party "team player," but he was not the captive of a deeply felt political ideology. Instead, what deepened within him was a visceral commitment to the victims of social injustices not represented by well-financed organizations. Injustices suffered by farm workers, coal miners, draftees in Vietnam, residents of large-city ghettos, and the rural poor ate at the politician who was born into all the advantages of wealth. He would temporize on various specific political maneuvers, such as whom to support among rivals in a party primary. But as William Shannon observed a year before Kennedy's death, "Once he identifies an injustice, Kennedy loathes it with rare intensity and works relentlessly against it."[12]

America's unhealthy tolerance for various forms of economic and racial inequity increasingly guided Kennedy's public life and contributed to a deepening despair noticed by more of his friends. He closed one of his books with a catechism of the wrongs that generated the passion in his politics:

There is discrimination in New York; Apartheid in South Africa; serfdom in the mountains of Peru. People starve in the streets of India; wealth is lavished on armaments everywhere. These are differing evils, but they are the common works of man. They reflect the imperfection of human justice; the inadequacy of human compassion; the defectiveness of our sensibility towards the sufferings of our fellows.[13]

Tracking the roughly parallel careers of Robert Kennedy and Richard Nixon provides an interesting contrast. Both began their early careers as prosecutors of spies or criminals and carried within them deep suspicions of communist activity inside and outside the United States. Nixon's political maturation as vice president and as a defeated presidential candidate contributed to a long-term distrust of social misfits who could endlessly provoke national confrontations and undermine social order. His adoption of the potent imagery of the silent majority was a safe gesture of reassurance to the political mainstream, a reminder that their values would not be eroded by "the other America" of the poor and disenfranchised.

Kennedy increasingly worked from the other side of these fears. He came to see America's underclass as heirs denied their rightful inheritance. He admired youthful political activists, even those who worked against him and for Senator Eugene McCarthy in the 1968 presidential primaries. In contrast, Nixon was deeply suspicious of the motives of any youthful political activists and carefully screened their access to him. He also found a responsive chord in simplistic appeals for "law and order," an appeal that had less attraction for Kennedy if legal maneuvers were used to create an unjust order. Similarly, Nixon easily retreated to his earlier anticommunism to justify American involvement in the Vietnam War. Although Kennedy also prospered from the same anticommunist rhetoric, he viewed such a well-born benchmark as too facile a rationale for such a complex issue. By early 1967 he went so far as to concede that troop increases instigated by his brother had been a mistake. He had no stomach for a land war that pitted Asian peasants against American military power.

His certainty about good and evil, right and wrong, justice and injustice sometimes led him into settings that others with a greater sense of political risk would have carefully avoided. For example, although he became an opponent to the Vietnam War effort managed by the Johnson administration, he frequently asked his university audiences to consider the injustices inherent in the widespread exemptions that kept them out of the military. The war was a mistake, he said, but it was compounded by the fact that America's poor too often were sent off to fight in place of middle-class students with college deferments. In a question-and-answer session at the University of Oklahoma, Kennedy prodded his audience into considering the unsettling consequences of their own support for the war. He began by asking how many of them favored the student deferment. Most responded favorably. How many supported increased spending and support for the war? Again, a large percentage affirmed their support. "Let me ask you one other question: . . . How many of you who voted for the escalation of the war also voted for the exemption of students from the draft?" An observer at the meeting noted that the audience sat in stunned silence.[14] Kennedy had made his point. On many campuses he similarly put his audience's feet to the fire over the same moral dilemma.

Several years earlier Kennedy had the opportunity to use his rhetoric of moral confrontation but on an even grander scale. He received an invitation from the multiracial National Union of South African Students to speak. It was an offer he readily accepted, even though the South African government seriously considered withholding the necessary visa. In a vain attempt to minimize reports of the visit, visas were denied to many American journalists who also wanted to make the trip. Pretoria produced yet another self-inflicted wound—a pattern for which it was justly famous—when it used its catchall Suppression of Communism Act to place the organization's leader under house arrest.[15] The act prohibited the leader from attending meetings but was much more successful in making him a martyr and increasing world interest in the upcoming visit.

For several days Kennedy toured the country and spoke on a number of campuses, including the Universities of Capetown and Stellenbosch. The occasion of his first speech at Capetown was to honor what the student organization called the Day of Affirmation, a period set aside to affirm support for equal rights in a country with official segregation.[16] Knowing that the speech would be widely reported in the United States as well as Africa, Kennedy chose his words with tact, never more so than in an opening with a carefully measured surprise:

I come here . . . because of my deep interest and affection for a land settled by the Dutch in the mid-seventeenth century, then taken over by the British, and at last independent; a land in which the native inhabitants were at first subdued but relations with whom remain a problem to this day; . . . a land which was once the importer of slaves, and now must struggle to wipe out the last traces of that former bondage. I refer, of course, to the United States of America.[17]

This approach of using the United States as an example of a nation with racial frictions was repeated in all of Kennedy's remarks throughout the country. He had not come to South Africa, he said, to lecture its people on how they should conduct their civic affairs. But, of course, that was precisely his objective. The opening references to America's racial problems cleverly sanctioned his criticisms of apartheid and oppression everywhere. They also allowed him to remind his listeners that blacks in America now sit on the highest courts, successfully compete for positions as astronauts, and win Nobel Prizes. He hardly had to add that changes in South Africa needed to start with similar steps.

It is from numberless diverse acts of courage and belief that human history is shaped. Each time a man stands up for an ideal, or acts to improve the lot of others, or strikes out against injustice, he sends a tiny ripple of hope, and crossing each from a million different centers of energy and daring those ripples build a current which can sweep down the mightiest wall of oppression and resistance.[18]

If those words were not direct enough, Kennedy could be more blunt. The next day he queried an Afrikaner audience at Stellenbosch University, the alma mater of many of the nation's political leaders: "If blacks are not 'inferior' to the whites, why don't they take part in your elections? . . . Why don't you allow them to worship in your churches? What the hell would you do if you found out that God was black?"[19] It was not that Kennedy was saying anything that this audience had not heard before. The voices of dissent had been numerous in South Africa and included many in the large audiences he addressed. The vital difference was that it was a Kennedy who drew the world's attention to the continuing affront of apartheid. The brother of the martyred John Kennedy and a serious contender for the presidency had a stature that was hard to ignore. Moreover, the confrontational context of his visit dramatized what defenders of Robert Kennedy sought to remind his many critics: that political power energized by conviction and high principle can be a powerful tool for change. His Capetown speech carried its own warning that just principles sometimes demand an existence that is separate from the refuge of friends and country. His speech included an inadvertent obituary, premature by only a few years:

Few men are willing to brave the disapproval of their fellows, the censure of their colleagues, the wrath of their society. Moral courage is a rarer commodity than bravery in battle or great intelligence, yet it is the one essential, vital quality for those who seek to change the world which yields most painfully to change.[20]

## BUSH MEETS RATHER

The images of political campaigns that stay with large numbers of voters are not drawn from sustained debates or generous excerpts of speeches. Instead, they arrive as combative television commercials or vignettes of political theater that have been compressed for presentation in the network newscasts. Thus, when George Bush joked in a preprimary Republican debate that he would rather be watching "Jake and the Fatman" on another channel, he could not have been accused of expressing an alien view. Bush and virtually every national politician with an itch to reach the American public knew that success on television increasingly depends on the brief "sound bite."[21]

In 1988, candidate Bush tested this premise with decidedly mixed results in a tense interview with CBS News anchor Dan Rather. The occasion was a nine-minute live segment on the "CBS Evening News" that neither man could have predicted would become the political story of the week. The segment moved "Nightline's" Ted Koppel to query Marvin Kalb about Dan Rather's psychological makeup. *Newsweek* ran a lengthy four-page spread entitled "The Great TV Shout-Out" and went so far as to commission a poll to measure American attitudes toward Rather and Bush. In describing what they called the most recent instance of "video arm wrestling," they quoted Bush's surprisingly hyperbolic statement that it was "the worst time I've had in 20 years in public life. . . . But it's going to help me because that bastard didn't lay a glove on me."[22]

What had galvanized the 10 million viewers of the "CBS Evening News" and the even larger audience that read about the exchange? Most of the interview was taken up with attempts by the anchorman to pin Bush down on what he knew about the arms-for-hostages Iran-Contra scandal. Rather knew that large numbers of Americans were suspicious of the Reagan administration's claims that neither the president nor Vice President Bush had explicit knowledge of the scheme initiated by CIA (Central Intelligence Agency) director William Casey and White House aide Oliver North. He tried to force Bush to describe where he was in the murky loop of contacts who organized the sale of weapons to Iranians to gain their help in releasing hostages held in Lebanon. Bush would only repeat his contention that he had fully answered questions about his role in the affair.

When Bush and his aides planned for the interview, they were determined not to let it be dominated by questions on the Reagan administration's biggest blunder. This was the main reason they insisted on a live interview. Bush felt he could better control the exchange with Rather if the interview could not be subsequently edited for later broadcast. The network's news executives reluctantly agreed and began planning their own strategy. Like a politician facing a big debate, Rather was rehearsed repeatedly by staffers on questions to pursue.[23] In addition, CBS decided to introduce the interview with a taped background report on Bush's possible role in the guns-for-hostages deal, creating sufficient public doubt to require him to move beyond his previous statements noting that he had limited knowledge of the plans and that his private conversations with Reagan would not be disclosed. According to Peter J. Boyer, CBS's strategy "was to hit Mr. Bush with the toughly worded taped report, putting him off balance, and then keeping him on the air with Mr. Rather for as long as it took to obtain the answers they were seeking."[24]

The usual response of a political figure facing tough questions by a well-liked journalist is patiently, but consistently, to divert the inquiry into a different and more promising direction. To show anger is possibly to lose the goodwill of the audience. But Bush was in a different situation. On this January day he could afford to stonewall on some of the questions and, at the same time, unleash a degree of controlled anger. The reasons ironically had as much to do with the *ethos* of Dan Rather as the previous comments of the vice president. One factor was Rather's legendary persistence as a questioner of the powerful; he was perceived as so aggressive at times that *not* to react to his aggression would seem unnatural. In the same year, Michael Dukakis made this mistake of underreacting when he kept his placid rhetorical style in response to a question about what his reactions would be if his wife were raped.[25] There was also widespread speculation in the national press about Rather's alleged bouts of "unstable" behavior and temper tantrums. This gossip was largely unfounded, but reports about the volatility of the man who replaced the fatherly Walter Cronkite had appeared in both serious and superficial analyses of CBS News. They struck a chord with many Americans who remembered his heated exchanges with President Richard Nixon during the Watergate affair and a more recent episode when he stormed off the set of the "CBS Evening News" after a sporting event cut into its time. This latter instance forced the entire network to go black for seven minutes, an event as unexpected in broadcasting as a drop in profits.[26]

A final factor also made it prudent for Bush to risk matching Rather's tough and "unfair" questions with even sharper responses. However unfair the perceptions were, given his heroic war record, Bush had acquired the image of a meek New England Walter Mitty and a lackluster campaigner. The conventional wisdom among analysts in 1988 was that campaign manager Lee Atwater served up blistering and often unfair attacks against Michael Dukakis in order to compensate for the mild Bush persona. Where Bush might describe a hopeless situation as being "deep in doo doo," Atwater could draw on his self-professed "redneck" roots to find the less euphonious four-letter equivalents.

Even so, the sharp responses of the vice president during the interview were still a surprise. The old political cliché that it is dangerous to attack anybody who buys ink by the barrel still has merit in the video age. In the short term, however, Bush was able to make his anger and Rather's aggression the key issue of the exchange, diverting attention from the more difficult issues surrounding the Iran-Contra affair. The initial taped report that set up the interview had its effect of focusing attention on the affair, but it also gave Bush the short time he needed to formulate an approach that would work for the length of the interview. Referring to the report, he began by saying, "You've impugned my integrity by suggesting, with one of your little boards here, that I didn't tell the truth." He noted that congressional investigators had not found reasons to doubt his own accounts of minimal involvement in the affair. "I want to talk about why I want to be President. It's not fair to judge my whole career by a rehash on Iran." And then making Rather's persona part of the context of the exchange, Bush referred to the anchor's widely publicized protest over the tennis match that intruded on his airtime: "How would you like it if I judged your career by those seven minutes when you walked off the set in New York?"[27] Within the space of a few minutes the egos of each man had been plundered. Only precious seconds remained to salvage control—if not dominance—of the situation. As the interview lurched on, the vice president tried one last time to explain his role in the affair:

*Bush*: You know what I'm hiding? What I told the President. That's the only thing. And I've answered every question put before me. Now if you have a question, please—

*Rather*: I do have one.

*Bush*: Please.

*Rather*: I have one.

*Bush*: Please fire away.

*Rather*: You have said that if you had known this was an arms-for-hostages swap that you would have opposed it. You also said that—

*Bush*: Exactly.

*Rather*: . . . that you did not know—

*Bush*: May I answer that.

*Rather*: That wasn't the question; it was a statement—

*Bush*: It was a statement—

*Rather*: Let me ask the question, if I may first.[28]

Rancorous exchanges between public figures are common in parliamentary systems. But Americans have little stomach for such face-to-face verbal combat. Afterward, the network and many of its affiliates received hundreds of complaints from irate viewers.[29] Rather felt it was necessary the following night to state to his viewers that he "did not mislead the Vice President about the subject of the interview" and that "I of course respect the Office of the Vice Presidency—the institution and the Vice President."[30]

For all the momentary intensity of such video moments, there is not much evidence to suggest that instances like this change many minds. Bush's attack on Rather created a euphoria among his supporters and others with deep-seated suspicions of the television network. But the doubts of Bush's detractors also remained and were later confirmed by his widely reported comment that the "goddammed network" would no longer get "inside stuff" from him.[31] The interview was a diversion, a momentary spark of expressive entertainment in an otherwise bleak campaign largely given over to negative television commercials.

## CRONKITE MEETS DALEY

No one could recall a political convention like it. Arguably not since the end of the Civil War had Americans been forced to confront divisions so deep and severe as those in the final year of Lyndon Johnson's presidency. Johnson announced his decision not to seek reelection in March 1968, convinced he could not salvage the credibility necessary to carry out his Vietnam policy. In addition to the Vietnam stalemate, he and the nation had to confront the assassinations of Robert Kennedy and Martin Luther King, Jr., widespread urban violence, and an economy stretched to its limits. Many specific moments in this period could serve as representations of the crosscurrents of America's turmoil, but one of the most ominous was a stormy midweek session of the Democratic Convention.

The capstone of the party gathering was supposed to be the August 28 ritual of formalizing the Democrats' national ticket of Hubert Humphrey and Edmund Muskie, but for millions of television viewers the street fighting in downtown Chicago was to color the remaining business of the party on that Wednesday night. Thousands of demonstrators—many of them students and others from various activist groups—had come to Chicago to protest a Vietnam policy that had become as divisive in the party as it was across the nation. The organizations that went to Chicago to bear witness against the Johnson administration had a diversity reflected in their names. Among them were the Chicago Peace Council, the Lutheran Action Committee, the American Friends Service Committee, the Medical Committee on Human Rights, Women's Strike for Peace, Students for a Democratic Society, and the Youth International party.[32] Their members ranged from middle-class college students pledged to work for peace candidate Eugene McCarthy to professional dissidents like Abbie Hoffman and Jerry Rubin, who were not always careful to honor the line that separated peaceful from violent protest.

In many ways the character of the crowds who had come to Grant Park and the streets of the Loop were probably not all that different from the larger numbers of prodemocracy students who massed in Beijing's Tiananmen Square twenty-one years later. In both instances the largest factions sought to dramatize peacefully their grievances against governments that had designed a future they did not want to share. Unlike the 1989 massacre in Beijing, no one was killed in Chicago. But both protests provoked clumsy military responses against unarmed civilians that would horrify millions of television viewers looking on. Party leader Deng Xiaoping was humiliated by thousands who camped in front of the Forbidden City at what was to be the capstone of his career, a fact that was all too obvious when Soviet leader Mikhail Gorbachev was forced to alter planned events during a visit that accidentally coincided with the protests. Similarly, Mayor Richard J. Daley took the presence of "troublemakers" in his city as a personal affront. He supported Humphrey as the party's mainstream nominee and grew frustrated with several factions that wanted to turn the convention into a forum for reassessing the direction of the party. He felt free to use the Chicago police, private security guards, and the Illinois National Guard as agents to punish those who insulted and taunted his city. A national report later characterized the mayhem of indiscriminate beatings and arrests as a "police riot," with scores of injuries and even more wounds to American morale.[33]

The Chicago confrontation began around 8:00 P.M. when news reports offered the first of many unsettling images of violence that would challenge the ideal of orderly political change.[34] From his glass-enclosed booth over the convention floor, CBS's venerable Walter Cronkite reported that under cover of nightfall the Chicago police and the National Guard were organizing to control a large crowd of demonstrators in Grant Park, about five miles away. The hall itself, he noted, was "a fortress": safe from whatever attempts at disruption might develop. Like a Hitchcock drama where terror lurks just under the veneer of "normal" events, the reports from the network had an eerie sense of false normalcy. Somewhere just out of camera range the familiar rituals of the political process were yielding to violent conflict.

Adding to this news were additional unsettling reports that the convention itself had been infiltrated by supporters of Mayor Daley who would do for the convention what his city's police intended to do downtown. Many times throughout the evening, CBS Special Events coordinator Robert Wussler cut to reporters in the upper deck of the large convention hall who noted that the galleries had been packed by Daley workers and city employees. Dan Rather also interviewed McCarthy delegates, many breathless with anger, complaining that the convention guards stripped them of their newspapers and their banners. Their frustration was heightened by reports that the same private guards allowed hundreds of Humphrey supporters to bring in whatever they wished.

In 1968, layers of suspicion blanketed the delegates and party leaders, many of whom expressed fading hopes of unifying the "regular" and "peace" factions. On the crowded convention floor delegates wondered if the legitimate needs for security had given way to party-sanctioned harassment of dissident delegates and "hostile" reporters. At one point CBS covered the attempt by security police to remove a man later identified as Alex Rosenberg, a New York delegate. Had he slipped through security gates without using his pass? Viewers were shown pictures of the convention guards trying to remove him from his seat. When he resisted, network reporters converged in a gridlock of bodies that crowded the narrow aisle in front of the New York delegation. As the blue-helmeted Chicago police showed up to assist, Mike Wallace attempted to follow Rosenberg and his escort to the edges of the amphitheater. In the process Wallace was shoved by a guard, and a visibly angry Cronkite noted that the same treatment had been experienced by Dan Rather earlier, "except they didn't use their fists." When the scuffle moved out of camera range, Wallace continued to talk to Cronkite but in a curiously transformed way. No longer were the two reporters just covering another convention; they were now using their network microphones as communication lifelines in a war. This pattern was repeated in the week of the convention; reporters thrown into the chaos of events responded like soldiers at the front, reporting back on the movements of Daley's troops as they rounded up demonstrators, delegates, reporters, and bystanders. The convention became a combat story, less violent than Vietnam footage that ran every night on television but equally troubling because the battle was within America's borders and included celebrities and national leaders among its victims and villains.

At no time was this sense of confused narrative more apparent than between 9:30 and 11:00 P.M. Cronkite had been using opportunities between speeches to indicate that there was "trouble" downtown. "We understand that Vice President Humphrey is under siege tonight," he said, referring to clashes between police and demonstrators in front of his Hilton Hotel headquarters. Reports of massed forces using tear gas to break up groups of violent protesters were presented at various times in the evening. At 10:00 P.M., after Iowa governor Harold Hughes finished his speech putting Eugene McCarthy's name in nomination (quoting McCarthy: "Those who make peaceful revolution impossible make violent revolution inevitable."), Cronkite introduced videotaped scenes shot in front of the Hilton and rushed on the air. With other viewers he was seeing the footage for the first time. The tape showed people milling around in the streets. There were sounds of demonstrators yelling "Sieg Heil," underscoring pictures of police arresting and occasionally clubbing demonstrators. The camera work was choppy and had the quality of combat footage; poorly lit street scenes caught the movements of figures moving in and out of the shadows. Wussler then decided to return CBS's coverage to the podium while Georgia representative Julian Bond finished his seconding speech for McCarthy.

The strongest and most dramatic images of the night followed soon after. Cronkite again introduced taped footage of the downtown demonstrations, narrated this time by veteran reporter Burt Quint. Quint was seen standing in a cleared street, midway between people gathered on a sidewalk and police who were across the street and out of camera range next to the Hilton. This benign image hardly prepared the viewer for what was to follow. CBS cut to another camera showing National Guardsmen in even rows, their unsheathed bayonets affixed to long rifles aimed low. The soldiers were moving in short, cautious steps toward what appeared to be ordinary people on the sidewalks, but still at some distance. In these shots there was no violence, but a viewer could not help but wonder if the guardsmen were prepared to use their weapons on the crowd. The middle-aged and well-dressed people standing along the walk looked out of place in the same picture with the brown-fatigued guardsmen poised for what appeared to be imminent battle. Abruptly, CBS returned to the convention hall and to an interview between Dan Rather and Mayor Daley. Daley could not have been aware of the footage that viewers had just seen and would see again as the brief interview progressed:

*Rather*: Mayor, Sir? Mayor Daley, Walter Cronkite is reporting downtown the police have used tear gas and there is considerable turmoil around the Hilton Hotel.

*Daley*: The situation is well in hand. There was a demonstration by people who were violating the law and coming into hotels contrary to the hotel management and were creating acts of violence.

*Rather*: Did the hotel people complain, Mayor?

*Daley*: Everyone has complained. The guests complained about people being there all night. The police took the proper action to have them comply with the law.

At this point CBS changed the video to show pictures of the police and demonstrators, keeping the audio of the interview.

*Rather*: Well, Mayor, so far as you know the police did not respond with undue violence?

*Daley*: Our police department is the greatest police department in the United States and the men in there are all family men, decent men, and they don't respond with any undue violence.

*Rather:* What about these reports that downtown is strictly an armed camp? For a businessman coming to Chicago tomorrow should he cancel his reservations?

*Daley:* Totally propaganda by you and your station and eastern interests who never wanted the convention in Chicago, and a lot of other people trying to hurt the pure name of this great city.[35]

The power of television to juxtapose images from one setting with words from another is a potent editorial tool. Daley was left with the task of denying what a series of images affirmed. Even as he spoke, television was demonstrating that Chicago was an armed camp. Later, when Dan Rather asked delegate Shirley MacLaine what she thought about the scenes she had seen on a portable television next to her, the actress remarked, "It looks like . . . Munich." Delegates in the convention hall, watching television watch them, became increasingly aware that the confrontation outside was making a mockery of their proceedings.

Even as the parliamentary machinery of the party continued on through the evening, the official proceedings had become a great lie. McCarthy's defeated delegates and the sizable "peace" faction were prepared for that. What they would not accept, and what they communicated to CBS viewers, was their anger at the "overreaction" of the security forces inside and outside the convention hall. For them there was no unity. There was limited freedom of expression. The convention was not the enactment of the democratic process that it pretended to be. On this evening violence again appeared ready to wash over what was supposed to be the high ground of orderly political change. Even the normally reassuring Cronkite seemed unsure of how to cover a political event that had taken on overtones of an insurrection. He became only the most credible witness to the coercion of delegates by a mayor determined to use his police like an army and by some protesters prepared to incite a police riot while the whole world looked on. Hubert Humphrey liked to talk about the "politics of joy," but no slogan could have been more out of place as the party stumbled toward adjournment in the late hours of Wednesday night.

## PHILLIPS MEETS LINCOLN

He had little regard for the Constitution. He would have even been happy to see his home state of Massachusetts secede from the Union. And Abraham Lincoln, he once noted, was little more than "the white trash of the south spawned in Illinois."[36] But even with all of his heresies, Wendell Phillips was one of the most sought after public figures of his age. When he visited a town to lecture against the political incrementalism that preserved American slavery, it was the unusual person who did not crowd into the local Lyceum Hall to hear his jeremiads. Journalist Horace Greeley—no friend of Phillips—estimated that between 1861 and 1862 over 50,000 people heard the fifty-year-old abolitionist in person, with another 5 million reading his speeches in sympathetic newspapers. [37]

In the remarkable person of Wendell Phillips stood many of the ironies and ambiguities that dominated life in the Civil War era. Like the nation of deeply split factions that troubled him, he carried a number of contradictions that were not easy to square. He was born into wealth and could have lived comfortably without ever doing a serious day's work. But he became an early and undying champion for the victims of his day—especially slaves, poor laborers, and feminists. In private, the tall, middle-aged man behaved more like a quiet merchant than the rhetorical flamethrower he became in public. He was a major force in the abolition movement, pushing Lincoln and both political parties to square the continued existence of slavery with the moral imperatives of the Declaration of Independence. But like most Americans, the Boston Brahmin was suspicious of politics and defended his actions by reference to strongly felt religious beliefs. Even his religious piety had its contradictions: Phillips's venomous attacks on the "great brothel" of the South made a smoldering ruin out of the concept of Christian charity.

And yet, what causes he took on. His countless addresses against slavery confirm what is perhaps the highest achievement that history can record in behalf of a reformer: the eventual adoption of "extremist" positions by the American mainstream. More than 130 years later, the reasonableness of his principles remain just as potent:

Of all the institutions of slavery on the face of the earth, there are none so unmitigatedly bad, so inexcusably atrocious, so colossal in their felonious aspect, so diametrically opposed to the professions and practices of the people that encourage and support them, as the institution of slavery in the United States of America. There is no republicanism in America while slavery exists. The cause of liberty throughout the world is maimed and bleeding while slavery remains there. . . . While that institution lasts, the experiment of men to govern themselves has not been proved to be a successful one; for there is no virtue in loving freedom for ourselves. [38]

Phillips opposed not only slavery but the considerable legal framework that upheld it in the North. Fugitive slave laws that required the return of escapees were an anathema to all abolitionists, even though they were routinely enforced by President Lincoln and many local jurisdictions, including Phillips's own Boston. The "civilized" northern view held at the time was that while slavery was a regrettable feature of the South, to push too far by ignoring southern requests for fugitive slaves would result in straining important commercial ties. After all, the South's cotton was almost exclusively milled into fabric in the Yankee North.

Phillips would consider no such temporizing, even granting the economic stakes that influential northerners had in southern productivity and the occasional threats made on his life. He stood in countless meeting rooms and courthouse squares arguing against the constant stream of legal maneuvers that resulted in the return of runaways to southern owners.

One of Phillips's many public pleas for the freedom of slaves was given in 1842 before an angry crowd in Boston's venerable Faneuil Hall. Many were present to hear about the case of George Latimer, a jailed slave waiting to be transferred back to his southern owner and the certain punishment of a public flogging. Others had come to cause trouble, especially since one of the speakers was to be Charles Remond, a free black who dared to address a white audience as their equal. By the time of the meeting, Massachusetts chief justice Lemuel Shaw had already decided Latimer's fate. Concluding that the Fugitive Slave Law was constitutional, Shaw noted with "personal regret" that the escaped slave would have to be returned.[39]

It was not unusual that many within Phillips's audiences were unsympathetic to his views. Previous abolitionist speakers on this night had been shouted down amid cascades of boos and hisses from various parts of the hall. As Remond rose to make his remarks, the tension and noise grew even greater. After repeated attempts, he finally gave up amid a ceaseless din that included shouts of "Down with the damned nigger" and "Turn the darkey out."[40] Phillips then tried to address the meeting. "Fellow-citizens, I will ask your attention but a single moment. I wish only to bear my testimony in favor of liberty." Energized by the electric hostility, he castigated lawyers who made a comfortable living in the North by taking the cases of slave owners. "They are but your tools. You are the guilty ones." "I know I am addressing the white slaves of the North," he continued amid more boos. "Yes, you dare to hiss me, of course. But you dare not break the chain which bonds you to the car of slavery." Then, reaching for the assertion that many would find so reprehensible over the course of his career, Phillips attacked the Constitution—specifically, Article IV, Section 3— as the legal tool that sanctioned the return of slaves. "When I look upon these crowded thousands and see them tramp on their consciences and the rights of their fellow-men, at the bidding of a piece of parchment, I say, 'my CURSE be on the Constitution of the United States.' " As the crowd hissed their disapproval, Phillips shouted back, "Fools! You know not the inestimable value of free speech. Cowards! You dare not hear a colored man speak in these liberty-loving walls." He told them that they did not have to abet Latimer's victimization:

Fellow-citizens, no law binds our police to aid the slave-catcher, nor our jailer to keep slaves. If they act at all, they are volunteers. Shall our taxes pay men to hunt slaves? Shall we built jails to keep them? . . . The man in the free states who helps hunt slaves is no better than a blood-hound. The attorney who aids is baser still. But any judge who would grant a certificate would be the basest of all.[41]

Before the Civil War, Phillips was a true radical. He believed that politics was hopelessly corrupted by an imperfect Constitution and scores of malevolent factions, among them the immoral South, petty legislators, "the cotton press," and a temporizing president who placed saving the Union above the emancipation of slaves. He saw his role as far different from other public figures who must ride the slow-moving train of public opinion:

The reformer is careless of numbers, disregards popularity, and deals only with ideas, conscience, and common sense. He feels, with Copernicus, that as God waited long for an interpreter, so he can wait for his followers. He neither expects nor is overanxious for immediate success. The politician dwells in an everlasting now. His motto is "success"— his aim, votes. His object is not absolute right, but . . . as much right as the people will sanction. His office is not to instruct public opinion, but to represent it.[42]

Phillips thus bore the need for a flying wedge of bodyguards as an emblem of moral courage. The taunts of a hostile crowd were not an embarrassment but only an indication of just how corrupt the nation's civil life had become. He would rage at the shortsightedness of listeners who despised his talk of disunion and abolition and, in later years, suffrage and temperance. But his moral certainty also allowed him to take pleasure in these crusades. "Parties and sects laden with the burden of securing their own success cannot afford to risk new ideas," he noted. Thus, "in all modern constitutional governments, agitation is the only peaceful method of progress."[43] "The republic which sinks to sleep, trusting to constitutions and machinery, to politicians and statesmen, for the safety of its liberties, never will have any."[44]

The great agitator's motives were a mix of altruistic and commercial impulses. He deeply believed in his causes, but he also enjoyed the celebrity status that they gave him. He made a good living from his speeches, especially one entitled "The Lost Arts," a noncontroversial lecture detailing the extensiveness of technical knowledge prior to the age of science. By his own estimate he gave the talk thousands of times, gaining a total income from it in excess of $150,000.[45] Even this peculiar form of nineteenth-century entertainment could be a bargaining chip in the campaign to communicate his as his social agenda. Lyceums would normally have to pay for his entertaining lectures; if audiences wanted to hear him for free, they would have to agree to allow him to speak on the subject of abolitionism.[46]

Phillips's philosophical purity was severely tested in the Civil War. The coming conflict unexpectedly placed the long-time advocate of disunion on the horns of a practical dilemma. To support the war would mean affirming President Lincoln's contention that the South could not secede from the Union, something Phillips had long encouraged as a way to free the North from its guilt by association. But opposing the war presented the practical problem of opposing the military machine that could destroy the South's despised slave-based economy. Phillips initially believed that Lincoln was an apologist for southern values. But he seemed slowly to realize that the Civil War would eventually encourage the Union states to punish the Confederacy: something that abolitionist arguments by themselves had not been able to do. At times, he counseled patience to other colleagues who refused to believe that Lincoln would overturn the institution of slavery. At other times, even after the first and incomplete Emancipation Proclamation, he was intolerant of the president's political problems in winning the war while holding onto the support of key border states. Typically, Phillips expressed sadness over Lincoln's death but also noted that God "has withdrawn him at the moment when . . . the nation needed a sterner hand."[47]

## WHAT THESE CASES SUGGEST

There is no grand theoretical scheme that holds these cases tightly together, but they are still instructive for what they say about public confrontations. Four general features are especially worth noting, the most basic of which is the inestimable heuristic value of conflict. "The purpose of confrontation," wrote Walter Lippmann, "is to discern truth."[48] In ways that are both subtle and plain, spectators to conflict sometimes acquire knowledge and almost always gain the ability to ask the right questions. It is not an overstatement to say that we often do not know what to think until we hear a variety of views on an issue. Was George Bush sufficiently forthcoming on his involvement in the Iran-Contra affair? Did Wendell Phillips make a reasoned case against the Constitution and for disunion in the 1840s? The dialectic of conflict still fulfills its promise of providing opposing chains of reasons—"good" or otherwise—that invite judgments about their quality and force. To a large extent the attitudes we carry in support of our policy preferences are synthesized from the public discussion of others. There can be no guarantee that good ideas will flow from the brawl of any number of rhetorical incompetents, but discourse that promotes the rise of more competing discourse usually serves the cause of knowledge and, indeed, may generate it.[49] Organized dialectic is so much a part of modern Western life that we sometimes forget its common forms in the structured opposition of the courts, political parties, governmental branches, advertisers, and special-interest factions. As journalist Alistair Cooke has aptly put it, a "passion for the idea of contradiction" lies at the center of an open society.[50]

A second conclusion justified by these brief examples and the more detailed ones that follow is that confrontations are often more accidental than rhetorical. Some are the subject of great planning; others happen with little advance consideration by their participants. The Bush-Rather encounter, for example, illustrates a public challenge that each side anticipated. If the hostile tone of the interview was greater than either man wanted, the general nature of the accusations could hardly have been a surprise. By contrast, John Lennon and Yoko Ono seemed genuinely unprepared for their encounter with Al Capp. The meeting itself was planned, but at least the Lennons were probably not expecting it to move beyond the ritual expressions of support that characterized their other bed-in visitors. Indeed, the Lennons' publicity objectives depended on the sympathy of their contacts; the event they staged had a fragile absurdity that could not withstand serious queries about the sacrifices they were making in behalf of peace. Capp surely sensed this and clearly found the Lennons' bedroom a wonderful place to make *them* rather than "peace" the issue. This kind of loss of control of a situation is one of the reasons persuasive encounters carry great risks for their participants, an important characteristic we will come back to in the next chapter.

Third, persuasive confrontations do not just "happen"—they are usually depicted. They come to us through intermediaries in journalism and the arts who extend our knowledge to cultural events that go beyond firsthand experience. These mediators may include playwrights like Brian Clark or reporters such as Walter Cronkite. Their narratives gain our attention by entertaining us and by using conflict as it has always been used in narrative: to give events significance and immediacy. Clark's play, for example, modulates what has been in ordinary life a diffuse and relatively obscure debate over the medical ethics of life maintenance practices. Similarly, CBS director Robert Wussler could not help but conclude that he had—in the journalist's phrase—a "good story" in the unfolding chaos at the Democratic National Convention. Our innate need for narrative has become wedded to the equally strong impulse to turn confrontations into symbols of moral certainty and self-definition. As the example of Phillips and the abolitionists indicates, a conflict may be at least implicitly presented to its audiences as a test for their souls and a measure of their compassion. Storytellers who construct confrontations from fact or fiction are engaged in a timeless process of collective reassurance.

Finally, these instances also suggest a common feature of most public disputes—namely, their dramatic value cannot necessarily be equated with their social importance. It is by no means the norm for a great issue to provoke a great confrontation. That was the case in the abolitionist debate and to some extent with the issues that tore at the fresh wounds of the nation in 1968. But is is at least as common for the expressive and personalistic dimensions of a dispute to create public attention. If more people in the United States watch television's "Geraldo" or "Oprah" than "Meet the Press," it is because the substantive content of the first two shows is subordinate to their expressive functions; they are less about ideas and information than about the vicarious pleasures of emotional intensity. Guests typically do not need to be experts or even knowledgeable to appear on these programs; what is important is that they be carriers of anger, fear, remorse, or moral outrage.[51]

Political confrontations are often the functional equivalents of grand opera, where the texts are largely secondary to the aural wash of the music. Lyrics of any sort can rarely stand alone when stripped of their expressive sounds. In many cases, like Kennedy's South African trip, the actual substance of a message becomes secondary to the enactment of a spectacle of courageous opposition in the face of adversity. Kennedy's speeches to his hosts were actually quite subdued, especially in his intimations of moral equivalency between South Africa and the United States. What really accounts for the widespread coverage of the trip was the drama of opposites it represented. To be sure, Kennedy had within his power the ability to offend our expectations about what an advocate for racial freedom would say in the last bastion of state-sponsored segregation. But he predictably confirmed what we expected, giving concrete expression to contradictions that—on a purely substantive level—could have just as easily been stated from the United States. The value of the trip was in its drama, in its ability again to invoke the bitter irony of a black nation ruled by a white minority.

It remains in the next chapter to explore in more depth several psychological and social features common to the kinds of public encounters briefly summarized here. As is evident from these public transactions, instances where advocates face hostile listeners offer useful chances to look into the kind of society we are. They also provide an opportunity to examine the communication processes that quietly occur in these highly visible events. Both of these goals are central to this study.

## NOTES

1. John Kenneth Galbraith, A Life in Our Times (New York: Ballantine, 1982), pp. 30–31.

2. Herbert W. Simons, Persuasion: Understanding, Practice, and Analysis, Second Edition (New York: Random House, 1986), pp. 121–122.

3. This encounter is reconstructed from several sources, including Ellen Sander, "John and Yoko Ono Lennon: Give Peace a Chance," Saturday Review June 28, 1966, pp. 46–47; and the 1988 documentary film Imagine (Warner Brothers).

4. William F. Buckley, Jr., On the Firing Line: The Public Life of Our Public Figures (New York: Random House, 1989), p. 15.

5. Brian Clark, Whose Life Is It Anyway? (New York: Dodd and Mead, 1978).

6. Thorstein Veblen's concept of "trained incapacity" is discussed by Kenneth Burke in Permanence and Change: An Anatomy of Purpose, Second Edition (Indianapolis: Bobbs-Merrill, 1965), pp. 7–9.

7. Clark, Whose Life Is It Anyway? p. 28.

8. Ibid., p. 138.

9. Ibid., p. 142.

10. Richard Eder, "Stage: 'Whose Life Is It Anyway?' From Britain," New York Times, April 18, 1979, p. III, p. 15.

11. Jack Newfield, Robert Kennedy: A Memoir (New York: E. P. Dutton, 1969), p. 19.

12. William V. Shannon, The Heir Apparent: Robert Kennedy and the Struggle for Power (New York: Macmillan, 1967), p. 54.

13. Kennedy quoted in Newfield, Robert Kennedy, p. 69.

14. Arthur M. Schlesinger, Jr., Robert Kennedy and His Times, Volume II (Boston: Houghton Mifflin, 1978), p. 809.

15. Harriet J. Rudolph, "Robert F. Kennedy's University of Capetown Address," Central States Speech Journal, Spring 1982, p. 320.

16. Shannon, The Heir Apparent, pp. 136–137.

17. Kennedy quoted in Rudolph, "Robert F. Kennedy's University of Capetown Address," p. 825.

18. Kennedy quoted in Schlesinger, Jr., Robert Kennedy, p. 780.

19. Kennedy quoted in ibid.

20. Kennedy quoted in Rudolph, "Robert F. Kennedy's University of Capetown Address," p. 328.

21. One pattern of news reporting apparently much favored by former CBS News chief Van Gordon Sauter was to build a story around a brief but telling "moment." See Peter J. Boyer, *Who Killed CBS?* (New York: Random House, 1988), pp. 138–139.

22. Jonathan Alter and Howard Fineman, "The Great TV Shout-Out," *Newsweek,* February 8, 1988, p. 20. See also E. J. Dionne, Jr., "Bush Camp Feels Galvanized After Showdown with Rather," *New York Times,* January 27, 1988, pp. A1, A16.

23. Peter J. Boyer, "When One Ambush Meets Another," *New York Times,* January 27, 1988, p. A16.

24. Ibid.

25. "Transcript of the Second Debate between Bush and Dukakis," *New York Times* October 14, 1988. p. A14.

26. George Hackett, "Rather: Lightning in a Bottle," *Newsweek* February 8, 1988, pp. 22–23.

27. Peter J. Boyer, "Rather's Questioning of Bush Sets off Shouting on Live Broadcast," *New York Times* January 26, 1988, p. A19.

28. Ibid.

29. Boyer, "When One Ambush Meets Another," p. A16.

30. Ibid.

31. Alter and Fineman, "The Great TV Shout-Out," p. 20.

32. Report of the Chicago Study Team to the National Commission on the Causes and Prevention of Violence, *Rights in Conflict* (New York: Signet, 1968), pp. 6–27.

33. Ibid. p. xxii.

34. This narrative is based on the review of tapes of CBS coverage for August 28, 1968, the Museum of Broadcasting, New York, and a chronology of CBS coverage for that day in Thomas Whiteside, "Corridor of Mirrors," *Columbia Journalism Review* Winter 1968–69, pp. 35–54. For other views of this convention, see Theodore H. White, *The Making of the President, 1968* (New York: Atheneum, 1969), pp. 257–313; Norman Mailer, *Miami and the Siege of Chicago* (New York: World, 1968), pp. 83–223; and Lewis Chester, Godfrey Hodgson, and Bruce Page, *An American Melodrama: The Presidential Campaign of 1968* (New York: Viking, 1969), pp. 503–604.

35. CBS convention coverage, August 28, 1968.

36. Carl Sandburg, *Abraham Lincoln, Volume III* (New York: Dell, 1974), p. 618.

37. James Brewer Stewart, *Wendell Phillips: Liberty's Hero* (Baton Rouge: Louisiana State University, 1986), p. 227.

38. Phillips quoted in Carlos Martyn, *Wendell Phillips: The Agitator* (New York: Negro Universities Press, 1969), p. 242.

39. Stewart, *Wendell Phillips: Liberty's Hero* p. 120.

40. Willard Hayes Yeager, "Wendell Phillips," in *A History and Criticism of American Public Address, Volume 1,* ed. William Norwood Brigance (New York: Russell and Russell, 1960), p. 339.

41. Ibid., p. 340.

42. Phillips quoted in Richard Hofstadter, *The American Political Tradition, 25th Anniversary Edition* (New York: Knopf, 1973), p. 136.

43. Phillips quoted in Martyn, *Wendell Phillips: The Agitator* p. 584.

44. Phillips quoted in Hofstadter, *The American Political Tradition* p. 140.

45. Ibid.

46. Carl Bode, *The American Lyceum: Town Meeting of the Mind* (New York: Oxford, 1956), p. 206.

47. Stewart, *Wendell Phillips: Liberty's Hero* pp. 264–265.

48. Walter Lippmann, *The Public Philosophy* (Boston: Little, Brown, 1955), p. 128.

49. This is a short summary of a very complex point with a complex intellectual history. The role dialectic plays in formulating attitudes takes two contradictory directions. The Greeks such as Plato and Aristotle asserted that the presentation of one's views was a separate stage that occurred *after* preferences and contingent truths were arrived at. For them, dialectic was one stage prior to advocacy. Others—particularly a wide range of social and democratic theorists—have described a more contingent "rhetorical knowledge" based on the synthesis of opposing views. For them, social knowledge and attitudes arise from public communication that serves to crystallize opinion. For different perspectives on these points, see Vasile Florescu, "Rhetoric and Its Rehabilitation in Contemporary Philosophy," *Philosophy and Rhetoric* Fall 1970, pp. 193–224; Robert Scott, "On Viewing Rhetoric as Epistemic," *Central States Speech Journal* February 1967, pp. 9–17; and Kenneth Burke, *A Rhetoric of Motives* (New York: Prentice-Hall, 1953), pp. 90–100, 183–189.

50. Alistair Cooke, Introduction to Buckley, *On the Firing Line* p. vii.

51. For a discussion of this point, see Joshua Meyrowitz, *No Sense of Place* (New York: Oxford, 1985), pp. 100–103.

# 2

# Persuasive Encounters: A Theoretical Overview

I had rather be their servant in my way
Than sway with them in theirs.[1]

*William Shakespeare*

When considered from its traditional model as an adjustive process, persuasion that is specifically addressed to a hostile audience looks like a strategic mistake. Our instincts tell us that bald challenges to attitudes that others firmly hold are almost certainly doomed to failure. We usually act on the assumption that any successful persuasive message will find as many ways as possible to soften differences that separate communicators. In this view, attitude change—if it comes at all—occurs only after careful adaptation has cleared a path of common ground that everyone can follow.

This valid assumption is partly what accounts for the drama of the encounters that follow, but it is at least partly mistaken. The purpose of the first half of this chapter is to trace in broad strokes two very different intellectual traditions that have been used to account for communication that deals with conflict. Most theories for predicting and analyzing persuasion fall into one of these patterns. The first focuses on the assumed requirement for *adaptation*, a requirement that seems to lie at the very nexus of successful communication. The second, resting on both old and new observations about the use of persuasive discourse as an advisory tool, challenges this requirement by providing psychological and ethical justifications for risking verbal conflict. Whether or not persuaders think in the terms of these traditions, most must still cope with the different options they represent. Each stands for a very different pattern of thought, and each leads to contrasting predictions about the risks and advantages of persuasive confrontations.

The second half of the chapter describes verbal conflict in terms of two key dimensions of audience involvement. One dimension explores the extent to which other secondary audiences will witness the conflict. The second estimates the degree to which an advocate in a dispute actually has control over the flow of ideas. In conflict arbitrated by debate, control over the form and substance of an exchange is shared by equal opponents. In what are defined here as persuasive confrontations, control resides largely with the persuader.

## THE PRESUMPTION FOR STRATEGIC ADAPTATION

Like the large-bodied bumblebee whose ability to fly on small wings seems to defy the laws of aerodynamics, the persuasive encounter is also not easily accommodated in the framework of accepted persuasion theory. One of the undisputed assumptions about communication that is meant to be heard by others is that adjustment and adaptation are fundamental processes. Under this broad presumption, there are many varied theories and vocabularies that describe the strategies of communicators, but nearly all students of human communication since the 1940s have portrayed successful interaction as a process of finding appeals and ideas that both advocates and audiences can claim to share. Critic and theorist Kenneth Burke signaled the centrality of this premise in 1951 when he contrasted the "old rhetoric" of "persuasion" with the "new rhetoric" of "identification." The old rhetoric, he noted, stressed the deliberate logic and formal appeals of messages. As in Aristotle's day, its best examples were found in the speeches presented to courts and legislative bodies. By contrast, the new rhetoric built on increased interest within the social sciences on the use of symbols to carry unconscious appeals meant to appease existing social values.[2] It found its best examples in less institutionalized settings where a good deal of persuasion takes place: in social movements, political campaigns, and even the jockeying for favor that is sometimes a party of daily conversation. To a significant extent, Burke and others fostered a view of language as a vehicle for transcending social and ideological differences. The key process they emphasized in this rebirth of interest involved the myriad ways in which communication is helped along by identification. Drawing heavily on anthropology's emphasis on the mechanisms that societies employ to create unity, they described what seemed to be a universal quest for symbols and rituals that cement feelings of membership and belonging. It became axiomatic that not only language develops on the basis of shared meanings but shared attitudes as well. Even the hierarchies of everyday life that represent the clearest opportunities for friction (i.e., between leaders and followers, teachers and students, workers and employers) are routinely oiled by the language of adaptation and compromise.[3]

A number of expectations were implicit in this approach: that successful messages will necessarily be shaped with careful attention to the circumstances in which they are presented; that human expression is best understood as a response to a particular situation with specific social and ideological requirements; and that our rhetoric is inevitably the product of the company we keep and the environments we inhabit. In Lloyd Bitzer's words, we live in a world of "rhetorical situations" where not "just any response" will do. Our behavior is governed in part by the expectations of others. Thus,

the speeches in the Senate rotunda three days after the assassination of the President of the United States were actually required by the situation. So controlling is situation that we should consider it the very ground of rhetorical activity, whether that activity is primitive and productive of a simple utterance or artistic and productive of the Gettysburg Address.[4]

The nearly universal compulsion to say and do "what is right" is evidence of a constant impulse to mediate our behavior through the filter of what we think others will want us to say.

At roughly the same time that scholars such as Burke and Bitzer were reviving interest in rhetoric as a socially adaptive process, many of their counterparts in the social sciences developed evocative vocabularies of their own to describe the conformist impulse in wide ranges of human action. Taking very different paths through the varied terrain of psychology and sociology, many influential researchers and writers arrived at generalized accounts of personal effectiveness based on models of self-initiated adjustment. For example, in the landmark *Presentation of Self in Everyday Life* Erving Goffman utilized the terms of the theater to describe the naturally changing roles of ordinary life.[5] In doing so, he convincingly argued that we are all "performers" governed by the constraints of the scenes in which we act and the audiences who witness our action. For Goffman "onstage" behavior is controlled by the sometimes precisely scripted roles audiences expect us to carry out: as teacher, student, waitress, boss, and so on.

Sociologist David Riesman's equally important contribution in *The Lonely Crowd* included the same key premise. His study was an ambitious attempt to document how Americans have changed over the years in their attitudes toward their environments. Describing nothing less than a "characterological" shift in American life, he argued that the collective American psyche has moved away from the "inner-direction" of our older and less urbanized forebears toward a uniquely modern "other-direction."[6] Where the inner-directed person tends to set his own course through life—even one that risks alienation from others—the other-directed person is far more susceptible to the flow of attitudes and values of those with whom he interacts. Riesman documented the extent to which the interdependencies of modern life have made Americans "more capable of and more interested in maintaining responsive contact with others both at work and at play."[7] If earlier Americans were more willing to stand firm in support of their own convictions, he noted, their modern counterparts seem to have a greater need to "fit in."

Both of these theorists remain influential because their descriptions of pliable behavior not only are vivid but also strike a chord of instance recognition. Our frequently expressed belief that many changes and transitions in life—marriage, divorce, self-destructive habits—require skills of "personal adjustment" is only the most visible recognition we give to the need for adaptive behavior. Even while we concede that the personality is not as easily remolded as wet clay, there is still a great deal of faith that productive change is within the grasp of almost any individual.

## Dissonance Reduction as Adjustment

On still another front at approximately the same time an influential group of experimental social psychologists led by Leon Festinger, Percy Tannenbaum, and others independently explored the motif of communication-as-adjustment in their own theory building.[8] Festinger's well-known dissonance theory, for example, is representative of an entire legacy of research completed in the 1950s and 1960s describing attitude change in terms of a natural impulse for psychological equilibrium. He developed what is still the most widely cited model of attitude change, nothing that a receiver's acceptance of a dissonant message may require adjustments in belief. These adjustments make it possible to hold new attitudes that will then fit in with other relevant ones that are already held. The theorized process is fairly simple. Dissonance, or mental stress, is created when a new attitude a listener is prepared to accept is shown to be noncongruent with other related attitudes already held. Thrust into a quandary of incompatible loyalties, a person may feel compelled to alter the intensity of his attitudes in order to reduce the dissonance. For example, news that a favorite politician has confessed to a disfavored activity—such as accepting money from a lobbyist— would create dissonance and, hence, the motivation to adopt new attitudes toward both the person and the act. The adjusted attitudes would lessen the tension created by the incompatibility of holding positive feelings toward a person who has engaged in criminal behavior.

Although dissonance theories have not been universally accepted among persuasion theorists,[9] they have the advantage of drawing on widely accepted expectations about how we maintain our internal equilibrium. It is easy to project that the politician's stock might suffer in such a development. It comes as more of a surprise that the theory also predicts that there might also be a simultaneous rationalization that the politician's crimes could have been worse. Even more, while the revealed inconsistencies in our lives may be checked by compensating changes in attitude, they may also be ignored through valiant efforts at rationalization. We may work to compartmentalize the various segments of our lives so that we are not confronted by their inherent contradictions. Or we may valiantly rationalize these contradictions.

Consider all these options as they are applied to Joseph Kesselring's classic comedy *Arsenic and Old Lace.*[10] The story flows from the absurd dilemma faced by a nephew who has discovered that his two kindly old aunts have been regularly poisoning their dinner guests. In the 1944 film adaptation directed by Frank Capra, Cary Grant's Mortimer faces the enormous task of reconciling his affection for this dotty pair of relatives with the shock that they have happily filled the basement with deceased elderly men. Dissonance initially reins for Kesselring's audiences, yet the unfolding circumstances of the play help them rationalize most of the sources of their and Mortimer's shock. These gentle women, they learn, only poisoned elderly and lonely men who had fallen on hard times, and then only with arsenic-laced brandy served after a very good meal. The women were not motivated by malice but by a big-hearted desire to give their unhappy guests their own version of eternal peace. Moreover, as another extenuating circumstance, they learn that a streak of insanity has run through the family, a fate that the adopted Mortimer has luckily escaped. In the end he succeeds in getting the two committed (along with a brother who thinks that he is Teddy Roosevelt) to what we are assured is a paradise of a rest home in the country. They are only too happy to go. Even this black comedy takes pains to remove the audience's dissonance while it gives them license to watch Mortimer's overly organized life come unglued. That he finds a way to put it back together again, finally discovering what the audience has long known, is the play's denouement. His perfectly normal psyche is a thermostat capable of self correction, successfully accommodating all the dissonant information built into the farce.

## Two Enduring Assumptions about Conflict

As a culture, we share a bias in favor of partly concealing differences behind an adaptive or conciliatory pose. One reason is obvious: Daily life would be uncomfortably tense without such an emphasis on agreement. But there are also two deeper reasons embedded in the American experience. One of these is the commonplace view that conflict is a momentary anomaly that is usually subject to resolution through hard work and compromise. We know that disagreements are common products of human organizations, but we also believe that they can usually be dealt with if the parties to a dispute have the requisite goodwill to solve them. Americans like to see themselves as relatively immune from the European pattern of lifelong divisions that result in permanent class, religious, and ideological factions. Faith in the values of an open society carries an equal faith in the possibility of using communication to overcome most disputes. Photogenic portrayals of an idealized America in political commercials are only the most romantic portrayals of this premise. Ads such as the widely copied "Morning in America" spots from the 1984 Reagan campaign used the reassuring symbols and old-time virtues of small-town America to evoke social harmony. Norman Rockwell evocations of barbershops situated on town squares, summer evenings spent on broad front porches, and simple church weddings quietly implied that the United States remains an inclusive society that will deny its promise to no group or faction.[11] Indeed, most forms of advertising have a similar investment in portraying a nation that has successfully transcended its differences.

Political scientist Mona Harrington calls this the "myth of deliverance," noting that at its core "is the conviction that human relations are, by their nature, harmonious, that *serious* conflict in human societies is unnatural and unnecessary."[12] Harrington implies that such a view places enormous responsibilities on the institutions that handle conflict, such as the courts or Congress, because they are thought to be the mediators that can apply reason and high principle to the resolution of even fractious issues involving class and status. Like philosopher I. A. Richards's belief that the study of communication should be devoted to underlying misunderstandings in language,[13] the myth of deliverance places great faith in the power of discourse to produce whatever adjustments are needed in order to change hardened attitudes.

A second commonplace view that also points to the possibilities of minimizing conflict is the general belief among communication and social theorists in the concept of homogeneity implied in words like *group* or *community*. These words presuppose that members of any society can be identified by their shared attitudes and ideological associations. It is hard to imagine discussing any communication effects and processes without reference to the idea that there *are* identifiable groups within a society that hold similar attitudes, circumstances, and patterns of thought.

A whole series of important consequences flow from our faith in this fundamental idea. We are quick to point out that individuals frequently self-select their group membership on perceptions of similarity. We also talk about "communities of discourse" when participants can be expected to understand and endorse the same terms in generally the same ways.[14] We further assume that people who come together under the umbrella of an organization or movement are essentially similar in their beliefs on certain relevant issues. For example, there is some safety in concluding that an antiabortion rally will be attended by members of the "pro-life community" or that the "academic community" will criticize efforts by legislators to increase tuition at certain colleges. Survey research data are full of conclusions about such apparently like-minded groups, including Vietnam veterans, gun owners, medical doctors, Protestant or Catholic leaders, or members of the National Organization for Women. Generalizing about group attitudes makes it possible to talk about more or less single-minded communities that are capable of responding *as units* to properly designed appeals.

Most of the time this habit of thinking in terms of group responses is helpful. But the price we pay in emphasizing group similarities is sometimes our neglect of the equally real variability within seemingly homogeneous groups. We frequently assume that in discussing like-minded communities we are really not dealing with thousands of different opinions on key issues but with *group* positions. Yet it is worth remembering what observers and historians of organizations continually reaffirm: that beyond the facade of official statements that tend to dominate public perceptions about organizations, there is usually a wide variability of attitudes among members.

There is also something useful in the reminder that we can insist too much on an ordered world of like-minded communities. There are significant dangers in oversimplifying the value of resolving conflict-producing differences, not the least of which is the possibility for intellectual growth that challenges to conformity can offer. In *The Uses of Disorder* urban theorist and critic Richard Sennett notes that the assumption of "solidarity" based on the kinds of commonplace views we have discussed can result in a "counterfeit sense of community." Part of the deception implied in these ideas is self-imposed. Individuals, Sennett notes, may "learn at a certain point in their own growth how to lie to themselves, in order to avoid new experiences that might force them to endure the pain of perceiving the unexpected, the new, the 'otherness' around them."[15] He cites what the small-group research of Irving Janus and others has demonstrated again and again—that "belonging" may be as much a matter of skillful personal denial as it is genuine solidarity.[16] Institutions naturally depend on perceptions of community to protect their own interests. The legitimacy of countless organizations and institutions requires the impression that their members are held together by common values and objectives. Although Sennett's arguments are much more complex than is suggested here, he makes a compelling case that adult maturity is easily arrested by the urge to seek the securities of a common identity. For him, the richest life is one that is probably lived entirely within a large city, where (with sufficient income) the sheer density of people and competing interests continually strengthens the individual's sense of identity. The inherently disordered and conflict-filled life of an urban area requires diverse personal contacts that act beneficially against our natural impulses to find more homogeneous surroundings. "Since men's full ethical nature is unstable, fragile, and involved in disorganized events," he notes, "only a society that is willingly unstable can provide, out of its own richness, a medium for growth beyond adolescence."[17]

We may routinely impose a conformist model on audiences, but the risk in doing so is to overestimate the extent to which the impulse for adaption drives persuasive communication. One of the conclusions that surfaces in the case studies that follow is how unpredictable the responses of presumably like-minded audiences can be. This is not to deny that human behavior is significantly shaped by the principle of adaptation; too much evidence exists to the contrary. Rather, if this principle becomes the only acceptable basis for explaining or judging discourse, it can have the effect of making communication born of conflict appear to be—at best, unusual or, at worst—the path to social destruction. For too many students of communication, notes Herbert Simons, "the effective persuader tends to be stereotypically depicted as a marvelously adaptable soul, one who, although not necessarily becoming a chameleon, nevertheless manages to move toward his audience psychologically in ways that cause his audience to move toward him."[18]

In the next section, we look at a second intellectual tradition that functions with a very different underlying principle, one that is generally more sympathetic to the expression of conflict.

## THE ADVISORY TRADITION OF MORAL RHETORIC

W. Lloyd Warner's exhaustive 1959 study of the "symbolic life of Americans" remains a fascinating look at the interplay between diversity and conformity in the rituals of public life. The sociologist's account of "Yankee City"—in reality, Newburyport, Massachusetts—begins during the years in which "Biggy Muldoon" polarized the city with antics designed to exploit his Irish working-class roots and to offend local aristocrats. Muldoon was probably a composite of several colorful New England politicians, including Boston's Frank Curley and Newburyport's Bossy Gillis. He made it clear to anyone who would listen that he relished his image as the city's "bad boy"; he was loved in part because he said he "hated" bankers, the police, "codfish aristocrats," and "foreigners" who refused to behave like "true Americans."[19] Biggy had unchangeable ideas about how privilege and corruption denied to people like himself the opportunities they rightly deserved. Nearly everything he did took on the character of a moral crusade against the rich and in favor of "the ordinary working man."

The road to his election as mayor began when he decided that his newly purchased Hill Street home could stand some drastic changes. Muldoon purchased the large mansion from a respected judge. Located in one of the nicest parts of town, its ancient elms and formal garden had long been a source of civic pride. Even so, he decided that it would make a wonderful gas station, and the battle that ensued virtually made him a public celebrity. When the horrified city fathers refused to allow the necessary permits to transform the house, he took it into his hands to make their opposition nothing less than an issue of class and status. His attacks were first directed toward the admired building itself and then toward the "aristocrats" who opposed him. Passersby soon found the old mansion draped with garish circus posters. Then slabs of stone from an old wall in the formal garden were removed and put to use on the front lawn as mock gravestones. Not surprisingly, many of Yankee City's distinguished citizens were prematurely given their last rites on the faces of the markers. He also rounded up a collection of chamber pots and hung them from the high ridgepoles of the house, fulfilling the worst stereotypes of the working-class Irish that were common at the time. The final indignity imposed on this cherished symbol was to cut down the old elms around it, leaving many of the residents of Hill Street in a state of trembling rage.

Even though Muldoon's tactics were excessive, the fact that he built his career on symbols of division rather than on symbols of unity illustrates an honorable tradition that sanctions dissent taken in the name of high principle. This tradition touches on the need to advise or warn audiences of dangers or problems they may be reluctant to hear. One of Warner's reasons for studying Muldoon and his environment includes this rationale. "Our political order," he notes, "permits ambitious individuals a choice among a number of career routes. They can accept the present world for what it is; they can attack its weaknesses and abuses and attempt to improve parts of the structure to conform to the precepts of justice and morality; or they can challenge the whole social and political order.[20] Muldoon chose a route somewhere between the second and third options, demonstrating how conflict perceived as the outcome of single-minded devotion to an ideal can carry its own social legitimacy. Most of his gestures telegraphed the egalitarian message that the city belonged as much to the "little man" as to the rich.

## Inner Direction as Moral Courage

In some ways, Muldoon is an apt example of what Riesman meant by an "inner-directed" person.[21] Where the more typical functionary might work for a more inclusionary "other-directed" style, he was only too happy to let the hardships and slights of his youth surface in a lifelong pattern of inviolate suspicion. Even the alienation of the rich had its advantages. His inner direction included what Riesman has described as a kind of psychic gyroscope of invariant beliefs that are not easily dismissed even in the name of social harmony. A sense of unchanging conviction makes such a person less vulnerable to the adaptive impulses common to other-directed types. In Riesman's words, "the inner-directed person could be 'at home abroad' by virtue of his relative insensitivity to others, [but] the other-directed person is, in a sense, at home everywhere and nowhere, capable of a rapid if sometimes superficial intimacy."[22] He is also careful to warn that these are not pure psychological states but broad categories intended to show how norms of behavior have changed. We are, he argues, increasingly part of a bureaucratized society that rewards the adaptability of other direction and penalizes dissent. The price of letting unaltered beliefs stand between us and the rewards of conformity have probably increased since the days of Biggy Muldoon.

Although his argument is more complicated than this, enough of Riesman's scheme is evident to see how it fits into an intellectual tradition that honors moral advocacy. If the adaptive impulse is an undeniable fact of life in a complex society, there are times when the apparent courage to challenge conventional attitudes carries its own rewards. Elements of this advisory tradition surface in a number of American attitudes: in the suspicions we have toward the person that places expediency above "doing what is right"; in fictional portrayals of dissenters who go against the grain of popular opinion; and in the common belief that "good reasons" can elude the sensibilities of even large numbers of people.

## Moral Courage and Dissent

Many disparate threads from the past and present are woven into the idea of moral advocacy. Aristotle was among the first to describe a special kind of communication—"epideictic"—concerned with advising audiences on the distinctions between "Virtue and Vice," the Noble and the Base."[23] He defined what has since become a common form of discourse, often labeled today as the "jeremiad." The jeremiad takes its name from the Old Testament prophet who warned that those who failed to keep their sacred covenant with God were doomed to face a deserved punishment. The jeremiads of the early American Puritans, for example, were sermons about the corrupting presence of sin and the necessity for repentance and reform. In Kurt Ritter's words, the minister "spoke as a scolding prophet—a voice in the wilderness."[24] Today we see its form in many secular contexts where audience members are encouraged "to view themselves as a chosen people confronted with a timely if not urgent warning that unless a certain course of atoning action is followed, dire consequences will ensue."[25] To cite a classic example, Fredrick Jackson Turner's 1893 Frontier Thesis carried a well-known warning to American historians about the dangers of neglecting the effects of westward expansion on the American psyche. This widely debated view, he admitted, was partly a protest against what he saw as the antiwestern biases of historians teaching in colleges along the East Coast.[26]

Extending beyond the jeremiad lies an even more extreme form of moral rhetoric described by Theodore Windt, Jr., as the "diatribe." Where the jeremiad offers specific proposals for the repair of the mistakes or moral shortcomings of an audience, the diatribe offers the less ceremonious equivalent of a kick in the shins. Windt traces this "rhetoric of last resort" over a time span that includes both the so-called Cynics of classical Greece and the comparatively recent student activists of the 1960s who were motivated by opposition to the Vietnam War. "For Cynics," Windt noted, "every question is an ethical question. Each problem, they contended, when stripped of its veneer of self-interest reveals a fundamental moral issue."[27] Their response to their world was basically to leave it: to wear simple clothes, live in communes, reject money, and give up on the possibility of finding political solutions for complex problems. Only by remaining apart from society could they create the moral consistency necessary to comment on the daily corruptions of the conventional life. Like the Puritan preachers who constructed their fiery jeremiads, they were not fully a part of the society but commentators on its excesses.

The moral diatribes of the Cynics and their modern counterparts rarely included the traditional conciliatory gestures of persuaders functioning as part of the system. In many cases the Cynics' objectives frequently included shocking their listeners into a recognition of the hypocrisies of their lives. Their methods included "fables, dialogues against imaginary opponents, topical references, parodies of serious poetry, obscene jokes, and slang phrases."[28] In some ways their strategies were not much different from some of the factions within the student movements, especially the "Yippies," who participated in confrontations such as those at the 1968 Democratic National Convention. Yippies delighted in a rhetoric of moral absolutism. The following passage from one of their publications was typical:

Who says that rich white Americans can tell the Chinese what is best? How dare you tell the poor that their poverty is deserved. . . . [L]augh at professors; disobey your parents; burn your money; you know life is a dream and all of our institutions are man-made illusions effective because YOU take the dream for reality. . . . Break down the family, church, nation, city, economy; turn life into an art form, a theatre of the soul.[29]

The details of these two forms are less important than the general sense of moral justification that underpins them. What is vital to both is the deeply rooted presumption that conviction may require rhetorical action that is both aggressive and uncompromising.

## Mythmaking and Heroic Dissent

All Western cultures reserve a place for stories and symbols of heroic dissent. Even in the most conformist of societies, myths selectively enshrine the ideal of courageous independence. They may range from the historic to the contemporary, from Martin Luther King, Jr. to Lech Walesa, from Patrick Henry to the crusading independent journalist I. F. Stone. To be sure, there is a good deal of romance in the heroic dissenter, especially given the likelihood that one group's visionary may be another group's out-of-touch radical. Even so, the perception that unpopular assertions can be justified on moral grounds is a powerful antidote to the routines of conformity. Consider the brief front-page quotes used by John F. Kennedy in *Profiles in Courage* to open various chapters in his hugely popular study of leaders in the Senate. In different ways each citation implies that greatness may require standing against the popular opinion of the moment. His chapter on John Quincy Adams opens with Adams's reminder that "the Magistrate is the servant not . . . of the people, but of his God."[30] The rhetorical signature that begins the chapter on Sam Houston suggests an especially stubborn defiance: "I *can* forget that I am called a traitor."[31] Similarly, Robert Taft is introduced with his own terse plea for the "liberty of the individual to think his own thoughts."[32] What Kennedy argued throughout the book he made explicit in his conclusion:

What then caused the statesmen mentioned in the proceeding pages to act as they did? It was not because they "loved the public better than themselves." On the contrary, it was precisely because they did *love themselves*—because each one's need to maintain his own respect for himself was more important to him than his popularity with others— because his desire to win or maintain a reputation for integrity and courage was stronger than his desire to maintain his office—because his conscience, his personal standard of ethics, his integrity or morality, call it what you will, was stronger than the pressures of public disapproval—because his faith that *his* course was the best one, and would ultimately be vindicated, outweighed his fear of public reprisal.[33]

One of the many cinematic counterparts to Kennedy's figures is the lone holdout in the jury deliberations portrayed in *Twelve Angry Men*. Hollywood has always been attracted to stories of independent figures who are able to stand against a tide of misguided or venal popular opinion. The 1957 film cast Henry Fonda as a quiet juror who discovers that he is the sole dissenter at the beginning of deliberations in a murder case. As the story unfolds, he has doubts about the prosecution's contention that an immigrant boy had murdered his father. Ever reasonable and coolheaded, his low-key but firm questions eventually force other members to consider overlooked evidence that eventually yields proof of the boy's innocence.

Fonda was only one of many Hollywood actors who found stardom in part because of the attractive independent-minded screen characters they portrayed. The same happened for Gary Cooper (*The Court-Martial of Billy Mitchell, High Noon*), Jimmy Stewart (*The Man from Laramie, Mr. Smith Goes to Washington*), Gregory Peck (*Only the Valiant, To Kill a Mockingbird*), and Al Pacino (*And Justice for All, Serpico*).

## Logic as the Engine of Conviction

Critic Wayne Booth is representative of an entire generation of communication analysts and ethicists who have devoted themselves to the question of when rationality requires dissent.[34] Their work is too diverse and involved to present in a brief space, other than to note that as a group they generally have held that the rules of logic ought to be superior and prior to more pragmatic goals that a persuader may have. They put forward the idea that an advocate's first obligation is not just to an audience but to the best reasons that can be found for a claim. In short, logic, not expediency, ought to be the engine of our convictions. Just as Copernicus found solid evidence against the conventional wisdom of his time that the earth was not the center of the universe, so too an individual may come to "know" what his peers still reject. The problem, as Booth sees it, is that faith in such a rhetoric of good reasons—a rhetoric grounded on the rules of logic and evidence—has been partially crippled by modern ideas about the subjectivity of most nonscientific knowledge. The cliché "You can't argue about religion and politics" speaks to the futility we often feel when confronted with attitudes contrary to our own. Booth notes that a kind of old-fashioned concern for determining when someone's rhetoric *logically* deserves our assent has largely "disappeared from most discussions of communication in our time."[35] The impulse to study persuasion as a process of adaptation has all but replaced it.

This lament from a former dean at the University of Chicago was more than just an abstract intellectual exercise. His own experiences in locating the rules of engagement for rhetorical opponents became very real when he encountered angry protesters who sometimes bypassed the normal channels for peaceful debate to shut down the university. By the middle of the 1970s most college campuses had been hit by protests not easily accommodated under the rules of rational debate.[36] Sit-ins, silent vigils, and efforts to prevent government members from speaking and recruiting were common. These sobering experiences led him to the conclusion that the rhetorical standards of institutions that ostensibly fostered the rigorous testing of ideas were not what they should have been.

The rationalist's hope that conviction should be the product of rigorous and orderly reasoning remains as old as Plato and is still largely unfulfilled. One problem rationalists face is that evidence about real human actions rarely adds up with the same certainty that comes with the computation of a math problem. What has *not* changed, as even the pessimistic Booth concedes, is the vague hope that the power of truly rational discourse can affect the thinking of even a majority. Our society's faith in reason has been shaken, he notes, but not destroyed. "One thing that we all believe, though many of us believe we have no good grounds for the belief, is that there really is a difference between good reasons and bad—which in my terms means a genuine difference between good rhetoric and bad."[37]

Evidence of such faith in reason is everywhere, but it is never more apparent than in our perceptions of criminality and justice. While the criminal justice system is much more than a processor of evidence, it is still easy to accept the view that issues of crime involve facts that must conform to strict rules of evidence. This partly explains the popularity of the crime story as such a durable genre. Guilt is a matter of the existence or absence of evidence; what makes the genre work is the fundamental faith we place in the premise that hard evidence will ultimately solve a case. Whether it is Arthur Conan Doyle's Sherlock Holmes or television's periodically revived Lieutenant "Columbo," the crime story routinely makes fact gathering the potent arbiter that certifies the rightness of unexpected conclusions. It serves as a reminder that good reasons can always be a license to stand against prevailing opinions.

Many pairs of words or phrases suggest the differences between the competing adaptive and advisory traditions we have reviewed here: compromise versus conflict, realistic pragmatism versus moral resolve, concern for audience acceptance versus conviction born of a sense of solid reasoning. It is important to realize that neither form deserves to have a monopoly on the analyst of persuasion. And in some of the cases that follow—notably, Edward Kennedy and Phil Donahue— elements of both traditions are ingeniously evoked at the same time. But what the disparate threads of these two patterns finally illustrate is that the kinds of confrontations considered in this book have their own legitimate social, moral, and logical bases. It would especially be a mistake to underestimate the extent to which some inner-directed advocates see themselves as moral agents charged with challenging rather than winning over audiences. Perhaps more than most of us, the individuals studied in this book are capable of drawing on reserves of unambiguous conviction to sustain them through the risks of persuasive confrontations.

## A TAXONOMY OF THE AUDIENCES TO ADVERSARIAL CONFLICT

Conflict that is expressed through communication emerges in many forums and is governed by a variety of variables. But it is possible to simplify some of these variables by focusing on two different but related dimensions.

The first involves the extent to which an exchange is seen or heard by others. At its most basic, conflict may involve discussion that is completely *private*, that is, witnessed only by the participants themselves. Its complexity increases as we move toward the *public* end of the dimension where others are functioning as observers or secondary participants. Consider a simple case. Two co-owners of a small business may engage each other in a debate over a choice to which both will be bound. Perhaps the issue is whether to invest in a new and expensive piece of equipment. They may argue their differing views alone, weighing various options and finally hammering out a decision away from their employees, customers, or spouses. But they could also do things differently, carrying on their discussion in public, perhaps in the presence of their employees or clients or even in front of a film crew doing a documentary on small businesses. Debates can fall anywhere between these extremes: observed by a limited number of people or presented to extended audiences who witness them through the mass media. It obviously makes a great deal of difference to all parties of a dispute if expectations of privacy are violated or if an audience of spectators is manipulated by one of the committed advocates. Such manipulation of this private-public dimension is part of the attraction that the spate of television shows devoted to talk and gossip have on millions. The producers of programs such as "Oprah" and "Donahue" frequently use the bait of the private secret to interest large numbers of viewers. Ordinary individuals are often coaxed onto these shows to "share" what are sometimes very personal traumas. For example, couples engaged in private counseling to curb their abusiveness toward each other and their children may volunteer to discuss publicly their most intimate differences and tensions.

A second dimension that defines the audiences for conflict is evident in the extent to which a persuader's comments are subject to the direct challenges of competing advocates. At one extreme is the concept of *debate* which is used here to designate conflict that proceeds on the principle that interested participants in a dispute will be able to make comments on each other's statements. Debates can be informal and private or formal and public, such as those presented for a television program audience. What all debates share is the expectation that participants with different views will have the option to comment immediately and directly on what has transpired. At the other end of the continuum from

Figure 2.1
A Taxonomy of Adversarial Relationships in Verbal Conflict

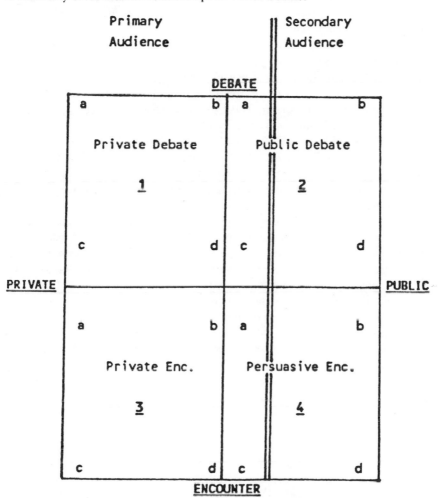

debate is the *encounter* which occurs in a setting where no formal role of opposition is assigned to (or emerges from) another person. The simplest kind of encounter occurs when a persuader is given an opportunity—usually a formal speech or direct access to a mass medium—to make a statement to a group whose members may disagree with what they hear but who are cast in the role of relatively passive listeners. Such a setting reduces the risk of challenge by an ideological opponent. Encounters thus allow advocates to gain a sustained hearing without the requirement to adjust their responses to the challenges of a specific rhetorical competitor. The simple model in Figure 2.1 shows the possibilities that emerge when these two audience-related continuums are combined.

Exchanges on the top *debate* cells (1 and 2) are largely governed by the interrogatories of formal opponents. Advocates in these settings must deal with counterarguments *as* they are making their own points. By contrast, the *encounters* in the bottom half (3 and 4) develop largely without such intervention. Although the audience and its views have probably been considered, no simultaneous opposition governs the flow of ideas. The lowercase letters in each cell suggest that there are degrees and permutations in each of these four settings.

To various extents, exchanges in the *private* cells (1 and 3) are limited to only one of a handful of participants. What generally makes an exchange private is the absence of significant numbers of spectators, especially the absence of news coverage that would expose the event to a secondary audience. By definition, *public* forms of conflict (2 and 4) reach larger numbers of witnesses, either immediate "primary" audiences of limited size (2–a, 2–c or 4–a, 4–c) or a secondary audience that learns about the event with the help of the media (2–b, 2–d or 4–b, 4–d).

Each of these two continuums is critical to our discussion because, as we shall see, what makes the persuasive encounter so risky is the fact that conflict must be handled by a communicator without the privacy that limits the damage caused by serious rhetorical miscalculations. What makes it potentially so rewarding is the absence of an immediate rhetorical competitor.

Consider how the nature of the audiences described by each of the quadrants defines a distinctly different environment for conflict.

1. *Private Debate.* As we have noted, differences of opinion are routinely handled in private, with messages directed to only one or a few others with different attitudes. Private debate is usually unstructured and casual. It may occasionally grow into a lengthy exchange of views, but in ordinary life it more frequently develops as a set of incomplete codes that signal differences without fully resolving them. Private debate typically occupies small amounts of the time spent together by friends, couples, siblings, and colleagues in the workplace. Like all forms of debate, the communication that takes place may involve as much expressive posturing as genuine problem solving; we often express our differences for the sheer pleasure of putting them on parade. Even so, such performances are still debates if interrogatories from one side of a dispute interrupt—and partly govern—the flow of ideas.

Countless instances of film and print fiction include scenes that speak to the universality of private conflict that sometimes spills into debate. To pick one narrow setting, it seems that life at sea has always been a preferred context for exploring confrontations. The inability of vessel-bound antagonists to escape each other has been evocative for writers of novels and screenplays, ranging from Herman Wouk's study of a crew who challenges the authority of their commander in *The Caine Mutiny* to the debate spurred by suspicions of race and status in Katherine Porter's *Ship of Fools*.[38] The heart of these and other stories lies in a series of private battles waged between a handful of adversaries. In Wouk's novel the decision to challenge the sanity of a captain starts as intense debate among a few of the officers, then spreads to a confrontation on the bridge of the ship, and finally ends in a formal military trial. In Porter's study of the transatlantic crossing of a German liner in 1933 the conflict is more subtle but no less real. The prejudice and suspicions that would eventually spill over into war are seen in miniature, in the happenstance that put fascists and their future victims on the same vessel.

2. *Public Debate.* Here, as in private debate, individuals representing different views are obliged to deal with the interrogatories of each side. The difference obviously lies in the presence of spectators, either as a primary audience sharing the same space at the same time or possibly as a secondary audience linked to the advocates through the mass media.

The existence of spectators has the obvious but important effect of enlarging the rhetorical and psychological stakes of an exchange. In a number of ways, audiences alter the rhetorical dynamics of what may still seem to be one-to-one communication. They make the expression of private or taboo feelings more difficult. They increase the likelihood that each of the participants will need to maintain his or her original positions in the interests of saving face. The presence of an audience may also have the unintended effect of turning public debates into gladiatorial exercises with a need for winners and losers and sometimes into senseless verbal retaliation. Such rhetorical fencing is now very common in broadcast political debates, but it is by no means limited to them. Even casual exchanges of views by public figures sharing the same forum can provoke differences that each advocate will try to use to his or her advantage. In his analysis of what he calls "dramatic encounters," for example, Orrin Klapp recalls the risk that every politician appearing on the platform with Louisiana governor Huey Long faced. Klapp notes that "it was hard to hold a 'safe' conversation with Huey in public, for he was always ad-libbing for the crowd; he was, to use an expressive phrase, always 'on the make.' "[39] Long enjoyed making a political point at the expense of an unwary stranger or guest.

One of the most infamous forums for contemporary political debate is "Question Time" in Britain's House of Commons. Most parliamentary systems have a similar period, but few seem so intense. During this brief but important weekly session, members of the House of Commons from the opposition parties are allowed to question the leaders of the government, including the prime minister. There is no equivalent process in the United States, one that would require a president to appear in the House of Representatives to answer questions from opposing party leaders. In the following 1978 exchange, Labor party prime minister James Callahan faced tough questions on levels of unemployment from the Conservative party leader—and future prime minister—Margaret Thatcher. As usual, the setting combined the cheerleading and rowdyness of a high school basketball game with the discussion of weighty matters of state. A BBC commentator provided the play-by-play:

*Speaker*: Mrs. Thatcher.

*BBC Commentator*: Mrs. Thatcher, the opposition leader, gets up to her dispatch box [podium], opposite the Prime Minister.

*Mrs. Thatcher*: Mr. Speaker, will the Prime Minister explain to the House why after four years of Labor Government the level of unemployment in this country . . . (shouts of "hear, hear," amid the steady din of other members expressing support or criticism for what follows) . . . is now worse than in any of our major industrial competitors. (More shouts and derision.)

*BBC Commentator*: A very short question; that's her habit.

*Mr. Callahan*: . . . part of the honorable lady's question in not true, as I think she will know when she looks up the figures. (More shouts.) . . . but of course unemployment is far too high in this country as it is throughout the western industrialized world, and it is my intention, with—I hope—the help of others in other countries to insure that there is a revival of world trade so we can get our own people back to work. Let me add one other thing. I think as a result of the sacrifices made by the British people over the last few years, it could be that next week's budget will provide a stimulus too.

*Mrs. Thatcher*: But does the Prime Minister not know that the figures I gave *are* true according to the Secretary of State for Employment: that the level of unemployment in this country is now worse than in that of any of our main industrial competitors, by quite a considerable margin? And will he explain why his policies have led to that result? (shouts and jeers)

*BBC Commentator*: The opposition leader is the one person who is allowed to follow up one supplementary [question] with another.

*Mr. Callahan*: If I look at the figures that I happen to have in front of me, I see that Canada is much worse. I take it that would be a major competitor. (shouts) I see that . . . (Shouts force him to pause.) I see that . . . I see that Italy is much worse. I take it that would be a major competitor. Oh, I see the major competitors are only those that the opposition selects. (Laughter and shouts of "hear, hear.") But I . . . (He tries to speak over general noise.) I hope that the opposition is going to accept that what we are facing is a world recession, (groans) and that a world recession demands collective international action if it is going to be overcome. And it is to that that we should be lending our efforts, together—of course—with the stimulus that we ourselves can give as a result of the success of the government's policies on inflation during the last twelve months. (Expressions of support and disbelief.)

*Speaker*: Mrs. Thatcher.

*BBC Commentator*: (over a torrent of shouting and yelling) For the third time Mrs. Thatcher comes back: the third question in a row . . . Labor [party] members getting up, not liking that . . .

*Speaker*: Order! . . . The House knows, I said before, that the Leader of the Opposition . . . (More shouts break out.) Order! . . . because it's a long established custom in this house (more protests) . . .

*BBC Commentator*: Mrs. Thatcher back in the box . . .

*Mrs. Thatcher*: According to a reply from the Secretary of State for Employment on the

30th of January, on a comparable basis the level for unemployment in Italy was 3.3 percent and [for] Great Britain 7.2 percent. We're suffering from the same world recession. *His* government is doing worse than other nations, with the single exception of Canada, which has less than half the population of ours. How does he explain this result? (shouts of support)[40]

It is little wonder that some Prime Ministers became physically ill before their weekly Question Time appearances. A process of public debate that denies the opportunity for uninterrupted speech and maximized give and take with a formidable opposition is not what many would voluntarily choose.[41]

3. *Private Encounter.* As we have seen, debates evolve when communicators view themselves as more or less equal participants in the discussion of their differences. Encounters are somewhat different. They also involve the expression of differences but in settings where—for a variety of reasons—the impulse or opportunity to match arguments with counterarguments never fully develops. The purest form of encounter is completely one way, when advocates know that there will be little or no competing commentary to alter or challenge their assertions.

What forecloses the possibility of debate? In private encounters the existence of a hierarchy or "pecking order" is usually the fundamental impediment. When rank defines a relationship, the possibilities for extended debate are usually limited. In place of an extended give-and-take among equals, the private confrontation involves more unilateral messages. In everyday life, such encounters develop largely within stratified organizations—especially businesses and public sector institutions—where responsibilities and decisions are based on hierarchical rather than democratic structures. Pay, status, job perks, and access may be governed by a pecking order that unambiguously defines authority. Thus, military recruits are not invited to negotiate the nature of their basic training, and students are not free to ignore the authority of an administrator who has imposed a punishment for an infraction of school rules. These relationships invite confrontations based on commands rather than extended dialogues. In most instances such relationships are harmless and even necessary. At their extreme, however, a superior's rhetorical domination of someone who is in no position to challenge it can be coercive and harmful.[42]

It is important to note that it is not *just* the superior who has the option of private confrontation. The arrows can flow the other way, particularly when members decide to communicate their displeasure with a particular aspect of an organization's decisions. These dissenting views are typically expressed at one time, without the expectation that they will form the basis of an ongoing debate. Dissent from a superior usually cannot be negotiated, but it can be expressed, sometimes with dramatic consequences.

Such an enforced substitution of an encounter for a debate was probably the only viable option open to Secretary of State Cyrus Vance as he prepared to resign over a major disagreement with President Jimmy Carter. Vance had grown frustrated with the administration's 1980 decision to go forward with a military plan to rescue some of the American hostages who were being held in Iran. Concern for the safety of the hostages had become a public obsession, forcing Carter and his aids to formulate a daring rescue plan by a Marine tactical unit. Vance privately stated his doubts about the scheme. But, as Carter later wrote, the secretary "was alone in his opposition to the rescue mission among all my advisers, and he knew it."[43] His options were limited by the circumstances of the moment. Presidents may talk of the need for vigorous discussion and "the airing of all sides" prior to a major decision, but few aides want to engage in extended debate with the president. Once Vance confronted Carter with his objections, his only other option was to put the matter behind him or resign. He stayed on for only a short time, long enough to see the rescue mission abandoned in the Iranian desert.

The pressure for conformity that exists as a countervailing force against private encounters has been the subject of study by organizational theorists for years. As Irving Janis has noted, organizations naturally have a "concurrence-seeking" bias that weighs in against potential dissenters, a fact of life that helps explain another ill-fated political fiasco approved by two presidents: the 1961 invasion of Cuba.[44] With the help of the Central Intelligence Agency, Americans had trained former Cubans living in the United States who were preparing a military invasion to reclaim Fidel Castro's island. It was a risky venture at best, made even more difficult by President Kennedy's understandable reluctance to use American power to overthrow a foreign government. It was decided to provide limited American air support for the invasion, but planning for the Bay of Pigs operation lacked the benefit of cogent dissent from Kennedy's aides.

The failure of [President] Kennedy's inner circle to detect any of the false assumptions behind the Bay of Pigs invasion plan can be at least partially accounted for by the group's tendency to seek concurrence at the expense of seeking information, critical appraisal, and debate.[45]

Like other types of verbal conflict, private encounters play an important part in fantasies communicated through the vehicles of popular culture. Americans generally assign a special place to individuals who have risked their personal safety to agitate for popular causes. When Poland's Solidarity movement used a picture of Gary Cooper in some of their 1989 posters, it struck a responsive chord. The sheriff of *High Noon* who was left to face a notorious outlaw was an ideal symbolic connection to the movement associated with Solidarity leader Lech Walesa. Many Americans probably identified similar strengths in the portrayals of struggling union leaders in the 1979 film *Norma Rae* and nuclear materials workers in the more recent *Silkwood*. Hollywood provides an important cultural yardstick for how we idealize the resolution of conflict in nondemocratic institutions. Norma Rae, portrayed by Sally Field, and Karen Silkwood, played by Meryl Streep, became heroes for the risks they took to confront the shortsightedness of their employers. Dramatizations of their private encounters made them legends. Heroes look all the more heroic for having maintained their convictions even in the absence of widespread public awareness.

4. *Persuasive Encounter.* The persuasive encounter differs in only one major respect from its private counterpart, but the difference has enormous consequences. By definition, persuasive encounters take place in the presence of witnesses, some of whom are the objects of the message and others who function as interested observers (4–a, 4–c). Robert Kennedy's addresses in South Africa cited in Chapter 1, for example, were given to local audiences composed of both hostile and sympathetic listeners. But it would be naive to conclude that he intended his comments to travel no further than the specific campuses on which he spoke. His travels were directed to several very distinct tiers of listeners and readers: to his audiences of students, to the South African government, and to citizens of other nations who might have brought pressure on Pretoria to reform.

In persuasive encounters the *primary audience*—the one to whom an advocate's message is ostensibly addressed—is sometimes unwittingly cast as part of the problem that gives urgency to the speaker's message. They can function as a kind of noncongruent backdrop that helps to define an advocate's place in a controversy. The fundamental object of the encounter may not actually be to change their attitudes as much as to create a spectacle that is worthy of news coverage. Such coverage guarantees exposure to a *secondary audience* (4–b, 4–d). There is almost always news value and curiosity in how an advocate will deal with supposedly hostile listeners.

One such instance represented in the next chapter is Senator Ted Kennedy's appearance at the college controlled by the Moral Majority's the Reverend Jerry Falwell. The liberal Kennedy believed that Falwell's advocacy of a religious test for candidates seeking public office was seriously out of step with the thinking of most Americans. An encounter in conservative Lynchburg was surely to his benefit. What better way to dramatize his message than to present it in front of his ideological opponents? If he failed to get many converts in Lynchburg, he gained national attention for giving the long-standing political rivalry between liberals and conservatives a newsworthy forum. Years earlier, John Kennedy had faced a similar group when he addressed a gathering of Houston ministers concerned about the possible negative effects of putting a Catholic in the White House. In 1960 this prejudice was a fundamental issue. But, as David Halberstam shrewdly observed,

the great inner truth about the Catholic prejudice . . . was not to hide it. Thus after getting the nomination in 1960 he was always looking for the right forum in which to confront the issue. His meeting in that year with the Houston ministers was an example of his mastery of a great new skill in televised politics: deliberately allowing someone else to rig something against you that is, in fact, rigged for you. . . . So instead of being thrown to the lions, John Kennedy was being thrown to the Christians, their turf, their anger; the angrier the questions, the ruder the hosts, the better for Kennedy, he would have the sympathy of the real audience, the one watching on television. The Houston audience was, much to its own surprise, a prop audience.[46]

The role of the mass media in creating persuasive encounters is often central to understanding their importance. Indeed, any persuasive message carried to a skeptical audience via the mass media at least nominally fits this category, even if there is no local "primary" audience. Most media forms cannot, or choose not to, handle genuine debates. The reasons are fairly simple. Very few editors or journalists are inclined to organize their reports around "long-form" discussions featuring major figures in a dispute. With some notable exceptions, different advocates are rarely given the same time and space to challenge each other's positions.[47] More basically, the very idea of an unstructured setting for dialogue violates the essence of print and television, the former with its emphasis on the sustained development of one author's view, and the latter with its demands for highly compressed and carefully paced messages. It is obvious that most forms of issue-centered media—editorials, news articles, television news reports, and commentary—cannot easily accommodate the two-way flow of ideas that is common to impromptu forms of communication. The Rather/Bush debate cited in Chapter 1 was "news" partly because it was the exception, an unscripted and "live" confrontation. Mass-mediated messages are usually immune to challenges that could alter the flow of their content. In their own time and space, they dominate rather than share their channels, a fact that has always made film, radio, and television effective avenues for commercial or political propaganda.

## The Limits of This Scheme

The symmetry of the four cells in Figure 2.1 should not imply that each of these forms occurs with equal frequency or that they represent the only mechanisms for handling conflict. In reality, most individuals deal with conflict by ignoring it or dismissing its relevance. To be intellectually engaged in a dispute requires a level of energy and a willingness to take risks that our fragile egos do not automatically provide. For this reason, theses settings represent only a small minority of instances in what is for most people a much larger arena of averted confrontations.

In addition, it would be a mistake to conclude that conflict occurs in the pure forms described above. Even carefully arranged political debates, for example, seldom achieve complete equality of participation. Dan Quayle learned that lesson in 1988 in a debate with Democratic vice presidential nominee Lloyd Bentsen. When Quayle volunteered that he had some of the same qualities and background of President Kennedy, Bentsen was able to achieve in seconds what an additional two hours might not have produced. "Senator," Bentsen began, obviously savoring Quayle's misguided vanity, "I served with Jack Kennedy. I knew Jack Kennedy. Jack Kennedy was a friend of mine. Senator, you're no Jack Kennedy."[48]

The four letters in the corners of each cell are meant to be reminders that specific events are usually hybrids. The location of 4–a, for example, suggests an encounter with perhaps some of the elements of a debate but no penetration into a secondary audience. Such was Ken Harrison's position in *Whose Life Is It Anyway?* In the context of the play, his encounter with the stern Dr. Emerson was part confrontation, part debate, but also largely private. By contrast, 4–d denotes an event—such as Robert Kennedy's South African trip—dominated by the speaker's message and relayed to a large secondary audience.

The value of all the models and schemes presented in this chapter is in understanding the partly concealed variables and unwritten rules of engagement that can shape public confrontations. More than anything else, they serve as a reminder that this book is about opportunities and audiences. The decision to stake out a controversial position in a public forum carries the prospect of using or misusing particular rhetorical opportunities. It is a decision that implies a host of contradictory demands and impulses: the recognition that the instinct for adaptation might defeat the more fragile sense of moral obligation; the prospect that failing with an immediate audience may be redeemed by the support of a secondary audience; and above all, recognition that persuasive encounters will probably test the goodwill of even the most tolerant listeners.

## NOTES

1. William Shakespeare, *Coriolanus* (New York: Signet, 1963), p. 95.

2. Kenneth Burke, "Rhetoric—Old and New," *Journal of General Education*, April 1951, p. 203.

3. A good overview of the merging of the observations of sociology and anthropology with rhetorical theory can be found in Hugh Dalziel Duncan, *Communication and Social Order* (New York: Oxford, 1968), Parts I–V.

4. Lloyd Bitzer, "The Rhetorical Situation," *Philosophy and Rhetoric*, January 1968, p. 4.

5. Erving Goffman, *Presentation of Self in Everyday Life* (New York: Anchor, 1959), pp. 17–76, 106–140.

6. David Riesman, with Nathan Glazer and Reuel Denney, *The Lonely Crowd, Abridged Edition* (New Haven: Yale, 1961), pp. 13–21.

7. Ibid., p. 23.

8. Leon Festinger, *A Theory of Cognitive Dissonance* (Stanford, Calif.: Stanford, 1957); Charles Osgood and Percy Tannenbaum, "The Principle of Congruity in the Prediction of Attitude Change," *Psychological Review* Winter 1955, pp. 42–55; Arthur R. Cohen, *Attitude Change and Social Influence* (New York: Basic, 1964), pp. 62–80. For a review of these and related "balance theorists," see Herbert W. Simons, *Persuasion: Understanding, Practice, and Analysis, Second Edition* (New York: Random House, 1986), pp. 57–67.

9. See, for example, Carolyn Sherif, Muzafer Sherif, and Roger Nebergall, *Attitude and Attitude Change: The Social Judgment-Involvement Approach* (Philadelphia: W. B. Saunders, 1965), pp. v–xv.

10. Joseph Kesselring, *Arsenic and Old Lace: A Comedy* (New York: Random House, 1941).

11. See Martin Schram, *The Great American Video Game: Presidential Politics in the Television Age* (New York: William Morrow, 1987), Parts 3, 4.

12. Mona Harrington, *The Dream of Deliverance in American Politics* (New York: Knopf, 1986), p. 16.

13. I. A. Richards, *The Philosophy of Rhetoric* (New York: Oxford, 1965), p. 3.

14. Edwin Black, *Rhetorical Criticism: A Study in Method* (Madison: University of Wisconsin, 1978), pp. 133–134.

15. Richard Sennett, *The Uses of Disorder: Personal Identity and City Life* (New York: Vintage, 1970), p. 39.

16. Ibid., p. 38.

17. Ibid., p. 135.

18. Herbert W. Simons, "Prologue," in *Perspectives on Communication in Social Conflict*, ed. Gerald R. Miller and Herbert W. Simons (Englewood Cliffs, N.J.: Prentice-Hall, 1974), p. 6.

19. W. Lloyd Warner, *The Living and the Dead: The Study of the Symbolic Life of Americans* (New Haven: Yale, 1959), pp. 16–50.

20. Ibid., p. 96.

21. Riesman, *The Lonely Crowd* p. 24.

22. Ibid., p. 25.

23. Aristotle, *The Rhetoric*, Book I, Chapter 8.

24. Kurt W. Ritter, "American Political Rhetoric and the Jeremiad Tradition: Presidential Nomination Acceptance Addresses, 1960–1976," *Central States Speech Journal* Fall 1980, p. 157.

25. Ronald Carpenter, "The Historical Jeremiad as Rhetorical Genre," in *Form and Genre: Shaping Rhetorical Action*, ed. Karlyn Kohrs Cambell and Kathleen Hall Jamieson (Falls Church, Va.: Speech Communication Association, n.d.), p. 104.

26. Ibid., p. 108.

27. Theodore Windt, Jr., "The Diatribe: Last Resort for Protest," *Quarterly Journal of Speech* February 1972, p. 5.

28. Ibid., p. 7.

29. Quoted in the Report to the National Commission on the Causes and Prevention of Violence, *Rights in Conflict* (New York: Signet, 1968), p. 68.

30. John F. Kennedy, *Profiles in Courage, Memorial Edition* (New York: Perennial Library, 1964), p. 27.

31. Ibid., p. 89.

32. Ibid., p. 185.

33. Ibid., pp. 209–210.

34. Wayne C. Booth, *Modern Dogma and the Rhetoric of Assent* (Chicago: University of Chicago, 1974), pp. ix–xvii.

35. Ibid., p. xiv.

36. See, for example, Wayne C. Booth, *Now Don't Try to Reason with Me* (Chicago: University of Chicago, 1970), Parts I, II, III; Robert L. Scott and Donald K. Smith, "The Rhetoric of Confrontation," *Quarterly Journal of Speech* February 1969, pp. 1–8; James R. Andrews, "Confrontation at Columbia: A Case Study in Coercive Rhetoric," *Quarterly Journal of Speech* February 1969, pp. 9–16; and Parke Burgess, "The Rhetoric of Moral Conflict: Two Critical Dimensions," *Quarterly Journal of Speech* April 1970, pp. 120–130.

37. Booth, *Modern Dogma* p. xiv.

38. Herman Wouk, *The Caine Mutiny* (New York: Doubleday, 1954); Katherine Anne Porter, *Ship of Fools* (New York: Signet, 1972).

39. Orrin E. Klapp, *Symbolic Leaders: Public Dramas and Public Men* (Chicago: Aldine, 1964), p. 71.

40. Transcription of Question Time, House of Commons, June 6, 1978, BBC Radio 4.

41. Gary C. Woodward, "Prime Ministers and Presidents: A Survey of the Differing Rhetorical Possibilities of High Office," *Communication Quarterly* September 1979, pp. 41–49.

42. For a case study of the effects of such coercive rhetoric, see Philip G. Zimbardo, Ebbe B. Ebbesen, and Christina Maslach, *Influencing Attitudes and Changing Behavior, Second Edition* (Reading, Mass.: Addison-Wesley, 1977), pp. 4–10.

43. Jimmy Carter, *Keeping Faith: Memoirs of a President* (New York: Bantam, 1982), p. 513.

44. Irving L. Janis, *Victims of Groupthink* (Boston: Houghton Mifflin, 1972), pp. 14–49.

45. Ibid., p. 48.

46. David Halberstam, *The Powers That Be* (New York: Knopf, 1979), pp. 325–326.

47. Some obvious exceptions include PBS's "The MacNeil-Lehrer News Hour," ABC's "Nightline," pro-con articles that appear in newspaper "op-ed" pages, and assorted radio talk shows. But it is important to note that very few media have the inclination or technology to handle genuine debate. They more typically provide short opportunities for encounters dominated by one side.

48. "Transcript of the Debate on T.V. between Bentsen and Quayle," *New York Times*, October 6, 1988, p. B22.

# 3

# Edward Kennedy: Behind Enemy Lines

I know we begin with certain disagreements; I strongly suspect that at the end of the evening some of our disagreements will remain. But I also hope that tonight and in the months and years ahead, we will always respect the right of others to differ—that we will never lose sight of our own fallibility—that we will view ourselves with a sense of perspective and a sense of humor.[1]

Edward Kennedy

In a speech that reporters variously called "improbable" and the equivalent of a "liberal Daniel venturing into a den of conservative lions," Senator Edward Kennedy addressed over 5,000 people at arch-conservative Liberty Baptist College in 1983. Reverend Jerry Falwell, the television evangelist and minister of the Thomas Road Baptist Church, built the school in 1971, partly to combat the kind of political liberalism personified by the Massachusetts senator. A page-one headline in the *Los Angeles Times* the day after the address proclaimed "Kennedy Lectures Falwell," and scores of newspapers and broadcasters followed suit with stories of this unlikely encounter. Seldom had a public event featured a speaker and audience separated by so wide an ideological gulf. With the election of Ronald Reagan in 1980, fundamentalist politicians gained a sympathetic advocate in the federal government. Opposed to almost everything advocated by many of them, Kennedy repeatedly challenged their political agenda that included federal support for school prayer, restrictions on abortions, increased military spending, and tax credits for private schools.

The invitation to address the college was triggered by an accident. A mass mailing from the Moral Majority urging thousands of Americans to join their cause inadvertently included the senator's Capitol Hill office. Always ready to poke fun at bureaucratic mistakes, Kennedy solemnly replied that it was not a surprise to find out that the Falwell organization was "not happy with Reagan." Falwell soon offered Kennedy a face-saving invitation to visit the campus, and to the surprise of many, Kennedy accepted. *Newsweek* described the address as "one of the best speeches he has ever given."[2]

Situated in the Blue Ridge Mountains on the edge of Lynchburg, Virginia, Liberty Baptist College (now "University") promises its 5,000 students academic programs "taught within the context of fundamental Christianity." Unlike Kennedy's Harvard, Liberty maintains a completely Protestant student body, requires church attendance, and bans fraternities, drinking, and mingling in its single-sex dormitories. Before Kennedy's speech, Falwell remarked to a friend, "Some of our people see him as the devil incarnate."[3] But the most liberal member of the Senate obviously sensed the possibilities of using this forum to discuss his views on religion and politics and received a standing ovation for his efforts.

The key to exploring this confrontation successfully lies as much in understanding the Kennedy image as the specific message he delivered in Lynchburg. Rarely have the personal strengths and weaknesses of a figure in American political history been so deeply entwined with his public record. By a mixture of design and accident, Kennedy's career is the product of public fantasies that stretch far beyond the issues for which he has been a passionate advocate. We start, then, with a look at the public persona that was an important context for this speech.

## THE KENNEDY ENIGMA

Few national politicians in America's recent past can claim anything like Ted Kennedy's roller-coaster ride of triumphs and defeats. Kennedy has given his friends a string of personal and professional victories to savor; but he has also provided his political enemies with an endless array of attractive targets on which to take aim. Every speech he gives takes place in the shadow of this dual legacy.

Edward Moore Kennedy is the youngest of four brothers and the only one to survive violent death through war and political assassination. He began his long career as a U.S. senator in 1963, eleven months before John F. Kennedy was assassinated in Texas and five years before Robert Kennedy was murdered while campaigning for the presidency in Los Angeles. Joe, Jr., the oldest son, had died in World War II, his plane shot down by enemy aircraft near the English Channel. "Unfortunately I'm an authority on violence and all it brings in pain and suffering," Edward Kennedy noted in a 1970 Earth Day speech at Yale. The remark was not in his prepared message, but he made it after he was interrupted by students who stormed the podium to urge violent action against the local police. This sudden seizure of the microphone took him by surprise, but the students' rhetoric of revenge struck him even more. The obvious pleasure they took in their rage was not unlike the moral certainty of a political assassin. After hearing them out, and haunted again by personal memories of senseless death, he strained to make his quivering voice finish the thought. "I do not believe that violence brings change. I believe violence brings self-indulgence . . . and there's no place for that in our society today."[4]

Even before his oldest surviving brother became president it was an obvious fact of political life that the family pedigree would carry enormous advantages and obligations. Joseph P. Kennedy had held several important posts in Franklin Roosevelt's administrations and had earned a reputation as a political and industrial opportunist. He relentlessly encouraged his sons to be ambitious, and he was not disappointed. Robert became attorney general and a close adviser in his brother's administration. This obvious nepotism created a flood of comments about aggressive exploitation of power by the Kennedys, but many Americans also had a grudging respect for the political dynasty they had created. In his first successful try for the Senate in 1962, Ted Kennedy shrewdly exploited his access to family and federal power with the campaign slogan "He can do more for Massachusetts."[5] It was a bitter campaign in which he defeated an opponent with an equally well known name, the nephew of the powerful speaker of the House of Representatives, John McCormick.

Aside from the fact that his three brothers had lost their lives in public service, two additional events shaped Kennedy's persona before 1983. One involved the circumstances surrounding the accidental death of Mary Jo Kopeckne fourteen years earlier. The second was the failed attempt to capture the Democratic party nomination in 1980 from President Jimmy Carter. The accident on Chappaquiddick Island raised serious doubts about what reporters euphemistically called the "character" issue, and the bruising campaign cast doubt on Kennedy's ability to match the political skills of his two youngest brothers.

## Chappaquiddick and a Troubled Persona

Every leader seeking national influence is the owner of both a complex personality and a public persona. Their persona includes the selective features of their personality that routinely surface in their public performances.[6] What we know about celebrities and persuaders is bound up in their persona, which ultimately acts as a filter through which all other information they communicate must pass. Politicians almost always have mixed personas; traits the public admires are usually balanced against both petty and substantial liabilities. The largely positive image of the amiable and even-tempered Ronald Reagan, for example, also had its darker side in the widespread impression that the former actor needed careful coaching from family and staff.

Every act Kennedy has undertaken since the Chappaquiddick affair has been tainted by different suspicions involving his honesty and judgment. With the exception of the Watergate debacle after 1973, perhaps no single event so persistently raised questions about the private ethics and public morality of a national leader.

Although all the details may never be known, the general facts of the accident are apparent. On July 18, 1969, Kennedy joined some of his staff members and former employees of Robert Kennedy for an evening party on Martha's Vineyard. Some of those who attended included the "boiler room girls": secretaries and assistants who had worked for R.F.K. when he was a New York senator and during his 1968 presidential campaign. The evening was intended to help ease the sense of loss they experienced by his recent death. Whether it was also another "fling" for a senator in an already strained marriage was to become the subject of endless speculation in the supermarket tabloids. Kennedy later explained that when he left the party, he offered to drive one of the women— Mary Jo Kopeckne—back to her cottage a few miles away. They never made it. Kennedy's Oldsmobile went off a narrow bridge over a tidal pond and Mary Jo drowned, unable to escape from the backseat of the car. In a speech to the citizens of Massachusetts seven days later, he offered this sequence of events:

The car overturned in a deep pond and immediately filled with water. I remember thinking as the cold water rushed in around my head that I was for certain drowning.... But somehow I struggled for the surface alive. I made immediate and repeated efforts to save Mary Jo by diving into the strong and murky current but succeeded only in increasing my state of utter exhaustion and alarm.[7]

That was sometime between 9:00 and 11:00 P.M. For reasons that are still not clear, Kennedy delayed seeking help. Twelve hours passed before he finally turned himself in at the Edgartown Police Station, eventually pleading guilty to the charge of leaving the scene of an accident.

Mary Jo's death created endless speculation. What members of the press had discussed among themselves suddenly became the presuppositions of many articles. Was his penchant for fast and reckless driving the cause of a senseless death? Were his motives less innocent than his professed intention of offering a ride to one of the "girls"? Was Kennedy's failure to report the accident immediately due to confusion or was it—like a decision he made in college to have another person take one of his exams—evidence of a failure to accept responsibility? He skillfully defended himself by making attacks on him also attacks on Mary Jo. "I know nothing in Mary Jo's conduct on that or any other occasion . . . that would lend any substance to such ugly speculation." He also emphatically denied that he was "driving under the influence of liquor."[8]

The political fallout from the entire episode was widespread. He was able to hold his seat in the Senate in 1970 but soon lost the valued position of Senate whip. Many supporters and Senate allies saw him as a less attractive advocate for their causes. The impression remained that if Kennedy was not legally guilty of a serious crime, his honesty and honor were at least suspect. The accident at Chappaquiddick gave new life to the cottage industry that prospered by exploiting suspicions about the "other women" and "ruthless opportunism" of the Kennedy brothers.

## The Struggle to Match the Legend: The Campaign of 1980

Because he decided to retrace the steps of two brothers by seeking elective office, Ted Kennedy set himself up for easy if not always fair comparisons. The public memory of J.F.K. and R.F.K. inevitably became selective. They were increasingly identified as realist-politicians who could make hard choices and stand by them. Popular books, films, and television movies drew heavily on moments from their public lives that amply displayed their intelligence, political savvy, and rhetorical eloquence. "Sound bites" of J.F.K.'s television press conferences and speeches have become video icons, touchstones to a mythologized Camelot remembered for its toughness and compassion. The president's inaugural address came to represent the transition of post–World War II American power to a younger, more activist generation. "Now the trumpet summons us again," began one of its most quoted lines, "not as a call to bear arms, though arms we need—not as a call to battle, though embattled we are—but a call to bear the burden of a long twilight struggle . . . against the common enemies of man: tyranny, poverty, disease and war itself."[9]

Throughout his own career Edward Kennedy has championed many of the same political issues, especially those that provide equal access to education and encourage federal activism to deal with social and economic injustices. But he has found it difficult to live up to the high expectations set by the selective public memory of his brothers. Many politicians are dull or inarticulate; the puzzling fact about Kennedy in the early 1980s was that he defied predictability. His 1980 keynote address at the Democratic Convention—traditionally one of the most widely reported speeches in an election year—was a rousing reaffirmation of the first principles honored by the party of Franklin Roosevelt. But the campaign during the key early Democratic primaries in the same year was a disaster. "Kennedy has always been one of the Party's most commanding speakers," Elizabeth Drew recalled at the time, "but, as was widely known, he can also stumble around and talk in semi-coherent half-sentences—and did at the outset of the campaign."[10]

Scores of confusing, vague, and shouted speeches were occasionally interrupted by moments of eloquence. The problem for Kennedy was that there was no convincing pattern of themes and no consistent rhetorical style that could provide an identifiable signature to his campaign. Patrick Devlin recalled that he frequently presented himself as "the shouter, the hopelessly inarticulate candidate who spoke in garbled sentences, the undisciplined stump speaker who often got more applause going into a speech than coming out. . . . I remember asking myself over and over as I watched Kennedy campaign, 'How can this man be so good and yet so bad?' "[11]

Typical of his problems in that year was an hour-long "CBS Reports" interview conducted by the veteran political reporter Roger Mudd. The prime-time Sunday evening broadcast was timed to coincide with Kennedy's official announcement that he would seek the Democratic nomination. Mudd's questioning was sometimes tough, touching on the considerable family turmoil created by Kennedy's separation from his wife Joan and her own problems with alcohol. But even straightforward questions exploring the candidate's presidential aspirations were answered in halting phrases and unconvincing platitudes. It was as if he had never heard the questions before or had not given much thought to a national agenda he wanted to enact as a contender for the most powerful office in the world. He was even tongue-tied on the much-discussed political violence that has haunted the Kennedy family:

*Mudd*: Of course, the risk of a third Kennedy assassination does cast a shadow over the Senator's candidacy. The senator himself, talking at his Cape Cod home, is aware of it.

*Kennedy*: I think anyone who—who had at least experienced the kind of past that I have would be quite foolish not to be mindful of the—of the dangers. I made a decision to remain in public life. I care very deeply about things that I believe in, but I don't have a —a false sense of—of—of danger on—I—I have a—a realistic assessment of it. I think if—and I'm not obsessed by it. I—I think if I was, I wouldn't be able to kind of perform in the —in the area of public life.[12]

Mudd, a longtime Kennedy friend, was privately shocked. "I was crushed at how little he gave and badly collected he seemed to be, and how in disarray he was and how weakly pulled together his thoughts were."[13]

Later Kennedy was better organized, and support for the campaign began to build. But the challenge to Jimmy Carter exacted a heavy price. By opposing the president's bid for a second term, he intensified divisions within the Democratic party. Clear proof of the damage was evidence in what should have been the party convention's high point after the renomination of Carter. Upon concluding his acceptance speech on the convention's final night, the president was left on the platform waiting for Kennedy to make a belated entrance to shake his hand. While millions of television viewers looked on, an embarrassed president of the United States played the role of a suiter left to wait too long for a suspiciously reluctant bride. No one could have missed the inescapable conclusion that the wounds in the party were deep and probably fatal to Carter's chances for reelection.

## THE PUBLICITY VALUE OF CONFRONTATION

In Washington, making news is a competitive enterprise. A federal legislator who is intent on pushing a particular political issue must not only compete with

131 others for the attention of the national press but also the president and other equally large egos in the executive agencies.

News organizations—especially television journalists—prize stories featuring oral combat. One important public forum open to a member of Congress is the committee hearing. Much of the work in the Senate and House occurs in committees jealously controlled by chairpersons with the power to "kill" or report out bills. These leaders also have the additional leverage of holding public hearings on future legislation. If they include the right mix of witnesses and advocates, hearings can be a useful way to publicize issues about which members feel strongly. The process of drafting and legislating bills is a well-known labyrinth of trap doors; few bills actually survive its rigors. But committee members who have little hope of seeing their projects enacted still use public hearings to dramatize particular harms or social conditions. Like many other Senate leaders, Kennedy has used hearings to keep his political wish list before the public: sometimes embarrassing a president reluctant to take bold action, at other times stealing some of the attention away from competing politicians with their own news agendas.

A good case in point is Kennedy's long-standing interest in proposals that would provide federal support for comprehensive medical care for all citizens. When he assumed the chairmanship of the Subcommittee on Health in 1971 he lobbied for various versions of a "Health Security Act" modeled after Social Security. Countless hearings have occurred in which individuals not covered under private health plans have testified about their inability to find and afford basic medical services. The drama of ordinary people caught in the web of a giant bureaucracy is always stirring—and all the more so if a president opposes legislation that would ostensibly help these victims. This was the case in 1978 when the Carter administration attempted to win Kennedy's support for a less expensive health plan. Kennedy's hearings had laid the groundwork for action, but he ultimately rejected a compromise with the president, even though—as Carter later recalled—"there was no prospect of congressional support for his own program."[14] But the confrontation still served the twin purpose of keeping the issue alive and maintaining the senator's persona as a committed advocate to the idea of uniform national health care.

Columnist David Broder notes that Kennedy is the "proprietor of one of the best publicity machines on Capitol Hill."[15] His staff is widely admired for its ability to prepare him for hearings, interview shows, and private meetings. The year before his Liberty Baptist speech, for example, he ranked second out of the 100 members of the Senate in the number of times he was mentioned on evening network newscasts. A year later he ranked first as the user of press conferences to explain his views and in the top three for the number of press releases made available to the press.[16] His frequent disputes with recent presidents on issues ranging from civil rights in Latin America to the appointment of federal and Supreme Court judges have enhanced his reputation as a "good story."

## THE RHETORICAL RISK TAKER

One of the most interesting features of Kennedy's public life is his willingness to cross a line that is rarely breached by other politicians. Unlike most of his counterparts who seek out friendly audiences, Kennedy has gamely appeared face to face before his critics. There is nothing especially foolhardy in this strategy; it creates dangers that can only be offset by a degree of political courage. These dangers became apparent in a dramatic 1974 confrontation over forced school busing in Boston.

Throughout the 1970s many residents in northeastern cities provided stiff resistance to court-mandated busing of public school students to achieve racial integration. The response of Boston's threatened white middle class was more intense than most. Kennedy was on record in favor of judicial decisions to desegregate individual schools that had been kept largely all white or all black by de facto segregation. His position was sharply at odds with the vast majority of constituents in the close-knit ethnic enclaves of central and south Boston. When a downtown rally was planned by busing opponents, Kennedy decided that he would attempt to appear. He was significantly at odds with many of his constituents, a fact that gave him some second thoughts. He must have wondered if any cause was served by meeting his opponents over so strong an emotional issue.

Personal events unrelated to the busing issue also made him hesitate. Reports hinting at his marital infidelity as well as Joan Kennedy's emotional problems continually dogged him. In addition, Ted, Jr., at twelve, had recently lost a leg to a rare form of cartilage cancer. Both traumas had weakened the resilient psychological armor that had served him so well in the past. Even so, he went ahead with his decision, knowing that the occasion would provide an opportunity to explain his support for judicial decisions balancing racial groups within specific schools. James MacGregor Burns described what followed after he stepped up to the microphone to address the angry crowd:

As Kennedy started to speak the crowd roared epithets and brandished signs: "IMPEACH HIM!" "SEND HIM TO ROXBURY!" "GET RID OF THE BUM." A woman shouted, "You're a disgrace to the Irish." A man tore the microphone out of Kennedy's hand; another man grabbed it and yelled for quiet, but no one heeded. Tomatoes and eggs sailed through the air and splattered on Kennedy's blue pin-stripped suit and onto his hair. The crowd began taunting him. "Why don't you put your one-legged son on a bus for Roxbury?" "Let your daughter get bussed there so she can get raped." "Why don't you let them shoot you like they shot your brothers?" The mob hounded him into the John F. Kennedy Building, shoving and kicking at him; then it pressed against a large plate glass window and shattered it with feet and fists.[17]

Kennedy finally gave up his attempt to be heard. "Anybody in public life has to expect this," he said afterward. Yet even this veteran political warrior must have grown weary of the hostile protesters that shadowed him everywhere—to political meetings, to visits at the homes of friends, even to church—in the months that followed.

More productive were other appearances that challenged the orthodoxies of a diverse range of hostile audiences, including a speech before a gathering of the Veterans of Foreign Wars urging that they reverse their decision to oppose amnesty for men who refused to serve during the Vietnam War. In 1973 he surprised and angered many of his supporters when he accepted an invitation to speak to supporters of former segregationist Alabama governor George Wallace. And in an antigun speech to the avidly progun National Rifle Association, he argued for legislation to reduce one of the highest murder rates in the world. "The question before us is a simple one," he told the gun users. "Are the possible minor inconveniences too great for the sportsman to bear if they can prevent children, convicted felons, and the mentally ill from mailing away for guns whenever the spirit moves them?"[18]

Biographer Burton Hersh has aptly described Kennedy as a "quiet brawler."[19] He sees no virtue in conflict for conflict's sake, but like most senators with high national visibility, he recognizes that the strategies of dissent or attack can help frame the public debate on national issues. Even powerful members of Congress know that their clout to get things done is based partly on their ability to influence the national news agenda.

## LIBERTY BAPTIST AND THE MORAL MAJORITY

People who write about politics frequently overstate the differences between various competing constituencies. But it would be a mistake to underestimate the huge expanse that separated Kennedy from his Lynchburg audience. In a very real sense Liberty Baptist's Moral Majority was a half a world away from Ted Kennedy's Boston, far more distant than the short Washington-to-Lynchburg flight provided to the senator on Jerry Falwell's private jet.

Liberty Baptist sits in a vastly different time and place from the mainstream of American life. Falwell once noted that he was trying to build a "fundamentalist Harvard" on the outskirts of Lynchburg, but it was to be a very different institution from the nation's first college. In 1983 the school accepted only "born-again" students who were prepared to give up many of the traditional perks of college life, including dancing, drinking, and movies. All who enrolled were expected to work at Falwell's Thomas Road Baptist Church and take courses in religious instruction. About 1,000 of the 4,300 students attending the college in 1983 were studying for the ministry.[20]

Falwell's school also symbolized the growth of what was for many political leaders a disturbing sense of absolute certainty about the "right" and "wrong" sides of complex political issues. His supporters represented a considerable political threat to many incumbents. In the last half of the 1970s and until 1988 the Moral Majority and other evangelical Christian groups were intensely active in local and national politics.[21] While most mainstream Protestant churches and some evangelicals maintained a clear separation of the church from political action, a number of fundamentalists including Pat Robertson, Falwell, and others increasingly argued that public policy and Christian morality were insep- arable. Issues such as rights for homosexuals, school prayer, and abortion were defined as both state *and* church issues. One of Falwell's first successes occurred in 1978, when he lent his support to the efforts of Anita Bryant to help defeat a gay rights ordinance and the Equal Rights Amendment in Florida.[22] From this start the Moral Majority and a loose confederation of allied organizations worked tirelessly to energize evangelicals across the nation to become involved in the selection of political candidates at all levels of government. They were helped enormously by like-minded industrialists such as Amway's Richard DeVos and by political professionals like direct-mail specialist Richard Viguerie. "Mo- rality ratings" of members of Congress were established, and the most liberal members were targeted for defeat.[23] An elaborate national network of churches became nominal parts of the movement, along with thousands of enthusiastic viewers of the "700 Club," "The Old Time Gospel Hour," and the Christian Broadcasting Network.

Dramatic evidence of the political gap between the world of the Moral Majority and Kennedy's beliefs is suggested in the annual ratings of members of Congress that are given by political action groups at opposite ends of the political spectrum. In 1983 Kennedy had received a high approval rating of 85 percent from the liberal Americans for Democratic Action; his Senate votes corresponded with their position most of the time. By contrast, the ideological twin of many of Liberty's staff and students, the Americans for Constitutional Action, gave him a dismal 5 percent rating. Similarly, on social and economic issues, he had a perfect score of 100 percent from the AFL–CIO but a low 22 from the U.S. Chamber of Congress.[24] Specific issues like the popular nuclear freeze resolutions that were introduced in Congress and local legislatures in 1982 and 1983 became measures of political purity. In contrast to many in the religious right, Kennedy supported the idea of an immediate stop to the building, testing, and deployment of American nuclear weapons.

The gap between Kennedy's and Falwell's personal histories was also enor- mous, even if partially concealed in the speech. A Catholic in a failed marriage, Kennedy was invited to address fundamentalists who were deeply suspicious about the mysteries and foreign rituals of the Roman Catholic church. He was the quintessential northeastern liberal—the champion of the use of federal power to ensure equal treatment for minorities such as homosexuals and blacks—but he was speaking to a predominantly white audience at a college started by a former segregationist. The speech pitted the defender of Americans pushing at the limits of social convention against an audience imbued with a strict code of piety. For most members of Kennedy's reluctant audience, the diversity of Amer- ican life required reform and forgiveness rather than a live-and-let-live tolerance. His belief that it was a grave error to provide a "religious test" for political ideas came to its hearers in sharp contrast to the Moral Majority's goal of defining political positions in terms of their biblical and moral correctness.

Then why did he face this audience? What did he seek to gain? First, he knew the event would be newsworthy, guaranteeing that even if the message was lost on the immediate audience, it would have an impact on others who learned about the speech the following day. Second, Kennedy could be reasonably sure that he would receive a respectful hearing. Falwell had been booed and shouted down when he tried to speak at Harvard University the previous April. "Hitler, Falwell, go to Hell" and "Racist, fascist pig" were a couple of the epitaphs hurled from some of the 1,000 Harvard students who heard him speak.[25] But Harvard's counterparts at Liberty were not likely to reciprocate. The same strict code of conduct that required men students to wear ties to class and forbid dating by freshmen and sophomore women would also ensure that there would be no public rudeness.[26] Third, Kennedy's passionate belief in pluralist politics made the speech a perfect opportunity. The Moral Majority had targeted a number of legislators for defeat by more conservative Christian politicians. Despite evidence today that the religious Right has had only limited success in defeating their enemies, there was proof enough in the stunning 1980 victory of Ronald Reagan. As Kennedy and his staff prepared the draft of the speech, their hopes were probably modest. Little did they realize just how well it would play to the 5,000 people who heard it first-hand and to the press that reported excerpts in the days that followed.

After he was introduced, Kennedy offered several humorous preliminary remarks. He noted, first, that a number of his friends were surprised that he accepted the invitation. "They seemed to think that it's easier for a camel to pass through the eye of a needle than for a Kennedy to come to the campus of Liberty Baptist College."[27] He also noted that he had offered Falwell a deal: If the leader of the school would lift the curfew for the upcoming Saturday night, Kennedy promised he would watch "The Old Time Gospel Hour" on Sunday morning. The audience thundered its approval. He then went on to observe that his speech would not be political. "Since I'm not a candidate for President," he noted, "it certainly would be inappropriate to ask for your support in this election, and probably inaccurate to thank you for it in the last one."

As is common with many national politicians giving major addresses, he used a TelePrompTer: a small video machine that projects the text of a speech on panes of glass fixed to both front corners of the podium. A mirrored finish on the speaker's side of the TelePrompTer reflects the one-inch-high letters of the text, whereas audience members see only transparent glass. Common in television, this device gives a speaker the freedom to look at the audience *and* the text of a message at the same time. Even with this help, however, Kennedy haltingly read through parts of the half-hour speech. At times the wording seemed unfamiliar; at other times a persistent cough interrupted the flow of ideas.

## THE SPEECH[28]

[1] I have come here to discuss my beliefs about faith and country, tolerance and truth in America. I know we begin with certain disagreements; I strongly suspect that at

the end of the evening some of our disagreements will remain. But I also hope that tonight and in the months and years ahead, we will always respect the right of others to differ—that we will never lose sight of our own fallibility—that we will view ourselves with a sense of perspective and a sense of humor. After all, in the New Testament, even the disciples had to be taught to look first to the beam in their own eyes, and only then to the mote in their neighbor's eye.

[2]   I am mindful of that counsel. I am an American and a Catholic; I love my country and treasure my faith. But I do not assume that my conception of patriotism or policy is invariably correct—or that my convictions about religion should command any greater respect than any other faith in this pluralistic society. I believe there surely is such a thing as truth, but who among us can claim a monopoly on it?

[3]   There are those who do, and their own words testify to their intolerance. For example, because the Moral Majority has worked with members of different denominations, one fundamentalist group has denounced Dr. Falwell for hastening the ecumenical church and for "yoking together with Roman Catholics, Mormons, and others." I am relieved that Dr. Falwell does not regard that as a sin—and on this issue, he himself has become the target of narrow prejudice. When people agree on public policy, they ought to be able to work together, even while they worship in diverse ways. For truly we are all yoked together as Americans—and the yoke is the happy one of individual freedom and mutual respect.

[4]   But in saying that, we cannot and should not turn aside from a deeper, more pressing question—which is whether and how religion should influence government. A generation ago, a presidential candidate had to prove his independence of undue religious influence in public life—and he had to do so partly at the insistence of evangelical Protestants. John Kennedy said at that time: "I believe in an America where there is no (religious) bloc voting of any kind." Only twenty years later, another candidate was appealing to an evangelical meeting as a religious bloc. Ronald Reagan said to 15 thousand evangelicals at the Roundtable in Dallas: "I know that you can't endorse me. I want you to know that I endorse you and what you are doing."

[5]   To many Americans, that pledge was a sign and a symbol of a dangerous breakdown in the separation of church and state. Yet this principle, as vital as it is, is not a simplistic and rigid command. Separation of church and state cannot mean an absolute separation between moral principles and political power. The challenge today is to recall the origin of the principle, to define its purpose, and refine its application to the politics of the present.

[6]   The founders of our nation had long and bitter experience with the state as both the agent and the adversary of particular religious views. In colonial Maryland, Catholics paid a double land tax, and in Pennsylvania they had to list their names on a public roll—an ominous precursor of the first Nazi laws against the Jews. And Jews in turn faced discrimination in all the thirteen original colonies. Massachusetts exiled Roger Williams and his congregation for contending that civil government had no right to enforce the Ten Commandments. Virginia harassed Baptist preachers—and also established a religious test for public service, writing into the law that no "Popish followers" could hold any office.

[7]   But during the revolution, Catholics, Jews and non-conformists all rallied to the cause and fought valiantly for the American commonwealth—for John Winthrop's "city upon a hill." Afterwards, when the Constitution was ratified and then amended, the

framers gave freedom for all religion—and from any established religion—the very first place in the Bill of Rights.

[8]   Indeed the framers themselves professed very different faiths—and in the case of Benjamin Franklin, hardly any at all. Washington was an Episcopalian, Jefferson a deist, and Adams a Calvinist. And although he had earlier opposed toleration, John Adams later contributed to the building of Catholic churches—and so did George Washington. Thomas Jefferson said his proudest achievement was not the Presidency, or writing the Declaration of Independence, but drafting the Virginia Statute of Religious Freedom. He stated the vision of the first Americans and the First Amendment very clearly: "The God who gave us life gave us liberty at the same time."

[9]   The separation of church and state can sometimes be frustrating for women and men of deep religious faith. They may be tempted to misuse government in order to impose a value which they cannot persuade others to accept. But once we succumb to that temptation, we step onto a slippery slope where everyone's freedom is at risk. Those who favor censorship should recall that one of the first books ever burned was the first English translation of the Bible. As President Eisenhower warned in 1953, "Don't join the bookburners . . . the right to say ideas, the right to record them, and the right to have them accessible to others is unquestioned—or this isn't America." And if that right is denied, at some future day the torch can be turned against any other book or any other belief. Let us never forget: today's Moral Majority could become tomorrow's persecuted minority.

[10]   The danger is as great now as when the founders of the nation first saw it. In 1789, their fear was of factional strife among dozens of denominations. Today there are hundreds—and perhaps thousands of faiths—and millions of Americans who are outside any fold. Pluralism obviously does not and cannot mean that all of them are right; but it does mean that there are areas where government cannot and should not decide what it is wrong to believe, to think, to read and to do. . . .

[11]   The real transgression occurs when religion wants government to tell citizens how to live uniquely personal parts of their lives. The failure of Prohibition proves the futility of such an attempt when a majority or even a substantial minority happens to disagree. Some questions may be inherently individual ones, or people may be sharply divided about whether they are. In such cases—cases like Prohibition and abortion—the proper role of religion is to appeal to the conscience of the individual, not the coercive power of the state.

[12]   But there are other questions which are inherently public in nature, which we must decide together as a nation, and where religion and religious values can and should speak to our common conscience. The issue of nuclear war is a compelling example. It is a moral issue; it will be decided by government, not by each individual; and to give any effect to the moral values of their creed, people of faith must speak directly about public policy. The Catholic Bishops and the Reverend Billy Graham have every right to stand for the Nuclear Freeze—and Dr. Falwell has every right to stand against it.

[13]   There must be standards for the exercise of such leadership—so that the obligations of belief will not be debased into an opportunity for mere political advantage. But to take a stand at all when a question is both properly public and truly moral is to stand in a long and honored tradition. Many of the great evangelists of the 1800s were in the forefront of the abolitionist movement. In our own time, the Reverend William Sloane Coffin challenged the morality of the war in Vietnam. Pope John XXIII renewed

the Gospel's call to social justice. And Dr. Martin Luther King, Jr., who was the greatest prophet of this century, awakened our national conscience to the evil of racial segregation.

[14]   Their words have blessed our world. And who now wishes they had all been silent? Who would bid Pope John Paul to quiet his voice about the oppression in eastern Europe; the violence in Central America; or the crying needs of the landless, the hungry, and those who are tortured in so many of the dark political prisons of our time?

[15]   President Kennedy, who said that "no religious body should seek to impose its will," also urged religious leaders to state their views and give their commitment when the public debate involved ethical issues. In drawing the line between imposed will and essential witness, we keep church and state separate—and at the same time, we recognize that the city of God should speak to the civic duties of men and women.

[16]   There are four tests which draw that line and define the difference. First, we must respect the integrity of religion itself. People of conscience should be careful how they deal in the word of their Lord. In our own history, religion has been falsely invoked to sanction prejudice and even slavery, to condemn labor unions and public spending for the poor. I believe that the prophecy "The poor you have always with you" is an indictment, not a commandment. I respectfully suggest that God has taken no position on the Department of Education—and that a balanced budget constitutional amendment is a matter for economic analysis, not heavenly appeals.

[17]   Religious values cannot be excluded from every public issue—but not every issue involves religious values. And how ironic it is when those very values are denied in the name of religion—for example, we are sometimes told that it is wrong to feed the hungry— but that mission is an explicit mandate given to us in the 25th Chapter of Matthew.

[18]   Second, we must respect the independent judgments of conscience. Those who proclaim moral and religious values can offer counsel, but they should not casually treat a position on a public issue as a test of fealty to faith. Just as I disagree with the Catholic Bishops on tuition tax credits—which I oppose, so other Catholics can and do disagree with the hierarchy, on the basis of honest conviction, on the question of the Nuclear Freeze.

[19]   Thus, the controversy about the Moral Majority arises not only from its views, but from its name—which, in the minds of many, seems to imply that only one set of public policies is moral— and only one majority can possibly be right. Similarly, people are and should be perplexed when the religious lobbying group Christian Voice publishes a morality index of Senators by their attitudes toward Zimbabwe and Taiwan.

[20]   Let me offer another illustration. Dr. Falwell has written—and I quote: "To stand against Israel is to stand against God." Now there is no one in the Senate who has stood more firmly for Israel than I have. Yet I do not doubt the faith of those on the other side. Their error is not one of religion, but of policy—and I hope to persuade them that they are wrong in terms of both America's interest and the justice of Israel's cause.

[21]   Respect for conscience is most in jeopardy—and the harmony of our diverse society is most at risk—when we re-establish, directly or indirectly, a religious test for public office. That relic of the colonial era, which is specifically prohibited in the Constitution, has reappeared in recent years. After the last election, the Reverend James Robison warned President Reagan not to surround himself, as Presidents before him had, "with the counsel of the ungodly." I utterly reject any such standard for any position anywhere in public service. Two centuries ago, the victims were Catholics and Jews. In the 1980s, the victims could be atheists; in some other day or decade, they could be the members of the Thomas Road Baptist Church. Indeed, in 1976 I regarded it as unworthy and un-American when some people said or hinted that Jimmy Carter should not be President because he was a born-again Christian.

We must never judge the fitness of individuals to govern on the basis of where they worship, whether they follow Christ or Moses, whether they are called "born again" or "ungodly." Where it is right to apply moral values to public life, let all of us avoid the temptation to be self-righteous and absolutely certain of ourselves. And if that temptation ever comes, let us recall Winston Churchill's humbling description of an intolerant and inflexible colleague: "There but for the grace of God—goes God."

[22]   Third, in applying religious values, we must respect the integrity of public debate. In that debate, faith is no substitute for facts. Critics may oppose the Nuclear Freeze for what they regard as moral reasons. They have every right to argue that any negotiation with the Soviets is wrong—or that any accommodation with them sanctions their crimes— or that no agreement can be good enough and therefore all agreements only increase the chance of war. I do not believe that, but it does not violate the standard of fair public debate to say it.

[23]   What does violate that standard, what the opponents of the Nuclear Freeze have no right to do, is to assume that they are infallible—and so any argument against the freeze will do, whether it is false or true. The Nuclear Freeze proposal is not unilateral, but bilateral— with equal restraints on the United States and the Soviet Union. The Nuclear Freeze does not require that we trust the Russians, but demands full and effective verification. The Nuclear Freeze does not concede a Soviet lead in nuclear weapons, but recognizes that human beings in each great power already have in their fallible hands the overwhelming capacity to remake into a pile of radioactive rubble the earth which God has made. There is no morality in the mushroom cloud. The black rain of nuclear ashes will fall alike on the just and unjust. And then it will be too late to wish that we had done the real work of the atomic age—which is to seek a world that is neither red nor dead. . . .

[24]   . . . As Pope John said two decades ago, at the opening of the second Vatican Council: "We must beware of those who burn with zeal, but are not endowed with much sense. . . . We must disagree with the prophets of doom, who are always forecasting disasters, as though the end of the earth was at hand." The message which echoes across the years since then is clear: the earth is still here; and if we wish to keep it, a prophecy of doom is no alternative to a policy of arms control.

[25]   Fourth and finally, we must respect the motives of those who exercise their right to disagree. We sorely test our ability to live together if we too readily question each other's integrity. It may be harder to retrain our feelings when moral principles are at stake—for they go to the deepest wellsprings of our being. But the more our feelings diverge, the more deeply felt they are, the greater is our obligation to grant the sincerity and essential decency of our fellow citizens on the other side.

[26]   Those who favor E.R.A. are not "anti-family" or "blasphemers" and their purpose is not "an attack on the Bible." Rather we believe this is the best way to fix in our national firmament the ideal that not only all men, but all people are created equal. Indeed, my mother—who strongly favors E.R.A.—would be surprised to hear that she is anti-family. For my part, I think of the Amendment's opponents as wrong on the issue, but not as lacking in moral character.

[27]   I could multiply the instances of name-calling, sometimes on both sides. Dr. Falwell is not a "warmonger"— and "liberal clergymen" are not, as the Moral Majority suggested in a recent newsletter, equivalent to "Soviet sympathizers." The critics of official prayer in public schools are not "pharisees"; many of them are both civil libertarians and believers, who think that families should pray more at home with their children, and attend church and synagogue more faithfully. And people are not "sexist" because they

stand against abortion; they are not "murderers" because they believe in free choice. Nor does it help anyone's cause to shout such epithets—or try to shout a speaker down—which is what happened last April when Dr. Falwell was hissed and heckled at Harvard. So I am doubly grateful for your courtesy here today. That was not Harvard's finest hour, but I am happy to say the loudest applause from the Harvard audience came in defense of Dr. Falwell's right to speak. In short, I hope for an America where neither fundamentalist nor humanist will be a dirty word, but a fair description of the different ways in which people of good will look at life and into their own souls.

[28]  I hope for an America where no President, no public official, and no individual will ever be deemed a greater or lesser American because of religious doubt—or religious belief. I hope for an America where the power of faith will always burn brightly—but where no modern inquisition of any kind will ever light the fires of fear, coercion, or angry division. I hope for an America where we can all contend freely and vigorously—but where we will treasure and guard those standards of civility which alone make this nation safe for both democracy and diversity.

[29]  Twenty years ago this fall, in New York City, President Kennedy met for the last time with a Protestant assembly. The atmosphere had been transformed since his earlier address during the 1960 campaign to the Houston Ministerial Association. He had spoken there to allay suspicions about his Catholicism—and to answer those who claimed that on the day of his baptism, he was somehow disqualified from becoming President. His speech in Houston and then his election drove that prejudice from the center of our national life. Now, three years later, in November, 1963, he was appearing before the Protestant Council of New York City to reaffirm what he regarded as some fundamental truths. On that occasion, John Kennedy said: "The family of man is not limited to a single race or religion, to a single city or country. . . . The family of man is nearly 3 billion strong. Most of its members are not white—and most of them are not Christian." And as President Kennedy reflected on that reality, he restated an ideal for which he had lived his life—that "the members of this family should be at peace with one another."

[30]  That ideal shines across all the generations of our history and all the ages of our faith, carrying with it the most ancient dream. For as the Apostle Paul wrote long ago in Romans: "If it be possible, as much as it lieth in you, live peaceably with all men."

[31]  I believe it is possible; the choice lies within us; as fellow citizens, let us live peaceably with each other; as fellow human beings, let us strive to live peaceably with men and women everywhere. Let that be our purpose and our prayer—yours and mine—for ourselves, for our country, and for all the world.

## POSSIBLE EFFECTS

Estimations of the impact of a single message on an audience are notoriously suspect, largely because one event is rarely capable of changing deeply felt attitudes. Persuasive effects are best understood as the products of *repeated* exposures to similar messages. Falwell clearly understood this pattern of incremental change. "If one liberal Pied Piper can come to Liberty Baptist College and in one speech steal away the spiritual and intellectual loyalties of our students," he noted, "then I and this college's faculty have not done our job."[29] Even so, Kennedy must have been pleased by the immediate public and press reception to his remarks. Although there were probably many students like the one who said that she disagreed "with everything" he had to say,[30] audience and press comments were usually more positive. One listener remarked afterward that she expected the senator's speech to be "a lot more radical than it was." Another noted that he "was surprised that he was so candid about what he believed."[31] Many listeners who had prepared themselves to dislike the Massachusetts Democrat seemed surprised by the conciliatory tone of his remarks. When his appearance failed to match what his detractors might have hoped, the result was probably to produce at least a temporary level of goodwill. Minutes after the speech one audience member noted, "My mind was changed toward him because of what he had to say, rather than listening to what everybody else had to say."[32]

Kennedy also had reason to be gratified about press coverage of the address. The immediate conservative audience was—to some extent—the right manufactured *context* rather than the sole *reason* for the comments. They gave the speech news value. The nation's largest news service, the Associated Press, carried the story, as did many other newspapers such as the *Chicago Tribune*, and *Philadelphia Inquirer*, and the *Los Angeles Times*.[33] Other news organizations focused precisely on Kennedy's main thesis: that groups like Falwell's Moral Majority were misguided if they intended to impose religious doctrine on complex political issues. The opening lines of paragraph 21 warning against a religious test for public office was the "sound bite" used in National Public Radio's coverage. Similarly, under the headline "Kennedy Lectures Falwell," the *Los Angeles Times* described portions of the speech emphasizing Kennedy's challenge to the Moral Majority and downplaying his more conciliatory remarks.

As to longer-term effects, a number of later events were probably altered by the speech and its extensive press coverage. This appearance paved the way for a second meeting in 1985, when Falwell and Kennedy addressed the annual meeting of the Religious Broadcasters Association. At that conference Falwell praised Kennedy for showing how it is possible to "prayerfully and intelligently" debate facts without name-calling and rancor: "I think we owe a lot of that instruction, information and example to the Senator Kennedys of our day who have been doing it that way for a long time."[34] In addition, one of Kennedy's objections to the Moral Majority was satisfied in 1986. Falwell changed his organization's name to the Liberty Foundation. No doubt sensitive to criticisms from Kennedy and scores of others about the presumption of a one-group "moral majority," he found it easier to adopt a term that carried less of a self-righteous tone. For a portion of Americans, the address probably also softened Kennedy's persona as an amoral political operator. But one of its most interesting effects might have been on the senator himself. It solidly committed him to active support for formal religion as a major force in the discussion of political issues. Perhaps more than many of his Senate colleagues would have wished, he affirmed the place of religious faith—if not coercive lobbying by organized churches—in a secular society.

## THE ANATOMY OF A SUCCESSFUL CONFRONTATION

The objectives and strategies in this lucid speech are never very far from the surface. There is no concealed magic at work; its plea for tolerance is skillfully and clearly drawn in observable stages. Kennedy began his remarks by professing goodwill toward the audience and by finding humor in what others had judged about their unlikely meeting. He offered a history lesson on the venerable American tradition separating church and state, without oversimplifying difficulties in drawing the line. The last half of the speech identified an ideal threshold that should separate legitimate political debate from what he viewed as more dubious religious tests of politicians and policy. Historical precedents were used to legitimize his ideas. He then amplified his theme with examples and simple references to values with wide appeal.

The speech is also interesting for what is not said. Kennedy shunned two nonproductive areas where little impact could probably have been made. He was careful to avoid making himself the issue. For example, there was no attempt to justify recent votes in the Senate. Nor did he make the speech a vehicle for arguing a political issue. A few lines of support in favor of a nuclear freeze are the closest he came to outright political advocacy [23]. He used most of his time to focus on the idea that the mixture of politics with organized religion usually ends up serving neither area very well.

The news media generally framed the Liberty speech for the public as a dramatic showdown between two political rivals, but that emphasis alone probably owed more to the possibility than the actuality of confrontation. No one present could have missed the gently worded but evident condemnation of the Moral Majority for concealing a political agenda behind a "self-righteous" false front of religious piety. (See especially paragraphs 2, 9–11, 19–26.) Yet, taken as a whole, the event serves as a good reminder that persuasion is as much a matter of accommodation as gladiatorial argument.

Press reports usually alluded to Kennedy's largely charitable attribution of the Moral Majority's motives, but most did not explore the sometimes ingenious ways he adapted his message to his audience. For example, Kennedy noted that the Moral Majority has itself been singled out for unfair attack—from groups as diverse as other fundamentalists [3] to audiences at Harvard [27]. Early on he made it clear that religious values are legitimate principles for anchoring public discussion of certain issues [12–15]. He stated several times that public dialogue has been enriched by the participation of religious leaders, ranging from Billy Graham to Pope John Paul to the Reverend William Sloane Coffin all of whom, not so accidentally, have taken positions at sharp odds with the views of the Moral Majority. He also established himself as a religious man. "I am an American and a Catholic"; he reminded them, "I love my country and treasure my faith"[2]. He skillfully used his own piety to combat what he believed to be their errant piety, thus taking away a key counterargument the Moral Majority has used against its foes, namely, that those who speak for "liberal" positions are "godless" and "secular."

## Building on Sturdy Commonplaces

A *commonplace* is a statement that expresses a value or first principle that is widely shared in a society or a tightly knit group within it.[35] The persuader's art frequently rests in the ability to identify commonplaces held in high mutual respect by both persuader and audience and in showing how they fit with an attitude the audience does *not* hold in high respect. Kennedy never allowed his message to drift very far from the safety of these core ideas, but he frequently suggested that they could be legitimately tied to his own conclusions. The four "tests" that he cited to separate "essential witness" from "imposed will" show a pattern of reasoning from nearly universal commonplaces to novel conclusions. The first starts from the universally accepted commonplace that "we must respect the integrity of religion itself"[16]. No one in the hall could have dissented from such a view, and yet Kennedy took this principle in a direction that challenged much of the political program of the Moral Majority:

People of conscience should be careful how they deal in the word of their Lord. In our own history, religion has been falsely invoked to sanction prejudice and even slavery, to condemn labor unions and public spending for the poor. . . . I respectfully suggest that God has taken no position on the Department of Education—and that a balanced budget constitutional amendment is a matter for economic analysis, not heavenly appeals.[16]

A second "test" worked in the same way. "We must respect independent judgments of conscience" is an irrefutable expression of goodwill and fair play. But Kennedy used this commonplace to suggest that the name of Falwell's organization implicitly denies the value of individual dissent and conscience:

Thus, the controversy about the Moral Majority arises not only from its views, but from its name—which, in the minds of many, seems to imply that only one set of public policies is moral—and only one majority can possibly be right.[19]

Having laid this groundwork, he made the only direct personal challenge to the minister of the Thomas Road Baptist Church in the entire speech: "Dr. Falwell has written—and I quote: 'to stand against Israel is to stand against God.' Now there is no one in the Senate who has stood more firmly for Israel than I have." Again, a key commonplace surfaced, this time the reminder that a different political position is not necessarily immoral: "Yet I do not doubt the faith of those on the other side. Their error is not one of religion, but of policy"[20]. One student's remark that Kennedy presented his ideas "in a way that was very easily accepted from a conservative point of view" illustrates how commonplaces can solidify support.[36]

While members of the audience expected that they would disagree with Kennedy, they were left with a sermon couched in the irrefutable mainstream virtues of tolerance, separation of church and state, and the principle of fair play. The ironic effect of the message's appeals to these core values created a subtle reversal of the participant's perceived roles. In the small world of this speech Kennedy became the protector of the status quo, whereas the Moral Majority emerged as the agent of unwanted change. Jerry Falwell was implicitly cast as a political radical tampering with cherished traditions that the senator sought to uphold.

## Hitting the Right Word Notes

There are other levels at which the speech probably affected the audience. A persuasive message is always more than ideas. As with all communication, some of the content that breaks through into consciousness is not in the accumulated meaning of complex sentences but in the potent meanings of discrete symbols. For example, we often read advertising copy selectively, focusing on verbal and visual images that strike a responsive chord. In an automobile ad, the "look" and demeanor of an attractive model may carry the message about what the car "says" about its owners. A car ad is usually not just about hardware, but about style communicated symbolically.

Similarly, a part of the way persuasion works is through key words that evoke images for which an audience has a strong sense of identity. A key word is a symbol—a noun, verb, or adjective—that has the power to economically call up strong positive or negative feelings when used in a certain context. Key words do more than name; they serve as condensations of strong emotions identified with special groups bound together by the same beliefs, experiences, or fantasies. They may act as in-group code words expressing bonds of kinship, as well as shared traumas and triumphs.[37] Kennedy's supporters, for example, probably responded (in this context) to "intolerance" as an especially apt representation of the danger the rise of the Moral Majority represented for liberals. For their part, the very different immediate audience no doubt found positive recognition in his use of the phrases "obligations of belief" and "essential witness." Both phrases are parts of a verbal signature that an overtly religious person might leave. Kennedy used their literal meanings to communicate a sense of piety and to signal an active faith that has not fallen into dormancy. Allies and skeptics of the senator undoubtedly heard other key words as well that offered treats and reassurances:

| Opponents of the Moral Majority | The Moral Majority |
|---|---|
| Tolerance and intolerance [1, 3] | Moral principles [5] |
| separation of church and state [5] | Women and men of deep |
| bookburners [9] | religious faith [9] |
| Pluralism [10] | Coercive power of the state [11] |
| Self-righteous [21] | Essential witness [15] |

Modern inquisition [28]

Fundamentalist [3]

Humanist [27]

Censorship [9]

Religious values [12]

Obligations of belief [13]

Evangelical Protestants [4]

At one point he made this kind of analysis of evocative words part of the overt content of the message. He focused on negative terms that had been the basis of a long process of name-calling by both liberals and conservatives:

Those who favor E.R.A. are not "anti-family" or "blasphemers" and their purpose is not "an attack on the Bible.". . . Dr. Falwell is not a "warmonger"—and "liberal clergymen" are not, as the Moral Majority suggested in a recent letter, equivalent to "Soviet sympathizers.". . . And people are not "sexist" because they stand against abortion; they are not "murderers" because they believe in free choice.[26, 27]

## Intentional Hedging?

Kennedy surely intended to mix together key terms representing the two different factions he sought to influence. Throughout the half hour, the speech was laced with symbols intended to appeal both to his immediate audience (i.e., "men and women of deep religious faith") and to the extended audience who may have harbored suspicions about "self-righteous" 'bookburners." Persuasion to hostile audiences usually contains such a stew of images, some of which are close to the author's ideology and some that have been borrowed from the internal vocabulary of the audience.

This is a point made in an extensive and thorough analysis of the speech by Robert Branham and W. Barnett Pearce.[38] They conclude that Kennedy's remarks are less notable as a defense of ideas than as an attempt to lessen hostility between the religious Right and political liberals. Their point that Kennedy and Falwell wanted to end senseless name-calling is a valuable one and is clearly evident in a number of passages (notably 1, 27, and 31). But their emphasis results in an underestimation of the consistently forceful argumentation that Kennedy developed. One of their main conclusions is that the message did not significantly challenge the actions of the Moral Majority. Instead of a message of confrontation, they argue, Kennedy put together a speech that would attempt to satisfy his supporters, the public at large, *and* the immediate audience in Lynchburg. His arguments were "masterfully ambiguous." He "does not offer significant challenge to the professed beliefs of his immediate audience."[39] They imply that Kennedy softened his arguments by allowing the speech to carry "different meanings for multiple audiences."[40]

The observation that politicians hedge on their beliefs to win as many supporters as possible is a familiar one and could be fairly adopted to some of Kennedy's earlier addresses.[41] But it is important here to distinguish between accommodation and ambiguity as different persuasive strategies. There can be little doubt here that Kennedy attempted to accommodate key principles he held in common with his audience, but it does not follow that the address was ambiguous. A speech that honors certain characteristics in an audience does not necessarily weaken the criticisms that may follow. Indeed, the reverse may be just as true; compliments may actually make criticism more meaningful. Compliments provide psychological rewards for their recipients that can later be bartered in the process of coaxing them to see "fair" criticism.

This principle can be considered from another angle. There is an interesting pattern in the message that follows a conciliation-contention sequence. (See especially paragraphs 2, 13, 15, 17, and 18.) Implied agreement about a common value is frequently followed by condemnation or disagreement on a related point. In ordinary life this pattern may take the form of the comment: "You are my best friend and nothing will come between us, but . . . " What follows after the opening assertion of friendship may be a criticism or a reprimand. For most listeners, the effect of such a sequence is cumulative rather than ambiguous. Such comments are not seen as ambiguous as much as they are viewed as part of the ritual of nonabusive conflict. For example, two major threads running through the speech are the contentions that "the city of God should speak to the civic duties of men and women"[15] and the very different point that a serious "transgression occurs when religion wants government to tell citizens how to live uniquely personal parts of their lives"[11]. Both ideas reappear several times, but they are not contradictory. Used together, the complementary first statement *sanctions* the criticism implied by the second statement. Together they defined a coherent position of criticism directed to some evangelicals, including—by inference—the Moral Majority. Kennedy used the speech to praise the use of religious values in the assessment of public policy. At the same time, however, he took pains to point out that religious beliefs should not be used to dictate what is right and fitting for others. "The proper role of religion," he noted, "is to appeal to the conscience of the individual, not the coercive power of the state"[11].

President Kennedy, who said that "no religious body should seek to impose its will," also urged religious leaders to state their views and give their commitment when the public debate involved ethical issues. In drawing the line between imposed will and essential witness, we keep church and state separate—and at the same time, we recognize that the city of God should speak to the civic duties of men and women.[15]

In short, while the theme of conciliation runs through Kennedy's remarks, that fact does not lessen the integrity of the address as a forceful refutation of several core beliefs held by many members of the audience. If the speech had a fault, it was perhaps that the threshold separating "witnessing" and "imposing one's will" was too subtle and too undeveloped for so brief a time frame. At its best, the speech was much more than a net of safe ideas designed to capture Kennedy's supporters and mute his political opponents. It remains as a model of how fundamental political differences can be defined in the context of shared values and principles.

## NOTES

1. Edward M. Kennedy, "Tolerance and Truth in America" (Speech at Liberty Baptist College, October 3, 1983). Mimeographed text. Text supplied by Senator Edward M. Kennedy.

2. "A Moral Victory?" *Newsweek*, October 17, 1983, p. 30.

3. Ibid.

4. Edward M. Kennedy, "Earth Day Address," April 22, 1970, reprinted in L. Patrick Devlin, ed., *Contemporary Political Speaking* (Belmont, Calif.: Wadsworth, 1971), p. 126.

5. Burton Hersh, *The Education of Edward Kennedy* (New York: William Morrow, 1972), p. 167.

6. For a more detailed discussion of the nature of the public persona, see Edwin Black, "The Second Persona," *Quarterly Journal of Speech*, April 1970, pp. 109–119.

7. Kennedy, "Statement to the People of Massachusetts," reprinted in Herbert W. Simons, *Persuasion: Understanding, Practice, and Analysis, Second Edition* (New York: Random House, 1986), p. 295.

8. Ibid.

9. John F. Kennedy, "Let Us Begin," reprinted in Theodore Windt, ed., *Presidential Rhetoric: 1961–1980, Second Edition* (Dubuque, Iowa: Kendall/Hunt, 1980), p. 11.

10. Elizabeth Drew, *Portrait of an Election: The 1980 Presidential Campaign* (New York: Simon and Schuster, 1981), p. 249.

11. L. Patrick Devlin, "An Analysis of Kennedy's Communication in the 1980 Campaign," *Quarterly Journal of Speech*, November 1982, p. 397.

12. "CBS Reports: Teddy," November 4, 1979.

13. Mudd quoted in Devlin, "An Analysis of Kennedy's Communication in the 1980 Campaign," p. 406.

14. Jimmy Carter, *Keeping Faith: Memoirs of a President* (New York: Bantam, 1982), p. 87.

15. David S. Broder, *Behind the Front Page* (New York: Simon and Schuster, 1987), p. 231.

16. Stephen Hess, *The Ultimate Insiders: U.S. Senators in the National Media* (Washington, D.C.: Brookings, 1986), p. 136.

17. James MacGregor Burns, *Edward Kennedy and the Camelot Legacy* (New York: W. W. Norton, 1976), p. 205.

18. Ibid., p. 223.

19. Hersh, *The Education of Edward Kennedy*, p. 440.

20. Ron Lee, "Falwell's College Strives to Become a Fundamentalist University Serving 50,000," *Christianity Today*, November 25, 1983, pp. 39–42.

21. In November 1987, Falwell announced his intention to retire from politics to devote all of his time to preaching. See Wayne King, "Falwell Quits as Moral Majority Head," *New York Times*, November 4, 1987, p. A14.

22. Robert C. Liebman, "Mobilizing the Moral Majority," in *The New Christian*

*Right: Mobilization and Legitimation*, ed. Robert C. Liebman and Robert Wuthnow (New York: Aldine, 1983), p. 59.

23. James L. Guth, "The New Christian Right," in ibid., pp. 24–35.

24. Alan Ehrenhart, ed., *Politics in America, 1986* (Washington, D.C.: Congressional Quarterly Press, 1985), p. 694.

25. Dinesh D'Souza, "Falwell at Harvard: Hisses and Jeers, and Even a Few 'Amens,' " *Christianity Today*, June 17, 1983, p. 41.

26. For a comprehensive overview of Liberty Baptist College and the Moral Majority in the early 1980s, see Frances FitzGerald, *Cities on a Hill* (New York: Simon and Schuster, 1986), pp. 121–193.

27. Kennedy quoted from a videotape of the speech "Contemporary American Speeches," Educational Video Group, 1988.

28. This slightly edited version of the speech is taken from a manuscript supplied by Senator Edward Kennedy. All paragraphs have been numbered. Just how much of the address studied here is the actual handiwork of the senator is difficult to say. Given the senator's high profile and schedule, it is doubtful that Kennedy was the only contributor here. Speech writers have long been a fact of life in most American political institutions. If their presence sometimes makes it difficult to guarantee the authenticity of a politician's verbal style, there is still the reasonable expectation that political speeches carry the general intentions and perspectives of their speaker–authors. For two different views on this problem, see Ernest G. Bormann, "Ghostwriting and the Rhetorical Critic," *Quarterly Journal of Speech*, October 1960, pp. 284–288; and Robert E. Denton, Jr., and Gary C. Woodward, *Political Communication in America* (New York: Praeger, 1985), pp. 263–269.

29. Quoted in Robert J. Branham and W. Barnett Pearce, "A Contract for Civility: Edward Kennedy's Lynchburg Address," *Quarterly Journal of Speech*, November 1987, p. 433.

30. Harriet Randolph, "Kennedy Lectures Falwell," *Los Angeles Times*, October 4, 1983, p. 7.

31. "All Things Considered," National Public Radio, October 4, 1983.

32. Ibid.

33. See, for example, Randolph, "Kennedy Lectures Falwell," pp. 1, 7; Jose Margolis, "Teddy Goes to Moral Majority Country to Praise and Condemn," *Chicago Tribune*, October 4, 1983, p. 14; and David Espo, "Kennedy Speaks at Falwell's College," *Philadelphia Inquirer*, October 4, 1983, p. 7A.

34. Branham and Pearce, "A Contract for Civility," p. 425.

35. For a discussion of commonplaces in persuasion, see Gary C. Woodward and Robert E. Denton, Jr., *Persuasion and Influence in American Life* (Prospect Heights, Ill.: Waveland, 1987), pp. 74–77.

36. "All Things Considered."

37. A useful overview of evocative words used as symbols of threat or reassurance is offered by Murray Edelman, *The Symbolic Uses of Politics* (Urbana, Ill.: University of Illinois, 1967), pp. 5–29.

38. Branham and Pearce, "A Contract for Civility," pp. 424–443.

39. Ibid., p. 432.

40. Ibid., p. 440.

41. See Kennedy, "Statement to the People of Massachusetts," in Simons, *Persuasion*, pp. 294–297.

# 4

# "This Just Might Do Nobody Any Good": Edward R. Murrow and the News Directors

Our history will be what we make it. And if there are any historians about fifty or a hundred years from now, and there should be preserved the kinescopes for one week of all three networks, they will there find recorded in black and white, or color, evidence of decadence, escapism, and insulation from the realities of the world in which we live.[1]

*Edward R. Murrow*

From the beginning of World War II until his death in 1965, no American broadcaster had ever known as much power or national prestige as Edward R. Murrow. He was an institution not only at CBS but to the nation as a whole. In a 1957 cover story, *Time* magazine called him "TV's top journalist" and the "VIP's VIP."[2] His lean features framed in the smoke of a cigarette instantly signaled his presence. Murrow was the rarest of intellects: a man who could translate his intelligence into remarkable fluency without sounding stuffy or borish. There are now Murrow schools of journalism and Murrow awards. Modern industry giants ranging from the British Broadcasting Corporation (BBC) to cable television's Home Box Office (HBO) have broadcast dramatizations of his unique and outsized career as a war correspondent and the conscience of electronic journalism. The major networks are now much stricter in what they will allow their best and brightest to do and say, but between 1939 and 1959, CBS gave Murrow much freer reign. He was a reporter, commentator, documentary producer, newscaster, and celebrity interviewer. In our time network superstars such as Dan Rather, Bryant Gumble, and Ted Koppel all have their own special functions. In Murrow's day he did them all.

This chapter explores Murrow's public reputation and the events that led up to a remarkable 1958 speech attacking his own industry. His message is still a timely reminder of the dilemmas poised when news is viewed as a commodity that must compete with entertainment for audience attention. It is also proof that the right message at the right time can endure as a touchstone for others still engaged in the same battles.

## THE 'SPINE' OF BROADCASTING

Most Americans first came to know Ed Murrow when CBS chairman William Paley hired him to report from Britain in the early days of World War II. His accounts of Nazi air raids, sometimes daringly broadcast from the roof of the British Broadcasting Corporation's office in central London, created an enormous following in the United States. For millions of listeners, they became stunning testimony of the courage of not only Londoners but of Ed Murrow as well. British leaders realized that no previous efforts to mobilize American public opinion to enter the war was as effective as the verbal imagery created by this correspondent. It was as if Murrow's resonant baritone and gift for clear narrative had been wedded to the cool persona of Humphrey Bogart. As writer Archibald MacLeish later noted in his own simple tribute, Americans were mesmerized by his accounts of German air assaults on the British Isles.

You burned the city of London in our houses and we felt the flames that burned it. You laid the dead of London at our doors and we knew the dead were our dead—were all men's dead—were mankind's dead. . . . Without rhetoric, without dramatics, without more emotion than needed be, you destroyed the superstition of distance and of time.[3]

Murrow reported first on radio and then on the new medium of television. He had misgivings about adapting his style of journalism to a video format, but somehow his concerns translated into the impression that he was not a performer but a communicator for whom ideas and issues always came first. He used this self-effacing style to good effect, exploring problems ranging from the excesses of Senator Joe McCarthy's paranoia over communism to an unrelenting 1960 study of the mistreatment of migrant workers in the United States.

The latter program, appropriately called "Harvest of Shame," was aired on the CBS television network the day after Thanksgiving. It was part of the landmark "CBS Reports" series produced by Murrow's longtime friend and colleague Fred Friendly and is an especially good example of why Murrow became America's most influential journalist. Typically, he focused his lean but unflinching commentary on a dark corner of American life. To much of the world, the inexpensive and plentiful food produced by American agriculture was a phenomenon to envy. But it came at a price. With the groundwork for the program laid out by

David Lowe—who traveled with the workers for nearly a year—Murrow took his viewers through dusty fields and migrant-worker camps from Florida to New Jersey. What they saw was not reassuring. The hour-long program confronted viewers with images of children working long hours in the fields and the prematurely aged faces of their destitute parents. They were often underpaid and forgotten. Their broken-down shacks without indoor plumbing and lack of schools only dramatized their poverty. It was obvious that prosperous growers used substandard labor camps to exploit the cheap labor of unorganized workers, a view of American agriculture that was at sharp odds with the reassuring symbols of Thanksgiving. The program also suggested that government agencies such as the Department of Agriculture had far more interest in farm owners than in their temporary workers. Friendly notes that it was

Murrow's kind of story, and as he stood in the rich Florida farmland describing the dawn shape up, all the anger and eloquence of Steinbeck's *Grapes of Wrath* seemed to emerge. Together Murrow and Lowe fashioned a document of man's exploitation of man that was full of anguish and outrage. When it was broadcast on the day after Thanksgiving, it shocked millions of viewers.[4]

For all its journalistic success, "Harvest of Shame" also illustrated a basic dilemma of broadcasting that still remains; namely, the more hard-hitting and journalistically sound a documentary is, the more it may seem to executives to undermine a network's commercial success. Any news program that criticizes a practice of an industry or a significant portion of the population is likely to alienate advertisers and their audiences. By criticizing the agriculture industry's use of cheap labor, "CBS Reports" predictably raised the hackles of several network sponsors. A tobacco company that carried advertising in the program made its displeasure known to CBS and felt obligated to apologize to growers for its participation.[5] This tension between advertisers and programmers constantly bedeviled Murrow throughout his career.

## THE "PERSON TO PERSON" MONEY MACHINE

From management's standpoint, the solution to the problem of unwanted controversy is simply to avoid it or trivialize it—a fact of life that explains why prime-time melodramas, video gossip programs, and simpleminded fantasies are still better vehicles for selling advertising minutes than hard-hitting documentaries. Murrow was both a victim of this dilemma and one of its best delineators. He gained varying degrees of support from CBS to produce radio and television programs on topics as diverse as police corruption, the dubious military justice system, and the dangers of smoking, but he also hosted a popular celebrity interview show entitled "Person to Person." The gulf separating that program from "CBS Reports" was as wide as a small ocean. "Person to Person" was better than most routine programs of its day, but it was still devoid of any serious content. Its celebrity interviews featured a half hour of painless and superficial pleasantries with the kinds of popular personalities who would today adorn the cover of *People Magazine*. Even when the guests were politicians or writers rather than film actors, the conversation never went much beyond what the rich and famous did for relaxation, what their work routines were like, and how they arrived at the name of the family dog. *New Yorker* critic John Lardner observed the program had "a ruthless way of impairing the dignity and impairing the personalities of some of the noblest thinkers at CBS."[6] Even Murrow was sometimes embarrassed by it.[7] The same journalist who had open invitations from heads of state and the admiration of leaders in politics and the sciences also made weekly appearances in which he would be called upon to admire the Hungarian salami stored away in Zsa Zsa Gabor's refrigerator.

"Person to Person" had huge weekly audiences, far larger than "See It Now" or "CBS Reports." The exposure gave Murrow clout with the network and a salary higher than CBS's chairman of the board. In addition, he kept several radio commentary programs that maintained the intellectual rigor that he prized. "Person to Person" was always his most popular effort but never his only one. It was only to coworkers and friends that the ever-brooding Murrow expressed concerns about the irony of his situation. He knew that high broadcast ratings did not always mean high purpose, but he also knew that networks constantly concerned about angering viewers and advertisers were likely to be more tolerant of a reporter who could point to popular success. "Listen," he once told a friend, "do you know what I can get away with because *Person to Person* is a big hit?"[8]

## THE PATRON AND THE IDEALIST

Murrow's patron throughout most of his life was board chairman William Paley. The son of a Philadelphia cigar maker, the outgoing Paley had built CBS from the humble origins of a few radio stations into a giant that challenged the reigning NBC radio network. He was a master salesman destined to make the new medium of television the ultimate merchandising medium of all time. While he privately accumulated one of the best private collections of modern art, he never lost his ability to judge the kinds of popular entertainment that would satisfy the escapist cravings of huge broadcast audiences. He drew on his early experience of selling La Palina cigars to establish the revolutionary idea that strategically placed thirty-second commercials could be worth thousands of dollars. Paley was unsurpassed in his skill of convincing skeptical industrialists that buying so ephemeral a quantity as time was actually a shrewd business decision. When he hired the former Washington State College speech student who had spent his summers working as a lumberjack, it was an unlikely marriage of commercialism and idealism. In 1935 Murrow had no interest in business and was planning a career as an academic. But Paley's money funded a new kind of news organization that would virtually reinvent the profession of journalism for the microphone and the small screen.

World War II made broadcast news a vital coequal with entertainment pro-gramming, and Paley generously funded CBS News by giving Murrow the freedom to hire talented newcomers to the air, including Charles Collingwood, Eric Sevareid, Howard K. Smith, William Shirer, and others. The quality and independence of this core staff set an early tradition of aggressive reporting and editorial independence. CBS's long-running "60 Minutes" and ABC's "Night-line" are most clearly the heirs to this tradition. But with notable exceptions, such as PBS's Bill Moyers, it is hard to identify many contemporary reporters who are given air-time to explore the same eclectic range of political and social issues.

For a considerable time the Paley-Murrow alliance remained strong, but it began to crack in the early 1950s and finally came apart in 1961. The journalist who had reported so vividly on Nazi death camps, on Britain's valiant battle to outlive German airstrikes, and on the remaking of the European map after the war now intended to bring the same intense reporting to national issues at home. But Paley was operating under different pressures. His CBS television network was launched with the firm goal of beating the better-financed and technically dominant NBC. Paley believed that Americans had grown weary of the world's political upheavals. The prospect of more sober voices telling the nation what was wrong with their society was not what he nor audience-research expert Frank Stanton had in mind for the 1950s. Stanton, who became president of CBS, was especially convinced that the future of radio and television was largely in entertainment for escape rather than news for information. As the decade un-folded, Murrow slowly became an outsider to this increasingly pervasive industry mind-set that relegated news and documentary programming to their roles as loss leaders for more profitable entertainment programs. Stanton's audience rating numbers were a constant reminder to members of the news division that they were far less popular with viewers than Burns and Allen or Jack Benny. The biggest blow came when "See It Now" was removed from the regular television schedule in 1958. The weekly half-hour program had been Murrow's prime outlet for creative interviews and documentaries, but it was clear that its focus on social problems and political controversies made advertisers nervous. Paley never questioned the value of CBS News, but he was unwilling to continue to give Murrow and others the airtime they had previously enjoyed. The issue came to a head in a showdown between Murrow and Paley in the chairman's office.

"Bill," Murrow pleaded at one point, "are you going to destroy all this? Don't you want an instrument like the See It Now organization, which you have poured so much into for so long, to continue?"

"Yes," said Paley, "but I don't want this constant stomachache every time you do a controversial subject."

"I'm afraid that's a price you have to be willing to pay. It goes with the job."[9]

If Murrow needed further evidence that the commercial success of television was threatening hard-hitting probes at the realities of American life, the end of "See It Now" provided it. Television critic John Crosby wrote that the show was "by every criterion television's most decorated, most imaginative, most courageous and most important program." He expressed dismay that CBS could not afford it but could justify a witless game show called "Beat the Clock."[10]

In his memoirs, Paley conceded that his differences with Murrow "were sometimes very strong," especially after Murrow's 1958 speech to the Radio and Television News Directors. "I was extremely hurt by it . . . ,[but] Murrow would not have been Murrow nor I myself if we had not had differences of opinion."[11] The address hit a raw nerve by representing American broadcasting as an industry that put its obligations to public service second to profits and by suggesting that its management was shortsighted. The long-simmering Murrow frustration at having an important news service tied to the vagaries of show business had finally surfaced in a public statement that implicitly made villains of Paley and other top network executives.

The year was 1958, and Murrow was at both the high point and the denouement of his career. His prestige had never been greater. It probably was no comfort to CBS management that their best-known journalist probably carried more credibility than most members of President Dwight D. Eisenhower's administration. But he was also slowed down by his feuds with Paley and Stanton and growing health problems. He was to later take some time off from broadcasting to join the Kennedy administration as director of the United States Information Agency. After Kennedy's assassination in 1963, he returned to private life and to semiretirement on his farm in upstate New York. By then Murrow had patched up some of his differences with Paley, hastened perhaps by the knowledge both shared that Murrow would not survive much longer. The famous trademark of a cigarette wrapped in the slim fingers of his left hand had finally taken its toll. Murrow died of lung cancer in 1965.

## BROADCASTING AND THE RTNDA

As one of the most visible members of a major news organization, Murrow regularly received invitations to address conventions and professional groups. He usually turned them down, but on short notice he decided to accept a request to address the October meeting of the Radio and Television News Directors Association at Chicago's Sheraton Blackstone Hotel. By modern standards the group was small: Perhaps 400 attendees and assorted guests crowded into the ornate Mayfair Room. Most of those attending were news executives, producers, and reporters from the nation's larger radio and television stations. The five-day convention held to the rituals of past meetings. News awards were presented to individuals and stations, and delegates attended several dozen meetings. An advertising agency vice president led a panel entitled "News: Radio's Most Salable Product." Reporters participated in sessions on "Small Station Election Coverage," "Legal Aspects of Campaign Coverage," "Covering Cape Canaveral," and "Why News Audiences Mean More to Advertisers."[12] Chicago mayor Richard Daley gave a welcoming address when the convention opened on Wednesday, and Murrow followed at 9:00 P.M. with an address that few could have anticipated.

The delegates were meeting at a time of unprecedented fortune and change in the broadcast industry. In 1958 nearly every American home had one television set. And although radio was in the midst of its own identity crisis—television had taken over much of its network talent—broadcasting as a whole was bursting with success. Annual television revenues exceeded $1 billion for the first time.[13] Ranking third only to the necessities of sleep and work, gazing at the small screen had taken its place as *the* dominant American pastime. On most evenings families could be found huddled in front of the glowing box, entertained by westerns, adventures, comedies, and game shows. A new crime-adventure program about the prohibition era called "The Untouchables" gave upstart ABC a big boost in its competition with CBS and NBC. "I Love Lucy" and a program about a talking horse called "Mr. Ed" continued to attract families and younger viewers. The newest video sensations, however, were game shows with fantastic dollar amounts riding on correct answers.

The "$64,000 Question" was true to its title: Ordinary people could win that amount by correctly answering a single question. The program mesmerized viewers, who rearranged PTA, church, and civic meetings to be home on Tuesday nights. What the audience did not know, but would learn in 1958, was that it and other popular quiz programs were rigged. After several years of rumors, congressional investigators learned that advertisers had the power to tell dull contestants when to lose and photogenic ones when to win. That revelation and the resulting public suspicions about broadcast ethics would devastate CBS and the rest of the industry.[14]

As popular as the game shows were, even more viewers were watching westerns, which galloped across the screen during nearly every hour of prime time. "Wyatt Earp," "The Rifleman," "Gunsmoke," "Death Valley Days," and "Have Gun— Will Travel" kept viewers occupied with simplified images and occasional facts about the Old West. With other half-hour slices of escape and fantasy, westerns created stiff competition for news divisions asked to produce documentaries and interview shows that could bring in audiences of equal size. Murrow and other "intellectuals" in broadcasting had barely concealed their disdain for these prime-time cartoons. But they were unable to refute the marketing logic that made escapist television so perfect a vehicle for selling large audiences to advertisers. Murrow's speech was a frontal assault on that reasoning.

Murrow was too sophisticated a newsman to miss the opportunity to extend the audience for his remarks. He treated the address as more than a routine appearance before a professional gathering. The preparation and delivery of the double-spaced text conformed to patterns used by politicians or presidents who were about to make a major policy address. Copies were distributed for 9:00 P.M.

release to the press and to CBS management back in New York.[15] He took special care to make arrangements with the journalism weekly *The Reporter* to publish the remarks. In addition, the *New Republic* and *Reader's Digest* (with its enormous national circulation) also reprinted sections of it. He knew that his half-hour sermon would itself become a news event.

## THE SPEECH[16]

[1]   This just might do nobody any good. At the end of this discourse a few people may accuse this reporter of fouling his own comfortable nest; and your organization may be accused of having given hospitality to heretical and even dangerous thoughts.

[2]   But the elaborate structure of networks, advertising agencies, and sponsors will not be shaken or altered. It is my desire, if not my duty, to try to talk to you journeymen with some candor about what is happening to radio and television in this generous and capacious land.

[3]   I have no technical advice or counsel to offer those of you who labor in this vineyard that produces words and pictures. You will forgive me for not telling you that the instruments with which you work are miraculous; that your responsibility is unprecedented; or that your aspirations are frequently frustrated. It is not necessary to remind you—the fact that your voice is amplified to the degree where it reaches from one end of the country to the other does not confer upon you greater wisdom or understanding than you possessed when your voice reached only from one end of the bar to the other. All of these things you know.

[4]   You should also know at the outset that, in the manner of witnesses before Congressional committees, I appear here voluntarily—by invitation—that I am an employee of the Columbia Broadcasting System, that I am neither an officer not a director of that corporation, and that these remarks are of a "do-it-yourself" nature. If what I have to say is responsible, then I alone am responsible for the saying of it. Seeking neither approbation from my employers, nor new sponsors, nor acclaim from the critics of radio and television, I cannot well be disappointed. Believing that potentially the commercial system of broadcasting as practiced in this country is the best and freest yet devised, I have decided to express my concern about what I believe to be happening to radio and television. These instruments have been good to me beyond my due. There exist in my mind no reasonable grounds for personal complaint. I have no feud, either with my employers, any sponsors, or with the professional critics of radio and television. But I am seized with an abiding fear regarding what these two instruments are doing to our society, our culture, and our heritage.

[5]   Our history will be what we make it. And if there are any historians about fifty or a hundred years from now, and there should be preserved the kinescopes for one week of all three networks, they will there find recorded in black-and-white, or color, evidence of decadence, escapism, and insulation from the realities of the world in which we live. I invite your attention to the television schedules of all networks between the hours of eight and eleven p.m. Eastern Time. Here you will find only fleeting and spasmodic reference to the fact that this nation is in mortal danger. There are, it is true, occasional informative programs presented in that intellectual ghetto on Sunday afternoons. But

during the daily peak viewing periods, television in the main insulates us from the realities of the world in which we live. If this state of affairs continues, we may alter an advertising slogan to read: "Look Now, Pay Later." For surely we shall pay for using this most powerful instrument of communication to insulate the citizenry from the hard and demanding realities which must be faced if we are to survive. I mean the word—"survive"—literally. If there were to be a competition in indifference, or perhaps in insulation from reality, then Nero and his fiddle, Chamberlain and his umbrella, could not find a place on an early-afternoon sustaining show [a sustaining program is run without advertising and usually deals with political or national issues]. If Hollywood were to run out of Indians, their program schedules would be mangled beyond all recognition. Then some courageous soul with a small budget might be able to do a documentary telling what in fact we have done—and are still doing—to the Indians in this country. But that would be unpleasant. And we must at all costs shield the sensitive citizens from anything that is unpleasant.

[6]   I am entirely persuaded that the American public is more reasonable, restrained, and more mature than most of our industry's program planners believe. Their fear of controversy is not warranted by the evidence. I have reason to know, as do many of you, that when the evidence on a controversial subject is fairly and calmly presented, the public recognizes it for what it is—an effort to illuminate rather than to agitate. . . .

[7]   The oldest excuse of the networks for their timidity is their youth. Their spokesmen say: "We are young; we have not developed the traditions nor acquired the experience of the other media." If they but knew it, they are building those traditions, creating those precedents every day. Each time they yield to a voice from Washington or any political pressure, each time they eliminate something that might offend some section of the community, they are creating their own body of precedent and tradition. They are, in fact, not content to be "half safe."

[8]   Nowhere is this better illustrated than by the fact that the Chairman of the Federal Communications Commission publicly prods broadcasters to engage in their legal right to editorialize. Of course, to undertake an editorial policy, overt and clearly labeled, and obviously unsponsored, requires a station or a network to be responsible. Most stations today probably do not have the manpower to assume this responsibility, but the manpower could be recruited. Editorials would not be profitable; if they had a cutting edge they might even offend. It is much easier, much less troublesome, to use the money-making machine of television and radio merely as a conduit through which to channel anything that is not libelous, obscene, or defamatory. In that way one has the illusion of power without responsibility.

[9]   So far as radio—that most satisfying and rewarding instrument—is concerned, the diagnosis of its difficulties is rather easy. And obviously I speak only of news and information. In order to progress it need only go backward—to the time when singing commercials were not allowed on news reports; when there was no middle commercial in a fifteen-minute news report; when radio was rather proud, alert, and fast. I recently asked a network official, "Why this great rash of five minute news reports (including three commercials) on weekends?" He replied: "Because that seems to be the only thing we can sell."

[10]   In this kind of complex and confusing world, you can't tell very much about the why of the news in broadcasts where only three minutes is available for news. The only man who could do that was Elmer Davis, and his kind aren't about any more. If radio news is to be regarded as a commodity, only acceptable when salable, and only

when packaged to fit the advertising appropriation of a sponsor, then I don't care what you call it—I say it isn't news. . . .

[11]   One of the minor tragedies of television news and information is that the networks will not even defend their vital interests. When my employer, CBS, through a combination of enterprise and good luck, did an interview with [Soviet premier] Nikita Krushchev, the President [Eisenhower] uttered a few ill-chosen, uninformed words on the subject, and the network practically apologized. This produced a rarity. Many newspapers defended the CBS right to produce the program and commended it for initiative. But the other networks remained silent.

[12]   Likewise when [Secretary of State] John Foster Dulles, by personal degree, banned American journalists from going to Communist China and subsequently offered contradictory explanations . . . the networks entered only a mild protest. Then they apparently forgot the unpleasantness. Can it be that this national industry is content to serve the public interest only with the trickle of news that comes out of Hong Kong? To leave its viewers in ignorance of the cataclysmic changes that are occurring in a nation of six hundred million people? I have no illusions about the difficulties of reporting from a dictatorship; but our British and French allies have been better served—in their public interest—with some very useful information from their reporters in Communist China.

[13]   One of the basic troubles with radio and television news is that both instruments have grown up as an incompatible combination of show business, advertising, and news. Each of the three is a rather bizarre and demanding profession. And when you get all three under one roof, the dust never settles. The top management of the networks, with a few notable exceptions, has been trained in advertising, research, sales, or show business. But by the nature of the corporate structure, they also make the final and crucial decisions having to do with news and public affairs. Frequently they have neither the time nor the competence to do this. It is not easy for the same small group of men to decide whether to buy a new station for millions of dollars, built a new building, alter the rate card, buy a new Western, sell a soap opera, decide what defensive line to take in connection with the latest Congressional inquiry, how much money to spend on promoting a new program, what additions or deletions should be made in the existing covey or clutch of vice-presidents, and at the same time—frequently on the same long day—to give mature, thoughtful consideration to the manifold problems that confront those who are charged with the responsibility for news and public affairs.

[14]   Sometimes there is a clash between the public interest and the corporate interest. A telephone call or a letter from the proper quarter in Washington is treated rather more seriously than a communication from an irate but not politically potent viewer. It's tempting enough to give away a little air time for frequently irresponsible and unwarranted utterances in an effort to temper the wind of criticism.

[15]   Upon occasion, economics and editorial judgment are in conflict. And there is no law which says that dollars will be defeated by duty. Not so long ago the President of the United States delivered a television address to the nation. He was discoursing on the possibility or probability of war between this nation and the Soviet Union and Communist China—a reasonably compelling subject. Two networks—CBS and NBC—delayed that broadcast for an hour and fifteen minutes. If this decision was dictated by anything other than financial reasons, the networks didn't deign to explain those reasons. That hour-and-fifteen minute delay, by the way, is about twice the time required for an ICBM to travel from the Soviet Union to major targets in the United States. It is difficult to believe that this decision was made by men who love, respect, and understand news.

[16]  . . . There is no suggestion here that networks or individual stations should operate as philanthropies. But I can find nothing in the Bill of Rights or the Communications Act which says that they must increase their net profits each year, lest the Republic collapse. I do not suggest that news and information should be subsidized by foundations or private subscriptions. I am aware that the networks have expended and are expending very considerable sums of money on public affairs programs from which they cannot hope to receive any financial reward. I have had the privilege at CBS of presiding over a considerable number of such programs. I testify and am able to stand here and say that I never had a program turned down by my superiors because of the money it would cost.

[17]  But we all know that you cannot reach the potential maximum audience in marginal time with a sustaining program. This is so because so many stations on the network—any network—will decline to carry it. Every licensee who applied for a grant to operate in the public interest, convenience, and necessity makes certain promises as to what he will do in terms of program content. Many recipients of licenses have, in blunt language, welshed on those promises. The money-making machine somehow blunts their memories. The only remedy for this is closer inspection and punitive action by the FCC. But in the view of many this would come perilously close to supervision of program content by a Federal agency.

[18]  So it seems that we cannot rely on philanthropic support or foundations subsidies, we cannot follow the "sustaining route," the networks cannot pay all the freight, and the FCC cannot or will not discipline those who abuse the facilities that belong to the public.

[19]  What then is the answer? Do we merely stay in our comfortable nests, concluding that the obligation of these instruments has been discharged when we work at the job of informing the public for a minimum of time? Or do we believe that the preservation of the Republic is a seven-day-a-week job, demanding more awareness, better skills, and more perseverance than we have yet contemplated?

[20]  I am frightened by the imbalance, the constant striving to reach the largest possible audience for everything: by the absence of a sustained study of the state of the nation. Heywood Broun once said, "No body politic is healthy until it begins to itch." I would like television to produce some itching pills rather than this endless outpouring of tranquilizers. It can be done. Maybe it won't be, but it could. Let us not shoot the wrong piano player. Do not be deluded into believing that the titular heads of the networks control what appears on their networks. They all have better taste. All are responsible to stockholders, and in my experience all are honorable men. But they must schedule what they can sell in the public market. And this brings us to the nub of the question.

[21]  In one sense it rather revolves around the phrase heard frequently along Madison Avenue: "The Corporate Image." I am not precisely sure what the phrase means, but I would imagine that it reflects a desire on the part of the corporations who pay the advertising bills to have the public imagine, or believe, that they are not merely bodies with no souls, panting in pursuit of elusive dollars. They would like us to believe that they can distinguish between the public good and the private or corporate gain. So the question is this: Are the big corporations who pay the freight for radio and television programs wise to use that time *exclusively* for the sale of goods and services? Is it in their own interest and that of the stockholders to do so? The sponsor of an hour's television program is not buying merely the six minutes devoted to his commercial message. He is determining, without broad limits, the sum total of the impact of the entire hour. If he always, invariably reaches for the largest possible audience, then this process of insulation,

of escape from reality, will continue to be massively financed, and its apologists will continue to make winsome speeches about giving the pubic what it wants, or "letting the public decide."

[22]   I refuse to believe that the presidents and chairmen of the boards of these big corporations want their "corporate image" to consist exclusively of a solemn voice in an echo chamber, or a pretty girl opening the door of a refrigerator, or a horse that talks. They want something better, and on occasion some of them have demonstrated it. But most of the men whose legal and moral responsibility it is to spend the stockholders' money for advertising are removed from the realities of the mass media by five, six, or a dozen contraceptive layers of vice-presidents, pubic-relations counsel, and advertising agencies. Their business is to sell goods, and the competition is pretty tough.

[23]   But this nation is now in competition with malignant forces of evil who are using every instrument at their command to empty the minds of their subjects, and fill those minds with slogans, determination, and faith in the future. If we go on as we are, we are protecting the mind of the American public from any real contact with the menacing world that squeezes in upon us. We are engaged in a great experiment to discover whether a free public opinion can devise and direct methods of managing the affairs of the nation. We may fail. But we are handicapping ourselves needlessly.

[24]   Let us have a little competition. Not only selling soap, cigarettes, and auto-mobiles, but in informing a troubled, apprehensive, but receptive public. Why would not each of the twenty or thirty big corporations which dominate radio and television decide that they will give up one or two of their regularly scheduled programs each year, turn the time over to the networks, and say in effect: "This is a tiny tithe, just a little bit of our profits. On this particular night we aren't going to try to sell cigarettes or auto-mobiles; this is merely a gesture to indicate our belief in the importance of ideas." The networks should, and I think would, pay for the cost of producing the program. The advertiser, the sponsor, would get name credit, but would have nothing to do with the content of the program. Would this blemish the corporate image? Would the stockholders object? I think not. For if the premise upon which our pluralistic society rests—which as I understand it is that if the people are given sufficient undiluted information, they will then somehow, even after long, sober second thoughts, reach the right decision— if that premise is wrong, then not only the corporate image but the corporations are done for.

[25]   There used to be an old phrase in this country employed when someone talked too much. It was "Go hire a hall." Under this proposal the sponsor should have hired the hall; he has bought the time; the local station operator, no matter how indifferent, is going to carry the program—he has to. Then it's up to the networks to fill the hall. I am not here talking about editorializing, but about straightaway exposition as direct, unadorned, and impartial as fallible human beings can make it. Just once in a while let us exalt the importance of ideas and information. Let us dream to the extent of saying that on a given Sunday night the time normally occupied by Ed Sullivan [the host of a variety program] is given over to a clinical survey of the state of American education, and a week or two later the time normally used by Steve Allen is devoted to a thoroughgoing study of American policy in the Middle East. Would the corporate image of their respective sponsors be damaged? Would the stockholders rise up in their wrath and complain? Would anything happen other than that a few million people would have received little illumination on subjects that may well determine the future of this country, and therefore the future of the corporations? This method would also provide real competition between

the networks as to which could outdo the others in the palatable presentation of information. It would provide an outlet for the young men of skill—and there are some even of dedication—who would like to do something other than devise methods of insulating while selling. . . .

[26] It may be that the present system, with no modifications and no experiments, can survive. Perhaps the money-making machine has some kind of built-in perpetual motion, but I do not think so. To a very considerable extent the media of mass communications in a given country reflect the political, economic, and social climate in which they flourish. That is the reason ours differ from the British and French, or the Russian and Chinese. We are currently wealthy, fat, comfortable, and complacent. We have currently a built-in allergy to unpleasant or disturbing information. Our mass media reflect this. But unless we get up off our fat surpluses and recognize that television in the main is being used to distract, delude, amuse, and insulate us, then television and those who finance it, those who look at it and those who work at it, may see a totally different picture too late.

[27] I do not advocate that we turn television into a twenty-seven-inch wailing wall, where longhairs constantly moan about the state of our culture and our defense. But I would just like to see it reflect occasionally the hard, unyielding realities of the world in which we live. . . . The responsibility can easily be placed, in spite of all the mouthings about giving the public what it wants. It rests on big business, and on big television, and it rests at the top. Responsibility is not something that can be assigned or delegated. And it promises its own reward: good business and good television.

[28] Perhaps no one will do anything about it. I have ventured to outline it against a background of criticism that may have been too harsh, only because I could think of nothing better.

[29] Someone once said—I think it was Max Eastman—that "the publisher serves his advertiser best who best serves his readers." I cannot believe that radio and television, or the corporations that finance the programs, are serving well or truly their viewers or listeners, or themselves.

[30] I began by saying that our history will be what we make it. If we go on as we are, then history will take its revenge, and retribution will not limp in catching up with us.

[31] We are to a large extent an imitative society. If one or two or three corporations would undertake to devote just a small fraction of their advertising appropriation along the lines that I have suggested, the procedure would grow by contagion, the economic burden would be bearable, and there might ensue a most exciting adventure—exposure to ideas, and the bringing of reality into the homes of the nation.

[32] To those who say, "People wouldn't look, they wouldn't be interested, they're too complacent, indifferent and insulated," I can only reply: "There is, in one reporter's opinion, considerable evidence against that contention." But even if they are right, what have they got to lose? Because if they are right, and this instrument is good for nothing but to entertain, amuse, and insulate, then the tube is flickering now and we will soon see that the whole struggle is lost.

[33] This instrument can teach, it can illuminate; yes, and it can even inspire. But it can do so only to the extent that humans are determined to use it to those ends. Otherwise it is merely wires and lights in a box. There is a great and perhaps decisive battle to be fought against ignorance, intolerance, and indifference. This weapon of television could be useful.

[34]   Stonewall Jackson, who knew something about the use of weapons, is reported to have said: "When war comes, you must draw the sword and throw away the scabbard." The trouble with television is that it is rusting in the scabbard during a battle for survival.

## IMMEDIATE REACTIONS

Most of the news directors seemed surprised but generally pleased by what they had just heard: surprised, because Murrow's criticism went well beyond the gentle "suggestions for improvement" that are usual for such occasions; and pleased, because many had themselves engaged in the same kinds of battles for airtime. News executive William Small, who helped arrange the convention, no doubt reflected the reaction of a large portion of the audience when he noted that 'his heresy had charm, his dangerous thoughts were prophetic but there was no rancor, no hate, just a little despair."[17] While one biographer described the "roaring acclamation" of the audience,[18] there was no reason to believe that one speech reshaped the broadcast policies of the major networks. A few weeks after the address, Murrow remarked to a friend that "what happened as a result was exactly what I predicted—nothing. Lots of requests for copies, but no action."[19]

In more subtle ways, however, the speech did have its effects, both negative and positive. Together, these effects represent a reasonable list of what a successful confrontation might hope to achieve. In a long summary of Murrow's remarks, the trade magazine *Broadcasting* reported that Murrow "chastised" newsmen "for being derelict in their duties to inform the public."[20] *Time* was more hostile than when it presented its favorable cover story of the CBS commentator the year before. *Time*'s publisher, Henry Luce, apparently saw a dangerous precedent in a star employee's public criticism of management decisions. A short account of the speech started with a tone of condescension: "The familiar, somewhat pompous figure with the familiar, somewhat pompous voice rose up before his fellows one day last week and, in his measured prose, indicted the whole breed."[21]

Even more alarmed were William Paley and other senior CBS officials. Murrow was a national institution; his comments could not help but anger the CBS hierarchy. One corporate insider said the chairman of the board was "furious about that speech. . . . Ed had been part of management but chose to go outside. When somebody—not just staff, talent, but part of management—does that, it's seen as a breach of faith."[22] Years later Paley wrote that he

did not believe television was overlooking any "mortal danger," and I didn't agree with Murrow's gloomy thesis at all. I wished he had come to talk to me about it. How much time should be given to news and documentaries in the prime evening hours has always been one of the thorniest questions in broadcasting.[23]

## PUBLIC UTTERANCE AS ENACTMENT AND SCRIPTURE: LONG-TERM EFFECTS

The rarest attribute of any persuasive effort is longevity. The fact that most messages do not reside very long in our memories leads nearly all advocates to focus on short-term results. But three decades after this address, its basic theme and the Murrow legend are still with us.

The staying power of the speech benefited from a nearly perfect alignment of subject, advocate, and time. Messages by well-known figures carry not only their explicit meanings, but meanings that are also derived from our knowledge of their prior biographies. On rare occasions a single event may emerge as an expression and summation of the accumulated *ethos* of a person's public career. These events may be explicitly rhetorical and symbolic; what they all share is the power to invoke a panoramic sense of perspective about a person or group. Thus, a key playoff game won by the Chicago Cubs may be judged against the content of their faithful and long-suffering supporters. Similarly, the bravado and despair of Tchaikovsky's Sixth Symphony may be redoubled by a listener's knowledge of the composer's personal agony at the time it was written. (He died, perhaps by his own hand, just days after conducting its 1893 premier.) In similar fashion this speech was a flattering enactment of what many Americans firmly believed about Murrow: that his treatment by CBS management had only toughened his resolve to communicate even unpleasant truths about his industry. If politicians and other rhetorical opportunists needed to be reminded that there is a difference between *standing for* something and *being* something, Murrow was generally not troubled by such a distinction.[24] The speech was the product of his experiences and faithful to his persona. It laid bare the conflicts of an industry still in its adolescence.

For these reasons the address is still a touchstone in continuing debates about the role of commercial values in the production of pubic affairs programming. It gave specific form and legitimacy to advocates of journalistic independence. Broadcast journalists, academics, and critics still quote Murrow's words as reminders of broadcasting's public responsibilities. The man who had flown bomber missions over Germany and had given America its first taste of war in Europe provided a durable public service creed. It was as if one of baseball's best players had also refined the game and written its best handbook. Later players would have to measure up and would have to seek respectability by comparing their work against his. A remarkable number of major network television news figures and analysts—Dan Rather, Fred Friendly, Av Westen, Robert MacNeil, Gary Gates, Roger Mudd, and many others—have specifically cited Murrow's 1958 warning as part of their own professional credo.[25] It sanctioned the continuing battle for airtime by scores of other broadcast journalists, and it gave scriptural legitimacy to the Murrow legacy. As Dan Rather noted, the standards of Murrow were the best standards of the industry; he was the measure of one's own professional worth. "Murrow was a master," Rather noted after taking over "CBS Reports." "I made it a project to go through the film library and look at every show Murrow did." It reminded Rather of something he already knew: "I was able to say, 'You're not that good and you are never going to be that good. But console yourself. Neither is anyone else.'"[26]

This "benchmark" feature of the address is especially evident in various episodes within the recent history of CBS News. Far more than the other networks, its members have been involved in highly publicized adversary relationships with CBS's leadership. In 1966, for example, Murrow's long-time ally Fred Friendly resigned as CBS News president in a widely publicized feud over how much airtime the network would provide for the coverage of Senate hearings on American Vietnam policy. Like Murrow, Friendly thought the network should have altered its daytime programming to cover important national events. When management declined to take his advice, he quit. Part of his decision to take a stand against management was the precedent established by the venerated Murrow. A brilliant showman to the end, Friendly made certain that sections of the Murrow address were in the letter of resignation that he distributed to the press.

My departure is a matter of conscience. At the end of the day it is the viewer and the listener who have the biggest stake in all this. Perhaps my action will be understood by them. I know it will be understood by my colleagues in news and I know Ed Murrow would have understood. A speech he delivered to the Radio-Television News Directors Association in 1958 spelled it all out.[27]

Several other episodes of rebellion suggest that others had not missed the significance of Murrow's willingness to take on management. After Murrow had left CBS to join the Kennedy administration, one of his replacements on "CBS Reports" was Howard K. Smith. Smith was firmly in the old mold; he viewed himself as both a reporter and a commentator. One of the programs he narrated was a hard-hitting look at Alabama's response to the civil rights movement in 1961. Among other things, it featured dramatic footage of Birmingham sheriff "Bull" Conner unleashing his police dogs on black children engaged in a peaceful civil rights march. Nothing from the period demonstrated as well or as graphically the racist limits of southern justice. Smith—himself a native of Louisiana—decided to close the hour with the famous caution against timidity issued by British statesman Edmund Burke: "The only thing necessary for the triumph of evil," Burke noted, "is for good men to do nothing."[28] The quote was Smith's way of pointing to the need for moderate whites like himself to come to grips with the ugly realities of American racism. CBS executives decided that it would be editorializing rather than reporting to use the quote; he would have to find another way to end the program. Smith fought the decision but was fired after confronting Paley over the issue.

A different type of episode in 1975 involved Daniel Schorr, a reporter who specialized in stories of internal dissent within the presidency. Schorr was never very popular with government leaders in the United States and Europe but was especially despised by the Nixon inner circle. With some justification he had informally told a gathering of students at Duke University that he had "suspicions" that CBS was downplaying Richard Nixon's Watergate troubles out of fear of retribution from federal agencies.[29] The comments—which Schorr later admitted were not very well thought out—also implied that Walter Cronkite and others had been given the word to ease up on the administration. They were picked up by the press, embarrassing the network and angering his colleagues. They also resulted in a predictable reprimand from CBS News executives. Schorr probably had several motives. It was also widely known that he had been the subject of an earlier massive FBI investigation authorized by the White House with the apparent goal of intimidation.[30] When the story came out, the lame explanation offered by Nixon aides was that their arch enemy was being considered for an administration position. But it is also likely that another leading CBS journalist was responding to the special license for independence that was part of the Murrow-friendly imprint on the news division.

The most recent episode in this lineage of dissent surfaced in an incredible series of events in 1986. Management at the network had just been shocked by a takeover attempt by the Turner Broadcasting Company, the operators of the successful Cable News Network. In order to save itself, CBS refinanced its holdings to make the company too big to be eaten by the smaller corporate shark. The long-term consequences of this strategy were twofold. Management had to impose severe economies on the entire company. And many key executives were transferred or fired as divisions in publishing and other areas were sold off. The effect all this had on morale was predictable. At one point pessimism was so rampant among staffers and the news division's management that some actually considered making an offer to purchase CBS News in order to preserve its integrity. Several key news employees invoked the memory of Murrow by going public with their criticisms of the unpenitent board of directors—a rare occurrence in most companies but something that people have come to expect from disgruntled CBS employees. In a widely read statement published on the editorial page of the *New York Times*, anchorman Dan Rather was brutally frank in his assessment of an order by the company's new head, Laurence Tisch, to cut 200 news staff positions. Tisch, he wrote, "told us to be the best. We want nothing more than to fulfill that mandate. Ironically, he has made the task seem something between difficult and impossible." Rather's article was appropriately entitled "From Murrow to Mediocrity?"—closely adhering to the arguments expressed in the 1958 speech and urging the network to continue "in the tradition of Edward R. Murrow":

Are we a business or a public trust? This answer is both. But how is it going to work? Which comes first? We in CBS News are painfully struggling with these questions. . . . Anyone who says network news cannot be profitable doesn't know what he is talking about. But anyone who says it must *always* make money is misguided and irresponsible.[31]

## THE POLITICS OF EMBARRASSMENT

A central feature of most persuasive encounters is the persuader's attempt to create a tension between what an audience presently believes and what it *ought* to believe. But Murrow was doing more here than prodding the immediate audience. The arrows of his remarks went in at least two different directions—not only to those members of the industry who were guilty of inverting their public service and commercial priorities but also to the management of his own company. Given the recent cancellation of "See It Now" and Murrow's not-so-concealed frustrations with the network, the speech suggested the alienation of one of CBS's most valued and credible human assets. In spite of his expressions of goodwill toward the network[4], the remarks were interpreted as a public renunciation and were all the more newsworthy because of it. Since he was not protecting his own organizational interests, Murrow's rhetoric begged to be interpreted as a statement of conscience.

He took the shortest possible route to humbling all the leaders of the broadcasting establishment by implying that no other major American industry created so much wealth from so modest a typical product. Given the recent quiz show scandals, his comments hit extremely close to a sensitive nerve. No wonder William Paley and other executives at CBS were angry. At the same time that he was criticizing management for pandering too much to the lowest standards of programming, he was also offering praise for the good sense and maturity of ordinary people [6, 32]. As he put it, the "American public is more reasonable, restrained, and more mature than most of our industry's program planners believe"[6]. There may have been more truth to the broadcasters' assessment of low public interest in news programming than Murrow was willing to concede, but it was surely in his interests to place greater responsibility on the broadcast executives and greater faith in the public.

## A TIMELY JEREMIAD

Up to this point we have emphasized the extent to which Murrow's speech and persona have influenced others in his time and after. But taking the measure of any message of warning ought to also include an assessment of how accurate its predictions actually were.

Murrow was normally not the kind of person who understood the world in terms of conspiracies, but these remarks were an exception. "This nation," he noted, "is now in competition with malignant forces of evil who are using every instrument at their command to empty the minds of their subjects, and fill those minds with slogans, determination, and faith in the future." In the prime-time schedule there was "only fleeting and spasmodic reference to the fact that his nation is in mortal danger"]5]. Intentionally, perhaps, he never named the "menacing" foes, although his language matched the standard anticommunist rhetoric he sometimes criticized in the politicians of his day. Even so, his jeremiad served his purpose by creating a sense of urgency. The profits for the networks may lie in escapist programming, he argued, but the future of nation depended on informed public opinion[25]. He was too diplomatic to turn his speech into a diatribe against specific low-brow programs with high ratings. But at one point he cited a programming decision that suggests how prescient his fears were.

Not so long ago the President of the United States delivered a television address to the nation. He was discoursing on the possibility or probability of war between this nation and the Soviet Union and Communist China—a reasonably compelling subject. Two networks—CBS and NBC—delayed that broadcast for an hour and fifteen minutes. If this decision was dictated by anything other than financial reason, the networks didn't deign to explain those reasons. . . . It is difficult to believe that this decision was made by men who love, respect, and understand news.[15]

Murrow had cited the problem correctly; he had only misidentified the enemy. Although it would be unfair to expect that broadcasters should carry the whole burden of anticipating future events, his concerns about the paucity of public discussion on national goals were soon to be borne out. American commitments in Southeast Asia would evolve into a brutal but undeclared war.

It is interesting to note what did *not* happen in the mass media—especially network television—in the first phases of American involvement in Vietnam. Soon after this speech, and in ways that are still not clear, the foreign policy establishment within the Kennedy administration made decisions about the necessity to send American "advisers" and experts into a number of Asian nations, especially South Vietnam.[32] It is now apparent that throughout the early 1960s American promises of troops and supplies occurred without much public debate and with relatively little television discussion. Intractable political turmoil in this part of the world—especially in Korea during the early 1950s and Laos somewhat later—provided a context for viewing the containment of Vietnamese communism. The long-term stalemate created by superpower involvement in Asian politics made it easier to lose track of the threads of diplomatic and military decisions that were shaping the Vietnam quagmire. What Americans learned from television came largely from official sources within the Kennedy and Johnson administrations, sources whose views were rarely evaluated or challenged in prime time.[33] Programs devoted to exploring what decision makers and their critics were thinking were usually relegated to dayparts when relatively few people were watching. As was noted above, Fred Friendly quit as president of CBS News when network officials refused to carry Senate hearings on the war. Reruns of "I Love Lucy" ran in place of a rare Washington policy debate that took place before the Senate Foreign Relations Committee. At the same time ABC and NBC briefly experimented with half-hour programs on the conflict that, by 1966, resulted in approximately 200 American deaths each week.[34] But both discontinued even these modest efforts, leading NBC's Robert MacNeil to observe that "the United States was engaged in a major war and the nation's most important news medium was not even reviewing the war week by week."[35]

Vietnam reporting in early evening and prime time began to change after 1966, when the heroic efforts of television journalists such as Jack Laurence and

Morley Safer became instrumental in dramatizing the horrific effects of guerrilla warfare. By then, television was making extensive use of film footage that was shipped out of the war zones and relayed back to New York in time for the evening newscasts. If it was never easy to achieve, "shooting bloody" in Vietnam became a form of spot news that lent itself to television and began to change attitudes toward the war. Americans were shocked but also fascinated by graphic footage of dramatic helicopter rescues, maimed soldiers, and the corpses of American and Vietnamese boys concealed in lush green fields. Television was much better at showing the costly effects of a policy than explaining the rationales of those who shaped it. Tragically, the vivid combat coverage was rarely matched by vigorous public discussion of Vietnam policy until after the Tet Offensive in 1968. By then the nightly portrayals of death and futility had had their effect, but too late to save the 20,000 Americans who had been killed in action. Few of those early casualties probably ever saw an extended television discussion about the wisdom of waging a land war in Southeast Asia.

If Murrow did not achieve what he ideally wanted—to alter the American agenda through the medium of television—he at least raised the right questions to the right audience. He suppressed whatever doubts he might have had about the capacity of the general public to watch news programming, focusing instead on the misplaced priorities of broadcast executives. The immediate audience in Chicago surely liked what he had to say; most of them saw Murrow as a prestigious ally. As an advocate of programming devoted to serious public discussion, he laid out a statement of principles that others could later use in their own feuds with the television "money machine." When considered from the perspective of the general public, this persuasive encounter is most memorable as a courageous reminder that television's enormous profits and large audiences carry certain obligations. Along with a similar message delivered by a Federal Communications Commission (FCC) commissioner three years later,[36] Murrow's effort surely helped heighten expectations about the "public trustee" role of television news. It was probably an added bonus that he made some of the industry's leaders slightly uncomfortable with their success. "I've always been on the side of the heretics," he explained to a friend after the speech, "because the heretics so often proved to be right."[37]

## NOTES

1. Edward R. Murrow, "A Reporter Talks to His Colleagues," *The Reporter*, November 13, 1958, p. 32.

2. "This Is Murrow," *Time*, September 30, 1957, p. 48.

3. Quoted in Fred W. Friendly, *Due to Circumstances beyond Our Control* (New York: Vintage, 1967), p. xvi.

4. Ibid., p. 121.

5. Ibid., p. 122.

6. John Lardner, "The Air," *The New Yorker*, November 14, 1959, p. 234.

7. A. M. Sperber, *Murrow: His Life and Times* (New York: Freundlich, 1986), p. 519.

8. Ibid., p. 426.

9. Friendly, *Due to Circumstances*, p. 92.

10. Erik Barnouw, *Tube of Plenty: The Evolution of American Broadcasting* (New York: Oxford, 1975), p. 237.

11. William S. Paley, *As It Happened* (New York: Doubleday, 1979), p. 318.

12. "RTNDA Convention to Review Canon 35," *Broadcasting*, October 13, 1958, p. 92.

13. Alexander Kendrick, *Prime Time: The Life of Edward R. Murrow* (Boston: Little, Brown, 1969), p. 412.

14. For an overview of these scandals, see Barnouw, *Tube of Plenty*, pp. 184–186, 246.

15. Sperber, *Murrow*, p. xix.

16. This is a slightly abridged version of the speech taken from *The Reporter*, November 13, 1958, pp. 32–36. Used by permission of the Edward R. Murrow Center of Public Diplomacy, Tufts University.

17. William Small, *To Kill a Messenger: Television News and the Real World* (New York: Hastings House, 1970), p. 4.

18. Sperber, *Murrow*, p. xviii.

19. Quoted in Kendrick, *Prime Time*, p. 416.

20. "RTNDA Stages Political Bout on Chicago Convention Program," *Broadcasting*, October 20, 1958, p. 86.

21. "Decadence and Escapism," *Time*, October 27, 1958, p. 60.

22. Quoted in Sperber, *Murrow* p. xix.

23. Paley, *As It Happened*, p. 315.

24. Murrow was not without his critics. He was criticized by some for devoting so much of his time to the generally lightweight program "Person to Person." See, for example, Gary Paul Gates, *Air Time: The Inside Story of CBS News* (New York: Harper & Row, 1978), p. 30. Also, although he received generally favorable reactions from his brief leadership of the United States Information Agency after 1961, he was roundly criticized for one of his first acts. "Harvest of Shame" had been purchased by the BBC for broadcast in the United Kingdom. However, Murrow asked the British network's director general to cancel the show because of what it revealed about working conditions on larger American farms. For two different accounts of this incident, see Eric Barnouw, *The Image Empire: A History of Broadcasting in the United States, Volume III* (New York: Oxford, 1970), p. 180; and Robert MacNeil, *The People Machine* (New York: Harper & Row, 1968), pp. 313–314.

25. See, for example, Av Westen, *Newswatch: How TV Decides the News* (New York: Simon and Schuster, 1982), p. 15; Dan Rather and Mickey Herskowitz, *The Camera Never Blinks* (New York: Ballantine, 1978), p. 294; MacNeil, *The People Machine*, p. 18; and Gates, *Air Time*, p. 26.

26. Rather and Herskowitz, *The Camera Never Blinks*, p. 332.

27. Friendly, *Due to Circumstances* p. 251. See also pp. 249–253.

28. Gates, *Air Time*, p. 38.

29. Daniel Schorr, *Clearing the Air* (Boston: Houghton Mifflin, 1977), pp. 116–117.

30. Robert Metz, *CBS: Reflections in a Bloodshot Eye* (Chicago: Playboy Press, 1975), pp. 362–363.

31. Dan Rather, "From Murrow to Mediocrity?" *New York Times*, March 10, 1987, p. A27.

32. For a survey of this period, see Jim Heath, *Decade of Disillusionment: The Kennedy-Johnson Years* (Bloomington: Indiana University, 1975), pp. 90–92, 133–142. A thorough chronology of the decision making of this period can be found in David Halberstam's study *The Best and the Brightest* (New York: Random House, 1972).

33. See Small, *To Kill a Messenger*, pp. 109–110; and Edwin Diamond, *The Tin Kazoo: Television and the New Politics* (Boston: MIT, 1975), pp. 114–116.

34. MacNeil, *The People Machine*, p. 67.

35. Ibid., p. 68.

36. See Newton N. Minow, "Address to the 39th Annual Convention of the National Association of Broadcasters," Washington, D.C., May 9, 1961, reprinted in Glen E. Mills, *Reason in Controversy* (Boston: Allyn and Bacon, 1964), pp. 271–282. To a gathering of broadcasting leaders, the Federal Communications Commission chairman offered a challenge and coined a new phrase in the space of a few sentences: "I invite you to sit down in front of your television set when your station goes on the air and stay there without a book, magazine, newspaper, profit and loss sheet or rating book to distract you—and keep your eyes glued to that set until the station signs off. I can assure you that you will observe a vast wasteland" (p. 274.).

37. Murrow quoted in Kendrick, *Prime Time*, p. 416.

# 5

# The Theater of Conflict: "Donahue" in Russia

Ironically, television, which persistently plays to the defensive, overcivilized aspects of society, with its charades of hosts and guests, at the same time has done much to connect people with one another, to demystify strangers, to deisolate backward communities, and especially to help break down the walls that often exist between individuals.[1]

*Michael Arlen*

American television now has countless local and national copies of the "Donahue" program, the well-known hour-long talk show that specializes in three-way give-and-take between Phil Donahue, a studio audience, and a series of passionate advocates. Issues discussed on the program have always ranged from the bizarre to the ordinary, but for almost two decades the show's mix of ingredients has been extraordinarily successful. "Vintage Donahue," *Newsweek* once noted, is "part psycho-drama, part street theater, part group therapy and always, in the vernacular of the trade, 'pure television.' "[2]

In an attempt to export his successful formula of energizing a studio audience to consider its own norms and values, Donahue taped five episodes of his program in the Soviet Union in 1987. The syndicated shows were aired the following month on 187 stations across the country. Programs were devoted to family life, exchanges of views between citizens of the two superpowers, political dissidents, and a debate between American and Soviet journalists. By far the most interesting hour was Donahue's attempt to engage an audience of 350 Soviet teens in an exchange on sexual, religious, and political topics. The silver-haired fifty-one-year-old host kept the basic pattern of his program, making concessions only to fashion by dressing more casually in jeans and a red sweater. Like a relay runner ready to pass on a baton to a teammate, Donahue used the now-familiar portable microphone to give fleeting control of the program to audience members ready to express an opinion. He consciously sought to duplicate the dialectic of claim and counterclaim that is basic to the program.

This chapter explores the "Donahue" program from three perspectives. The first and largest section takes a broad look at the genre of the television talk show as a vehicle for public discussion. The second part includes the transcript of the program with Soviet teens as a specific case study. And the third closes the chapter with several observations on the persuasive possibilities and limitations created by the Soviet program's unique content and setting. Donahue's now much-copied brand of therapeutic confrontation offers some important lessons about the changing nature of television as a source of public discourse.

## FROM THE BIZARRE TO THE CONFRONTATIONAL: "DONAHUE'S" GENRE

The television talk show has been around at least since 1950, when comedians Jerry Lester and Morey Amsterdam served as hosts for NBC's "Broadway Open House."[3] A forerunner of the durable "Tonight Show," "Open House" represented a new kind of programming with greater risks and more spontaneity than was allowed in comedy, drama, and variety genres that early television had inherited from radio. Then, as now, talk shows usually required entertainers to serve alternately as "hosts" and "guests." The success of the conversation depended on how well the wit and guile of the celebrities could hold audiences and advertisers. David Letterman, Johnny Carson, and countless hosts of local shows still carry on this tradition, usually by providing entertaining diversions that have the effect of moving viewers away from the issues that divide communities, classes, and regions.

Over the short history of American television the discussion of "serious" issues has been the exception, usually confined to the Sunday network interview shows or the isolated efforts of David Susskind, Dick Cavett, William F. Buckley, Jr., and a few others relegated to the semianonymity of Public Television. In both their entertainment and informational forms, talk programs have traditionally shared key similarities. Guests are almost exclusively entertainers, newsmakers, or political leaders. If studio audiences are used at all, they are present to listen and adore rather than be heard.

Since its first broadcast in 1968, "Donahue" has rewritten some—but not all—of these basic rules. Like its older daytime counterparts anchored by Mike Douglas and Merv Griffin, "Donahue" has always contained consistent amounts of celebrity gossip and tabloid content. The program has also elevated public discussion of American sexual practices to the level of a master theme for daytime television. Nearly every possible transgression of traditional sexual mores has been endlessly explored. Homosexuality, transvestism, and incest are as basic to "Donahue" as presidential speeches and Beirut bombings are to the "CBS Evening News." But unlike most of its competitors, a significant percentage of programs illuminate important cultural changes and social issues.

One of the first taboos "Donahue" attacked was the long-held belief that the audience should be present only to express its approval for the host and his guests. In the "Donahue" format the audience is essential to the show. Encouraged during the initial warm-up to respond to the discussion that will follow, many willingly oblige by asking the most penetrating questions. Television critic Marvin Kitman notes that "Phil's audiences are the best thing about his segments; their eyes are open . . . and the sharpness of their questions suggests they have been bussed in from University of Chicago graduate seminars."[4] It is to Donahue's credit that he can coax out of ordinary people a kind of commonsense critical thinking that would give comfort to a Jeffersonian populist. His audiences provide plenty of reasons to refute the assumption widespread within the television industry that telegenic communication is possible for only a talented few. "The average housewife is bright and inquisitive," he once noted, "but television treats her like some mental midget."[5]

Donahue emphasized the importance of the audience years ago by leaving the safe refuge of the interviewer's desk to join them. He conducts most of his shows—literally and psychologically—from the perspective of the audience. If at times his conscious efforts to identify with his largely urban female viewers seems contrived, there is little doubt that he has shifted the emphasis of many talk shows away from stage-managed discussions and toward the model of a more open-ended public forum. He has made his audiences cocreators of his programs: no longer outsiders looking in but participants with the intellectual capacity to move a discussion along.

The second taboo Donahue undermined was the conscious programming decision of the major television networks to stay away from forums that allowed issue advocacy. Even in the late 1980s, a discussion about difficult political and social issues might have been acceptable for ABC's innovative "Nightline" or stuffed into truncated two-minute segments on "Today" or "Good Morning America." But more sustained discussion of one issue was thought to be risky. On almost any commercially sponsored news show, even a five-minute segment devoted to one issue is considered extravagant. Television programmers have long concluded that informational shows at the fringes of the broadcast day can never compete with game shows and soap operas. At their best, goes the traditional reasoning, "talking heads" might draw modest numbers of predominantly male viewers attracted to "serious" topics but not stay-at-home women. Most networks remain skeptical that daytime viewers will choose "Donahue" over steamy "soaps," which is why most of the weekday informational talk shows are still produced by syndicators rather than the major television networks.

The fact that "Donahue" has survived so long is evidence of its commercial success. But perhaps Donahue's imitators provide a better sign of the importance of his formula. "Phil really opened the door for everybody," notes the distributor of "Oprah Winfrey." "He aired topics that nobody touched before him, that people couldn't talk about on the air."[6] Yet "Donahue" is a strange mixture of the trivial and the significant. Low "Donahue" features television actors striving to be profound about the banal characters they play in the glacier-paced plotlines of daytime soaps. Low "Donahue" also spends time in the well-worn paths of celebrity talks—for example, with film actress Liz Taylor breathlessly reviewing the details of a divorce or a recently contracted waistline. But for each of these shows there is usually redemption in the high "Donahue" who uses relatively anonymous guests to bring issues to life: an FCC commissioner criticizing the lack of regulation over children's television programming, an atheist attacking tax exemptions for churches, or parents describing the warning signs of suicidal children. With some hyperbole Donahue once noted that "our program survives on issues. We discuss more issues, more often, more thoroughly than any other show in the business."[7]

A third barrier the program helped to conquer was the belief of most producers that a successful show needs people schooled as television performers. A typical segment of Merv Griffin's show for the late 1970s, for example, could include an appearance by Zsa Zsa Gabor. Again and again Griffin called on this former film actress to bless his audiences with her presence. She was but one example of many celebrity guests with nothing much to say but safely locked into the talk show circuit simply for being well known. By contrast, informational talk shows have been more willing to devote an hour to an issue and to give more unstructured time to ordinary people outside the usual circles of celebritydom. Talking on subjects ranging from the crisis of farm bankruptcies to homelessness to the experience of coping with the knowledge that one is a carrier of AIDS, these advocate–participants have been given at least limited exposure in national forums like "Donahue." In most cases they represent constituencies who have little direct access to the public and only fleeting coverage on television news. Many remain the captives of a form of reporter-centered broadcast journalism that gives priority to the prominent role of the reporter/narrator. Because television gives very little direct access to the victims of social change and cultural upheaval, stories are typically constructed about them, leaving most as characters to be used in heavily scripted news narratives.

Part of Donahue's emphasis on ideas and nonexpert guests evolved out of necessity. Discussing topical issues with an audience was one of the few alternatives open to a new television host surviving in the media backwater of Dayton, Ohio. In his 1979 book he recalled the accidental evolution of the program's audience-centered format:

The show's style had developed not by genius but by necessity. The familiar talk-show heads were not available to use in Dayton, Ohio. Although we were able to attract a Phyllis Diller or a Paul Lynde during the summer months when the "Hollywood stars" worked the Kenley Theater, . . . after the biggies left town we were left with a lot of open dates to fill. The result was improvisation.

For example: a woman whose daughter was on a protest fast in the Green County Jail calling for an end to the Vietnam war:

*Audience:* What if she dies?

*Mother:* If she dies, she dies.

*Audience:* You have an obligation to her.

*Mother:* You have an obligation to the men coming home dead from this war.[8]

In Dayton the necessity to improvise meant that it was sometimes easier to explore an issue than to book a celebrity.

There is obviously a long history of public discussion of significant issues in the daily and periodical press. The persuasive essay remains the hallmark of countless newspaper opinion pages and "serious" magazines such as *The Nation, The New Republic,* and *Atlantic Monthly.* But making vigorous and frequently impassioned public debate the basis of a continuing television show was more than an incremental step in the late 1960s. In the very narrow framework of television, a major gulf had been bridged. A medium largely limited to escapist content and the selling of products now accepted programs centered on social issues and controversial ideas.

If there has been a negative side effect to the fall of these taboos, it is probably to be found in the countless local and national clones of the "Donahue" format. Like the supermarket tabloid that imitates the layout of a newspaper, many local and syndicated attempts to do an in-studio talk show imitate the structure but usually not the intent of "Donahue." Under various names such as "People Are Talking" or "The Morning Show," these programs have duplicated the look of an audience-based talk show but rarely use it to discuss issues. Perhaps every fifth program buys into respectability with an issue of genuine local importance, such as the growing problem of what to do with the mountains of solid waste accumulating in most urban centers. More typical are programs on astrology, sex-change operations, cosmetic surgery, and teenage prostitution. These and other "issues" are frequently favored under the pretext of "learning more about the subject," but most programs are transparent attempts to raise sagging ratings by pandering to an unquenchable public appetite for fetishes and fantasies. As former CBS News president Fred Friendly has noted, "Television makes so much money doing its worst, it can't afford to do its best."[9]

## THE RHETORICAL FORMULAS

High "Donahue" usually features a group of people who either have been harmed by the actions of powerful groups and institutions or have defied a long-standing cultural norm. These participants are sometimes cast as sympathetic victims, such as three women featured in a January 1988 program who had been disowned by their parents for marrying outside the Jewish Orthodox faith. Others may strain even Donahue's considerable skill at evoking tolerance, such as a recent program on women who have abandoned their families.

He usually starts by questioning guests on their "pain," "trauma," or "guilt." Members of the audience—and a few selected viewers who call in—are soon encouraged to ask questions and make judgments on what they have heard. A common sequence has audience members cautiously probing the wisdom of a guest's actions ("Have you tried to talk to your parents?" "How could you leave your children?"). Donahue frequently comes to the defense of someone who has offended a social norm. At other times he is the surrogate of puzzled or doubting audience members. Sometimes programs with only the thinnest pretext to serious discussion—for example, on the effects of being married to an older or younger spouse—can reveal interesting norms and social customs. As writer David Halberstam has noted, "More sociological information about modern-day mores gets exchanged on that program than anywhere else."[10]

### Implicit Appeals I: Civility in the Arena of Conflict

Donahue long ago lost his journalistic virginity by taking positions in programs that put him at odds with significant numbers of television viewers. His book, for example, describes a Catholicism gone dormant and a belief in feminism that is probably more virulent than that held by the women in his audiences. His programs sometimes frustrate conservatives opposed to an evident liberalism on social issues. Donahue's sympathy is apparent for homosexuals, transsexuals, drug users, and others who are at odds with mainstream American values. In the eyes of critic Frank McConnell writing in the Catholic weekly *Commonweal*, he is guilty of "pandering radical ideas" to his predominantly white, middle-class audience of women. "Controversial ideas are his joy and toy" and all the more annoying because they are offered up with an "alterboy sweetness" that reduces the idea and core assumption in the program—faith in the power of tolerance—to a simple theatrical ploy.

You can't watch Donahue for any length of time without realizing—first uncomfortably, then surely—that his enthusiasm for discussion, his consuming interest in fairness, his boyish eagerness to understand, is a performance. It is rather like watching Sammy Davis, Jr., sing "I've Gotta Be Me" in Vegas. All that existential heroism, one thinks; all that triumphant *selfhood*, winning through against any obstacle. And then one realizes that this riveting confession is part of the dinner show, repeating night after night.[11]

There can be no doubt that Donahue is the star performer in a "show," but his evident tolerance—whether sincere or contrived—offers its own useful rewards. High "Donahue" produces a remarkable degree of vigorous and orderly discussion. It provides an effective model for how to engage in a public exchange of views without allowing the heat of debate to consume the fragile framework of public civility. The best programs offer a range of positive lessons about the rules of fair-minded conversation. Some are obvious; others are quite subtle. In the best moments of this genre we are reminded that what a guest or studio audience member *says* matters more than who they *are*. In addition, one side of a dispute is seldom allowed to dominate a discussion. Questions soliciting information are frequently favored over empty, self-serving assertions. Perhaps the most important lesson of all is that Donahue shows a genuine understanding of the contingent nature of most claims made in the policy arena; he evinces an awareness that judgments about people involved in complex decisions (e.g., "Abortionists are murderers") are really about *preferences* rather than *truths*. All these routine preconditions for civil public discussion may seem obvious, but that does not diminish the fact that they are needed. There is no shortage of radio and television talk show hosts who poison the airwaves with exploitative programming.[12]

## Implicit Appeals II: Faith in the Power of Dialectic

At its best, the program has pioneered a pattern of unrehearsed television debate that is as close to the form of a philosophical dialogue—dialectic—as most Americans will encounter. We are most familiar with persuasive attempts today when they appear as messages organized *in our absence* and then delivered *without our overt feedback*. Television commercials, political speeches, or newspaper editorials, for instance, obviously come to us as complete "one-way" units of communication, seeking only our agreement. In many ways a higher form of persuasion is the conversation organized to explore one theme about which reasonable individuals differ.

This was the form of discourse preferred by the Greek philosophers prior to the rise of sustained one-voice argumentation common to the book or the essay. Plato's most interesting writings, for example, are his dialogues between Socrates and a variety of different advocates. Never mind that Plato functioned essentially as a playwright, reserving the best arguments for his teacher. The ideal of dialectic is apparent on every page, where the vigorous give-and-take of conversation between two intellectual equals merges persuasion into education. A dialogue of claims and corrections creates a continuing basis for actively testing the merits of ideas.

The ideal of dialectic is most clearly institutionalized in the court trial but with a costly difference. The process of a trial, including the examination and cross-examination of witnesses, ostensibly functions to review disputed facts in order to establish the guilt or innocence of a defendant. The arguments are directed to a jury sworn to weigh the evidence in the absence of their own biases. But an important difference between a practical trial and idealized dialectic is that the search for truth should transcend "winning" at all costs. The dialectician's goal is not to gain an advantage over opponents but to allow all parties to "discover" what they "know." The point was explained in Plato's *Theaetetus*, where Socrates equates the construction of self-knowledge with the midwife who assists with the birth of a child.

> The triumph of my art is in thoroughly examining whether the thought which the mind of the young man brings forth is a false idol or a noble and true birth. And like all midwives, I am barren, and the reproach which is often made against me, that I ask questions of others and have not the wit to answer them myself, is very just—the reason is that the god compels me to be a midwife, but does not allow me to bring forth. And therefore I am not myself at all wise, nor have I anything to show which is the invention or birth of my own soul, but those who converse with me profit. Some of them appear dull enough at first, but afterwards, as our acquaintance ripens, if the god is gracious to them, they all make astonishing progress. . . . It is quite clear that they never learned anything from me; the many fine discoveries to which they cling are of their own making. [13]

It would be futile here to try to settle the question about how often people enter into open debate with the goal of "discovery" rather than conquest. It is enough to note that the probing questions asked by Donahue and his audiences—notable for their lack of assertive dogmatism—are reasonably helpful components of the dialectic method. Given the paucity of similar examples in other mass media forums, the audience-centered format of the show is an object lesson in how to explore conflicting opinions on an issue in the spirit of open-ended inquiry.

The most popular venue for the discussion of issues in American life is the television newscast, but video journalism suffers from a chronic lack of time. The result is frequently to reduce an issue to a "package" of views presented in under two minutes. Most idea-centered stories are overlooked or condensed to such an extent as to be rendered meaningless. Even an imperfect dialectic is a useful antidote to the oversimplified one-sidedness of the prepared "pitch" and the unchallenged assertion contained in a thirty-second news "sound bite." For example, a 1988 "Donahue" program about "repeat offenders" engaged in violent assaults had the unsettling effect of reminding viewers that finding reliable methods for protecting themselves against violent crime is a long way off. A typical television news statement made by a mayor or police official might offer reassurance, but an hour-long flow of questions and answers can make the gritty realities of American crime painfully obvious. As the program unfolded, it became increasingly evident that neither a professional criminologist nor a police detective could offer the kinds of answers the audience wanted. In this particular program, there was no narrator to simplify the issue or to focus on a few reassuring words from those who are officially charged with controlling lawlessness. The constant presence of a "criminal's" observations throughout the show—in this case, a rapist released as an under-aged offender—sharply defined the limits of the experts' authority:

*Audience*: How can we protect ourselves from someone like this?

*Serial rapist*: You can't.

*Audience*: I can't? (gasps from others in the audience)

*Serial rapist*: You can't.

*Audience*: Well, we'll carry guns then from now on.

*Serial rapist*: There is no . . . surefire way in my belief for anyone to protect themselves [*sic*].

*Donahue* (frustrated): Nobody is asking for an ironclad guarantee in writing of not being victimized by this kind of person. What we do think we are entitled to receive from the people who have spent their own professional lives investigating this kind of horror is some free advice as to how we might be alerted to at least diminish our chances of being victimized.

*Police Detective*: (after a long pause) . . . You need to increase your awareness. That's it. It's the least preventable crime we have to deal with.[14]

The presence of an unrepentant offender (at best, a silent presence in most news narratives on crime) combined in the same forum with the "experts" to create a skeptical but wiser audience.

### Implicit Appeals III: Therapeutic Form and Narcissistic Content

No feature of television talk shows like "Donahue" is more striking than their implied appeal to an ethic of therapeutic self-disclosure. "Let's get it out in the open," Donahue and other hosts frequently advise participants. There is little doubt that these programs are on the air to entertain television audiences. But it is obvious by now that the language and demeanor of their hosts owe less to the mystique of the entertainer than to the image of the "caring" listener. The comic entertainer may win over an audience by finding humor in an infinite range of human failings and institutional absurdities. Parodies of the president, for example, are part of Johnny Carson's nightly opening monologue. The hosts of informational talk shows, by contrast, exist as professional empathizers. A joke or insult at the expense of an audience would be unthinkable. They function with a different set of rules, foremost of which is the belief that the personal and sometimes very private details of an ordinary life can be a window on the personal circumstances of millions of viewers. A therapeutic attitude immunizes such television against charges of exploitation by making "self-discovery" and "feeling good about oneself" unchallengeable benefits.

Therapeutic communication has a number of easily recognized features, among them: that accurate listening is as important as talking, that the communication of feelings is as important as the communication of facts, and that the public disclosure of private information paves the way to a healthier attitude about oneself and others. When topics focus on personal habits or behaviors, discussion is frequently about "dysfunctions," "guilt," or "fear." If the issue involves culturewide problems such as racism, a sociological vocabulary emerges in words such as "behavioral traits," "roles," and "learned behavior." In both cases the key underlying assumption is the same: No topic is too sensitive or private if public discussion helps to repair the fabric of one's life. During a program exploring discrimination among light- and dark-skinned black Americans, for example, Donahue consistently employed the therapist's line, urging the ethic of self-discovery for a largely black audience divided on just how significant the "problem" really was:

*Donahue*: I see this audience walking away from the reality of the discrimination that truly does exist in the black community.

. . .

*Audience*: I think that black Americans have a lot more to deal with than who is lighter than who. . . .

*Donahue*: But you can't fix this if you don't acknowledge that it's here.[15]

The empathy-rich communication of "Donahue," "Oprah," "Sally Jessy Raphael," and others clearly has both positive and negative consequences. Without a doubt, their self-help dialectic imitates an important and constructive type of interaction. In an age when so much public communication serves someone's vested public relations interests, even a mediated television dialogue with an empathetic listener can be a refreshing contrast. Donahue has a good ear for the passion, anger, and pain expressed by his guests and audiences. His frequent introjection, "I hear you; I hear what you're saying" may be a cliché, but it is the modus operandi of the therapist who is determined to put understanding ahead of judgment. He frequently takes the time to check his understanding of a point someone has made by trying to summarize it back to them accurately.[16] Even if the demands for rapidly pacing the show make the conversation less than ideal, there is nonetheless much to admire in his efforts to track the flow of ideas and feelings that surface within a typical hour. The true dialectician, Donahue hates speeches by anyone on the program. He is the model of a "nurturing" communicator who is able to use the give-and-take of conversation to cast light into the darker corners of well-worn issues.

If there is a negative consequence of television's adoption of the therapeutic model, it is not so much in attempts to duplicate the *form* of the sympathetic listener but in the talk program's obsession with subjects traditionally associated with the *substance* of therapy. Healing one's own physical or psychic wounds is—at best—a long and private process, usually shared by a limited number of caring friends or professionals. The examining room, the private conversation, and the counselor's office have traditionally been shelters from the public world. With these programs they are very much a part of it.

The "giving" personality has become the central figure in a strange kind of theater for self-help. Because content frequently follows form, the host anxious to win the thrust of an audience has made sympathy with their problems a standard feature of a carefully cultivated public persona. Programs may deal with subjects of no long-term consequence to an audience, but viewers are still willingly transformed into voyeurs witnessing telegenic images of pain, humiliation, and healing. The subjects occupying the greatest attention have increasingly little to do with vital public issues but everything to do with private choices and personal feelings. Revealingly, the first two questions Donahue asked one of the members of his Soviet audience dealt with when he first had sex and whether he used a contraceptive.

Ours is an era that revels in preoccupation with the self.[17] Even the considerable public achievements of individuals can seem insignificant in comparison with the facts of their personal biographies. A narcissistic culture defines human relations less in terms of the formal styles of public manners than in the riveting details of personal relationships. This "tyranny of intimacy," notes Richard Sennett, places a premium on "personality" as *the* defining feature of social relations. How a person "feels" or what someone "experiences" can matter as much or more than how well they perform their public roles.

"Intimacy" connotes warmth, trust, and open expression of feeling. But precisely because we have come to expect these psychological benefits throughout the range of our experience, and precisely because so much social life which does have a meaning cannot yield these psychological rewards, the world outside, the impersonal world, seems to fail us, seems to be stale and empty.[18]

The sexual activities of a senator may become more interesting than his political skill. The life-style of an actress may surpass interest in a specific performance she gives or in her gifts as a public performer. In much of the West there is a narcissistic quest to confirm that the rich and famous have suffered the same kinds of personal indignities that frequently interrupt the routines of ordinary lives. Guests on "Donahue" and other similar programs are invited to talk about the details of their first sexual encounter, their wedding night, an addiction to "one-night stands," or varied forms of humiliation at the hands of acquaintances, spouses, and parents.

Nothing, it seems, is off-limits. In 1988, for example, Donahue devoted a program to mothers who had actually killed one of their young children. The therapeutic frame of reference was perhaps the only perspective that could have made the program acceptable to a general television audience. Clinical rather than criminal explanations removed some of the weight of personal responsibility from the participants. The talk in that program was of "stress," "postpartum psychosis," and "hormonal imbalances." In the therapeutic mode of communication, the search for external causes partially replaces blame and personal accountability.

With subjects like these the line that separates useful information from blatant exploitation is very thin. Those who suffer from mental and physical problems may appear on a program ostensibly to offer useful information, but they may also serve the purpose of delivering a very large audience to strings of adjacent thirty-second commercials. Their secrets and misfortunes are easily transformed into a kind of public entertainment that is sanctioned by a therapeutic motive. Guests on informational talk shows seem to exist in a peculiar middle region that is neither public nor private. At times some are like the paper-gowned patient in the doctor's examining room: vulnerable to the need to sacrifice privacy for therapy. Others are more like the willing nightclub stripper who entertains through artfully calculated disclosure. Both are prepared to reveal secrets to expectant eyes but for very different reasons. No one would mistake a reluctant patient for a lusty stripper, but in the grayer world of talk show television, the pretense of respectablity easily conceals the dubious reasons for our rapt attention.

## THE SETTING

Donahue's program with Soviet teens was taped in a Moscow studio provided by Gostelaradio, the government agency in charge of broadcasting. At the agency's request a Soviet crew was used, but Donahue—sensitive to the possible charge that he was used by the Soviet media—noted that little else "was different from the way that we might want to show off our best side to a Soviet television crew." About 350 students were picked from two local high schools described by *Time* as among the "most prestigious."[19] The rapid pace of the show was preserved through the use of simultaneous English and Russian translations delivered through individual headphones. Even so, an impressive number of the students conversed with Donahue in English.

### The Audience

In his 1976 book *The Russians* Hedrick Smith wisely noted that "generalizing about Soviet youth is as impossible as generalizing about American youth."[20] Differences in regions, family backgrounds, and income levels make even simple stereotypes suspect. What few common denominators Smith found in the 1970s are probably still valid. Many feel what must be the universal pinch of generational differences. Students in large cities also appear to be as career oriented as their counterparts in Peoria or Philadelphia; joining the "right" organizations and applying to the best schools are usually important objectives. Most have become sexually active by the time they finish high school, in spite of the fact that those seeking an amorous adventure must be especially creative in a nation where so many families share crowded living spaces. David Shipler, who followed Smith as the *New York Times* Moscow bureau chief, reported many of the same patterns in his more recent book on Soviet life.[21] Soviet teens are like their American counterparts, but even in the early stages of *glasnost* there were subtle differences of emphasis.

## Soviet Defensiveness

One long-term characteristic just beginning to change in 1987 was the extreme reluctance of Soviet citizens to go on record criticizing anything but the most trivial cultural flaws. Virtually every Westerner returning from the Soviet Union recounts a wealth of stories about the daily grind of bureaucratic red tape that entangles everything from buying good shoes to finding a place to live.[22] Even party leader Mikhail Gorbachev has railed against low efficiency, poor production quality, and the indignities the vast official superstructure imposes on daily life. Yet most citizens remained defensive and wary around Western reporters; whatever criticism they harbored against state institutions were usually borne silently.

Shipler, for example, described a meeting he requested with about fifty members of the Communist party teen organization Komsomol. In the United States there is perhaps no counterpart that carries as much influence with so many younger citizens. In large cities it combines the activities and facilities of a well-equipped American YMCA with the public spiritedness of a service organization. Although it has lost some of its clout in recent years, Komsomol still provides the Russian equivalent of an "old boy" network, leading to admission to good schools and better jobs. As an extension of the party, many of its activities carry the zeal and moral commitment of a religious organization. Its evangelism, however, is not based in religious orthodoxy but in the political pieties of Soviet socialism. Komsomol members quote and misquote the scriptures of Marx and Lenin with a familiar kind of Sunday school certainty. Not surprisingly, Shipler found most of those he encountered were unprepared to hear questions challenging their government's foreign policy motives. More unusual was the extent to which they were not prepared for Shipler's unexpected criticism of American actions.

My simple effort to maintain that neither of our countries always acted out of the noblest of motives ignited an astonishment and rage that swept the entire room, twisting the youngsters' faces into hurt and anger. Unwittingly I had challenged a most fundamental vision of a world divided into good and bad, and the teenagers and adults were each struggling, fighting to retain that vision and keep it intact. It reminded me of the view from my teenage years in the 1950's, when the world was cut unambiguously by an iron curtain, and America still stood on the side of purity. . . .
. . . They were clearly put off-balance somewhat by my readiness to criticize American as well as Soviet behavior; I did not seem to fit the standard mold of propagandist.[23]

Donahue found less vehement denial in response to his own questioning, no doubt the effect of the *glasnost* that followed after Shipler's experiences in the early 1980s. However, he did find a continuing reluctance to criticize openly aspects of domestic Soviet life. In warming up his audience just before the taping began, Donahue grew frustrated at their passivity. He wanted to see some willingness for cultural self-examination, the kind that comes easy to Westerners who are encouraged to explore the inevitable gulf that separates cherished national ideals and the harder realities of daily life. "You are like sheep," he told them. "Are we going to spend the entire program listening to you tell [Americans] how wonderful everything is here?"[24] Their responses indicated a degree of patriotism that has long been out of fashion in the West, especially Europe. Britain, Italy, and France have long traditions of political turmoil created by students agitating for internal reforms. For Soviet youth in 1987 the pattern was still reversed; their beloved state provided genuine reassurance against external threats posed by the United States and other anti-Soviet nations.

### What Is Fit for Discussion?: A Reversal

A second interesting difference between American and Soviet youth could be seen in the relative status of religion and sex as topics for public discussion. Members of Donahue's Moscow audience were clearly embarrassed by his opening questions on when they first "had sex" and whether it was true that "most young women are virgins when they get married." These queries seemed as inappropriate in Moscow as they would have been had the topics come up at a gathering of the Moral Majority. After this frosty start, wrote *New York Times* reporter John Corry, "it was a relief to get on to the popular music" provided by a local rock group.[25]

Interestingly, these same Soviet teens exhibited a strong degree of publicly expressed certainty about the "waste" of religious training. Unlike American youth who are publicly more circumspect about the status of their own faith, some of these Soviet teens were surprisingly frank about why they do not believe in God. Several expressed a passing interest in the rituals of the church, but many criticized the "spiritual drug" of religious belief. Skepticism was obviously a sanctioned norm, even though the Soviet Union still contains an enormous number of devoted Christian and Muslim believers.

### THE PROGRAM[26]

[1]  *Phil Donahue*: Would you kindly stand for one second, please? You had sex when you were 18 years old?

*Audience*: Yes, that's when I started.

*Phil Donahue*: Did you use a contraceptive when you practiced sex at age 18?

*Audience*: Yes.

[2]  *Phil Donahue*: Did you take care of this matter yourself or did the girl insist that you do it?

*Audience*: Yeah, I knew about it before. Before that I knew quite a bit. I knew how, when, what, etc. I was well prepared.

*Phil Donahue*: Are most Soviet boys conscientious, like you, in protecting the girl from pregnancy?

*Audience:* Basically, yes. Why don't you ask the others?

*Phil Donahue:* Yes.

[3] *Audience:* You talk as though everybody here was already involved in that. I think when most of my girlfriends had gotten married at 18 or 20, they were virgins, and before marriage they did not engage in sex. They were waiting for that one special man, for that one special person, and they found that one special person. And most of their husbands also, for most of them their wife also was the first woman with whom they had ever had sexual relations.

*Phil Donahue:* Is that true with most girls? Most young women are virgins when they get married, in the Soviet Union?

*Audience:* Well, a great number of girls are virgins until marriage. They only really begin sexual life after marriage. I don't really know, maybe not everybody.

[4] *Audience:* You know, I just want to say that I think it's quite the opposite. You can't really say that it's very good if a girl when she gets married is still a virgin, because I think quite the opposite. She should be quite sure of what her husband is as a man, that he'll be a real partner for her; otherwise it could be a real tragedy. And sex for a married couple is extremely important. After all, sex is 80% of happiness for a married couple but, of course, that depends on each individual woman. But for me I think that's very important.

*Audience:* I think it is necessary to change the subject of conversation, because these questions are very deep to be concerned by us.

[5] Phil Donahue (speaking over tape): This is day two of our visit to the Soviet Union. In this hour Soviet teens give a powerful exchange on everything, from religion to war. But unlike American teenagers, areas they were reluctant to discuss included dating, school, and sexuality.

*Audience:* It's not a surprise that American students can't understand us, because they have many more problems than we have, the criminality, drugs, etc. Secondly, all boys and girls here are in somewhat different surroundings. This is new to them. They've never been on television and this is the reason why they can't immediately talk to you as they do in America, where they are probably more easygoing, and when they may even have [the] experience of being on television.

*Audience:* What can we do if everything is all right here? Should we create problems? We don't want to invent problems!

*Audience:* School is likewise, sometimes you are happy and sometimes you express just no particular emotions, and that's all.

[6] *Phil Donahue:* All right, I will listen to your advice and I will change the subject. We also will be hearing from Rondo, one of the most popular rock groups here in the Soviet Union. And we'll hear from them in a moment. First, I would like to ask you, do you have a favorite American rock group or rock personality?

*Audience:* Van Halen.

*Phil Donahue:* Yes.

*Audience:* (Unintelligible)

*Phil Donahue*: Let me practice moving about this large crowd here.

*Audience*: Lionel Richie.

*Phil Donahue*: Lionel Richie, yes.

*Audience*: Michael Jackson also.

*Phil Donahue*: Would you like to have Rondo perform? Please welcome Rondo. (Rondo performing, followed by commercials)

[7]  *Phil Donahue*: May I share with you, please, another stereotype notion that some Americans have of you. They think that people in the Soviet Union are not permitted to—are not encouraged to believe in God, and not encouraged, or are discouraged, from practicing religion. Do you believe in God? And do you practice religion, and is this important to you?

*Audience*: I personally don't believe in God because our science has proved that [he does not exist], I think. But there are people who do believe, and I think that they believe because they haven't found a solution to their problems perhaps, and they are trying to run away from them. I think that religion simply hampers people.

*Phil Donahue*: Yes.

*Audience*: I think that since the church and state here are separate, maybe you might go have a look at a church just if you're interested. I think all those old rites are extremely interesting. They are beautiful. For example, the Easter procession is very interesting simply because it's beautiful. You have to know what kind of rites existed in the country before the separation of church and state. In the past people did believe in religion, and after all, they had some reasons for doing so. But right now—

[8]  *Phil Donahue*: Isn't communism an atheist philosophy?

*Audience*: Of course it is an atheist philosophy, but in our country we have freedom for people to believe what they want, and a man can be a communist or he can be a believer. The law doesn't forbid that, and therefore, if he wants, he's free to go wherever he feels like.

*Phil Donahue*: Would you mind sharing with us your views on this issue?

*Audience*: You know, I personally very much love the past. I would have nothing against going and taking a look at those rites, but right now you've got all those really pious old women in the church and you try and avoid going so as not to get into conflict with them, because they are those old people who were sort of born from the beginning of the century, they are over 80, and they stick to their old beliefs. They still believe in those things and they don't accept the fact that practically no one believes in God anymore. And, therefore, they try to prevent young people from coming to church.

[9]  *Phil Donahue*: You don't believe in God?

*Audience*: Of course not. I'm a member of the Komsomol and therefore I don't.

*Phil Donahue*: But the Komsomol is the youth adolescent group that helps you devote your energies to the Soviet Union and to also understand its tradition and to be proud of it. Is that an accurate reflection of that organization?

*Audience*: Yes, it is a social organization. It's found throughout the Soviet Union. Consequently, for practical purposes, all of the young people are members of the Komsomol, those who want to be of use to their country, who want to actively work for their country.

*Phil Donahue*: Are all members atheists?

*Audience*: I really think so, yes.

[10]   *Audience*: That girl said that she was a member of the Komsomol, she didn't believe in God and she only finds the past interesting in terms of the church. Well, my father is a communist, he's [been] a member of the Communist Party from 1918 on. He joined the Party as soon as he could. But he's also very familiar with church rites. He knows all of those holidays very well because he has had to study that. He was the leader of an atheist group and had to do that [because] you have to know all those church rites if you're going to fight against them. In order to struggle against religion you have to get to know it first. And second of all, religion is more complex than one might think. It's more complex than we might understand and people can believe in God and not go to church, for example, or there might be people who believe in God but simply prefer to be quiet about it.

*Phil Donahue*: Why do you have to struggle against religion?

*Audience*: Because somehow religion numbs people's minds. It's opium for the people, because belief in God, I think, is pretty complicated. It's more complicated than simply going to church and beating your head against the floor there in prostrations.

*Phil Donahue*: Hang on just a moment.

[11]   *Audience*: I want to say that in your country a lot of people believe in God, but they don't reject the cruel films and the crimes. Why is there in your country very many cruel films, very many murders? And they believe, they go to churches, and they don't reject that cruelty. Why? Maybe it's not true? Maybe they don't believe; maybe it's all a mask.

*Phil Donahue*: All a mask.

*Audience*: Personally I don't believe in God, but I think church exists for those who have a weak character. The church is now against people; it fans wars.

*Audience*: I and all my friends simply don't believe in God because we don't see any need for it.

[12]   *Phil Donahue*: Is there anybody in this room who believes in God? One, two, three, four, five, six. You believe in God?

*Phil Donahue*: How do you explain you're in the minority?

*Audience*: I don't think that God exists sitting up there in the sky somewhere, but I think that faith is simply an integral part of the human soul and that each person in his soul believes in God, because I think you can't live without faith.

*Audience*: (Applause)

*Audience*: I think that you don't absolutely have to believe in God, but you have to believe in something. A person can't simply live without any kind of faith at all, and within each person I think there must be a kind of God. There has to be something for which he can live. You can't simply go ahead and live without having that internal God.

[13]   *Audience*: Our American comrades are somewhat disturbed apparently that our churches aren't being supported, but true belief doesn't require any support or propaganda. Personally, I don't believe in God, but I was interested in some Christian matters and I'm close to the position of Dostoyevsky who considers that God should be in your soul but not outside.

*Audience*: (Applause)

*Audience*: In the United States there is a somewhat distorted religion. Rock operas like Jesus Christ Superstar and all that, prove it. This doesn't seem to go together with the Christian principles.

[14]   *Audience*: Many have said that they don't believe in god; now why don't you raise your hands, those of you who were baptised. The majority. And you say that you don't believe in God, that your father was a communist. So what? Communism is not a religion.

*Audience*: It is also a religion!

*Audience*: It's an ideology.

*Audience*: What do you mean ideology? Isn't Christianity an ideology?

*Audience*: You were simply convinced of that. Somebody convinced you.

*Audience*: Have a good look. Isn't Christianity an ideology?

*Phil Donahue*: Yes, hang on.

[15]   *Audience*: Perhaps people don't always believe in God, but people always believe in something good. They believe in things that they can do. And if people believe they can't do something themselves, then they believe in something supernatural.

*Audience*: I agree because I think that you don't have to absolutely believe in some kind of an idol or something, but you have to believe in something good, something right, something just for yourself and for your friends. You don't have to look at somebody and say somebody is God. You can just use somebody as a model and say that that's the kind of person I would like to be.

*Audience*: Well, people say that communism is a kind of religion, like Christianity, but, after all, communism is based on scientific principles. And what about Christianity? Throughout time the church has simply been a screen and behind it have been more intelligent people who have been running things and running the lives of all those believers.

[16]   *Phil Donahue*: Please let this young woman speak.

*Audience*: In my point of view, religion is a kind of spiritual drug which can only simply help a weak person survive. But in the USSR young people are mostly attracted to the church because it's a kind of spectacle, because it's very pretty, it's beautiful. All of those rites on the holidays are beautiful in the Russian churches. And, for example, even when you get married in the marriage palaces, you can't compare that to getting married in the church, just because it creates a completely different kind of mood when you get married.

*Audience*: I think right now we're talking about religion, but I think that everybody believes in some kind of good. I don't think we should confuse believing in the good with faith in God. Those are completely different kinds of things. . . .

*Audience*: Communism isn't fostered in your country and religion isn't fostered here. Every country can adopt its own position and have different opinions. There are things that in a certain country are not being encouraged. There's nothing wrong in that. I don't see anything wrong in that.

*Phil Donahue*: And we'll be back in just a moment.
(Commercials)

[17]  *Phil Donahue*: Some of you feel that the American culture is too materialistic, and that we are only concerned about property and money. Is that so? What are your views about the American people?

*Audience*: I don't think that the American people are materialistic and uncouth. I have a very positive view of the American people. It's a people that defended its freedom, had great cultural achievements, and it could not be as gross and materialistic as you think we think.

*Phil Donahue*: So I'm wrong then about your perception of us?

*Audience*: I consider the American people as the closest to the Soviet people in spirit, and nobody in the world is as close to us as Americans and upon the way in which we behave towards one another. Everything depends. The Americans are very close to us. I like Americans.

[18]  *Phil Donahue*: If you like Americans and we are so close to you, then why have your governments spent so much money on armament, which we say we are developing because we don't trust each other?

*Audience*: Does your government spend less money on arms than we do? The more you spend, the more we spend. Everything is linked.

*Audience*: Common Americans approve such—(trying to speak English)

*Phil Donahue*: Would you care to speak in Russian?

[19]  *Audience*: Common, ordinary Americans, do they feel bellicose about us? Do they want to make war on us?

*Phil Donahue*: They do not want to make war on you, no. But we have spent billions of dollars on military armament in order to be prepared in the event of what we call the communist aggression.

*Audience*: (Laughter)

*Phil Donahue*: And the perception is that you want to export your way of life, your philosophy, and that it is the belief of some Americans that you in some places do this by military might.

*Audience*: So that means that they don't support that arms race or does it mean that they have a feeling of dislike for us? How do they feel about us?

[20]  *Phil Donahue*: How do Americans feel about you? I think millions and millions of Americans admire you. I think the vast majority of the people in the United States believe that you, like them, are people who are interested in peace, people who are compassionate, and people who want a safe world for your children. But there is some concern about the behavior of your government with the many, many missiles that are in place near Western Europe—Eastern Europe. With the many billions of rubles that you spend on military hardware, Americans are looking and saying we better be prepared in case you decide to be militarily aggressive.

*Audience*: But how many times has our government and Mikhail Gorbachev proposed disarmament? Why does your government and Mr. Reagan ignore those proposals? After all, we agree, we young people, we love each other, we have nothing against each other. We're ready to be friends.

*Audience*: I don't know how correct you are when you say that they admire us, but very often when they show broadcasts from America where they show interviews with kids, sometimes they don't know anything about us, they really know almost nothing about our countries, so I don't see how you can say that they admire us. Your authorities don't say anything about our country except anti-Soviet propaganda about war and things like that.

*Audience*: (Applause)

[21]  *Audience*: A few days ago I was talking with an American—I speak English very badly—but when we talked about art and science and things like that we understood each other very well. But as soon as we started talking about politics, it turned out that two different people were talking. He showed me an atlas that was published in America and it showed the Soviet Union as taking up the entire world. It's true that we take up a great deal of territory, but we don't cover the entire world. After all there's Africa, Antarctica and other countries.

*Audience*: (Laughter)

*Audience*: And then we do an umbrella, we are talking about SDI [the Strategic Defense Initiative undertaken by the Reagan administration], and he showed us that umbrella. Now, comrade Americans, why do you need an umbrella when there is no rain? That's it.

[22]  *Audience*: I don't know about all Americans, but we had an American boy, Gus, in our school and we talked to him about everything under the sun, music, art, anything you want. Now I don't consider that Americans are so anti-Soviet. American youth, on the contrary, are very close to us.

*Audience*: Why do you say that you want to know what our policy is, whether we disarm. . . . Your information media informed your people very badly about our positions. Your information media. We know that.

[23]  *Audience*: I just want to say that the ideology of our government, in addition to the fact that they tell us everything as it is about your country, they tell us not only the bad, they tell us the good. We know a lot about your writers, your actors, and different films, and when it comes to us they tell you practically nothing about us. And then you say you talk about the arms race, that we're after that and so on, but

those are only response measures to you. We're never going to be the ones to engage in a first strike.

Phil Donahue: That's what we say. We say we are not going to engage in a first strike and we are responding to your military build-up. And then you say, no we are responding to your military build-up, and the argument continues back and forth until we have 60,000 nuclear bombs in the world now, and the United States and the Soviet Union own most of them. When is this madness going to stop? Why won't we stop blaming each other and reach across this gap between East and West and start to talk to each other?

Audience: I want to say that I think that the whole problem here is that we can't meet more often with each other, just ordinary American people with Soviet people, and get together and just talk

[24]  Audience: I would like to say the way I feel about you Americans. I think you are marvelous; I think you are great, intelligent, kind people. I think you've got an absolutely marvelous cultural heritage. We love you, we know your culture, we know Hemingway and Salvadore Dali and think they are fantastic people. We love you, we respect you, we want to see you more and want to meet with you more.

Phil Donahue: Yes.

[25]  Audience: We say that your government is engaged in an arms race as a consequence of what our country does, but for a year and a half our country has had a moratorium on nuclear explosions. Why doesn't your country do the same thing?

Audience: (Applause)

Phil Donahue: Yes.

Audience: I try to speak to Americans. They are people, but they speak only about money. But I think it's only their trouble.

Phil Donahue: Money?

Audience: Money, only money. They speak only of money.

Phil Donahue: Yes.

[26]  Audience: What I would like to say is that the Soviet information media were enormously worried about the film AMERIKA which purports to show that our troops occupy your country. I would like to say that I am about to do my military service. I guarantee to you that I will not invade your territory with a machine gun if you don't invade us. And before that film has started being shown, I'll tell all Americans that I will never attack them personally.

Phil Donahue: And we'll be back in a moment.
(Commercials)

[27]  Phil Donahue: Are all of you prepared to serve in the Soviet Army?

Audience: I have already done my stint in the army and I'm going to a technical institute. When I went into the army I was sure of myself. Physically it may be difficult, but from childhood the feeling for our homeland is engrained in us, instilled in us, the sense of duty. I would like to know whether American youth have a sense of duty to their homeland, for living in that country. I am very happy, by the way, that I live in my country.

*Phil Donahue*: American youth do have a sense of duty to their country. But, as you know, America's recent history has been marked with some unhappiness and agony because of the Vietnam War, and there is still a great debate in the United States about whether or not we should have engaged in that war. That is the American tradition of arguing about the foreign policy decisions of our government. American thinks that you are not able to argue about these decisions and you must follow the dictates of the government without being able to argue about the rightness of the decisions. Let me get someone else who might want to get in. Yes.

[28]   *Audience*: The military service has problems: the problem of the limited contingent in Afghanistan, and people who go into the army sometimes get sent to Afghanistan and end their lives before they even start living. Many of us are afraid to go into the army because we are afraid that we will be sent to Afghanistan to be killed there. Many people have been killed there.

*Phil Donahue*: Who wants to speak to this?

*Audience*: As far as I know, and I have a lot of friends who are planning to go into the army, as far as I know, many of them want to go to Afghanistan in order to test themselves, to try and see what they are capable of.

*Audience*: (Applause)

*Phil Donahue*: Yes.

[29]   *Audience*: The problem of Afghanistan isn't a matter of desire but of duty. It's the internationalist duty of our youth, and boys go there not because they want to, but because their assistance is required there. That's why they go. You people say that Americans argue with their government. Now does that change anything? So they criticize and demonstrate. Does that make the government change its mind?

*Audience*: You said that we cannot argue against our government; we can, but I don't think that will yield any result.

*Audience*: What is in that government that one has to argue against and what are its decisions?

*Audience*: (Applause)

[30]   *Audience*: What are these decisions of a government that one has to argue against?

*Phil Donahue*: Whether or not the military conflict in Afghanistan is proper. Wouldn't that be one question? If I'm understanding this man, you don't want to go to Afghanistan as a soldier.

*Audience*: That's correct.

*Audience*: I can say one thing. I had a cousin who was killed in Afghanistan. Everybody speaks of internationalist duty, but I am ready to die for my homeland, quite honestly, but I'm not prepared to die for others. I've not the slightest intention of doing so. A very large number of boys who haven't even started living are dying in Afghanistan, and I'm against it.

[31]  *Phil Donahue*: If you were called by your government to go to Afghanistan as a soldier, would you go?

*Audience*: Of course, I have to do it, but in my soul I would be against it.

*Phil Donahue*: Yes. Let me get someone who hasn't had a chance. Yes.

*Audience*: I've already been in the army. I used to think that Afghanistan was terrible, but when you've done your service—towards the end of your military service—there is no such idea about giving your life. If you have to give your life, you do. But those who have been in the army will never say that. There are boys here who have done their military service; they understand it. It's their duty, a duty of a citizen of our country. Any soldier that you ask will be glad to go to Afghanistan if he's asked to go. There's no such discussion in the army. An order is an order and you carry it out.

[32]  *Phil Donahue*: This young man said he didn't want to go. In America many young people—if they have that opinion—are permitted to say so. Do you think that's a good idea?

*Audience*: I don't know. It may be a matter of age.

*Phil Donahue*: Wait a minute. Did I misunderstand you?

*Audience*: I didn't say that war was wrong. I said that the losses sustained by us are losses that are wrong. But the assistance that we give to Afghanistan is correct, our internationalist aid.

[33]  *Audience*: I have a question. How do you assess that war in Vietnam? Do you see it as a tragedy for the American people or not? I heard a song of the Paul Hardcastle group called "19," and the words of that song said that none of them were seen as heroes. They were all 19 and it really was a tragedy, as I understood it. Is that true? Was it really a tragedy?

*Phil Donahue*: Was the Vietnam War a tragedy?

*Audience*: Yes.

*Phil Donahue*: Well, we lost 58,000 young men and eight women, whose names appear on a Vietnam Memorial in Washington. And some Americans are saying why. Why?

*Audience*: I also would like to ask that question: Do you think it was a just war or not for the American people?

[34]  *Phil Donahue*: My personal opinion, which my country allows me to express, is that the Vietnam War, the United States decision to go to Vietnam to fight in this military conflict, was a mistake. I do not think the United States should have done that. Not everybody in America agrees with me. The Vietnam War split our country very badly. Even today arguments continue about whether or not we should have engaged in it. My point is that many people in the United States are saying at least we can argue about whether or not this particular foreign policy decision is a good idea. They see the Soviet Union as a place where no argument is tolerated.

*Audience*: I was also in the army and had many friends who went to Afghanistan and not one single one of them said that he was sorry he had been there. Everybody understood that what they did was for a just cause. They understood that they were doing their internationalist duty. These are my friends and that's the way they talked.

*Phil Donahue*: Yes. And we'll be back in just a moment.
(Commercials)

[35]   *Phil Donahue*: Very little time left. I just want to give some of you a chance to make your points. Yes.

*Audience*: Your society is interested in business. It's profitable for them to produce weapons, and that's why they try and propagandize and say that the Soviet Union makes weapons and turns some people against us.

*Audience*: Do we look like aggressors? On the contrary, we want to see Americans. You don't show them.

*Phil Donahue*: Do Americans look like aggressors?

*Audience*: No, I don't think so.

[36]   *Audience*: I would like to ask you, you and your friends here in the Soviet Union, do you believe in the possibility of communist aggression? Do you really believe that we would attack your country?

*Phil Donahue*: Well, Americans remember your Premier Khrushchev who said, "We will bury you." That's what Americans heard him say. Americans also looked up and saw the Soviet invasion of Czechoslovakia. Americans believe that the Soviet Union's presence is felt in Cuba, where Soviet missile bases were being constructed, before they were stopped by President Kennedy. I'm not here to call you names or to make criticisms, but to remind you that there is evidence that is available to the American people which suggests that you are not as a nation, as a government, always like doves. Do you understand that? So if Americans appear to be concerned, they can point to a number of instances which suggest that your words do not always match your policy.

[37]   *Audience*: We were just talking about this right now. I think this is the most controversial topic that we've been talking about today. Why don't we see Americans so we could know what they think. We know very little about Americans, I think. Would it be possible to have a broadcast?

*Phil Donahue*: So maybe there were some problems in the past with your media, with your information service, just as you have criticized ours?

*Audience*: Well, I don't know.

*Phil Donahue*: Yes, way back here.

[38]*Audience*: I think that communist aggression, as your country sees it, is impossible because for so many years now our government has been engaged in a unilateral moratorium. Moreover, your government has not been responding to this.

*Phil Donahue*: May I say that there are a number of Americans who admire your government for the moratorium. I do not speak for all Americans, no one person does, but, please, let me share with you the information that millions of Americans admire the Soviet decision to have the moratorium. Yes. With very little time left. Yes.

*Audience*: To admire isn't enough. You should support that moratorium in deeds.

*Phil Donahue*: Many Americans do. Let me get somebody else in.

[39]   *Audience*: You just said that your people have a right to dispute your government. Now where are these millions of Americans who are against the position of the government?

*Audience*: (Applause)

*Phil Donahue*: My good man, there are more public demonstrations in support of the moratorium and the peace movement in the United States than there are in the Soviet Union. I myself was in Central Park with almost one million people who were there to support peace, to support détente. So, please, don't believe that Americans who feel this way are hiding their feelings and not expressing them. Let me get to someone back here who hasn't had a chance. Yes.

[40]   *Audience*: I want to answer a question about my attitude towards Americans. I spent 10 years there and I like them and I think that they like us very much too. I saw their attitude toward us because I was in the hospital and I saw it.

*Phil Donahue*: What is the attitude?

*Audience*: They like us.

*Phil Donahue*: See. Please don't think of us as all being hawks who are somehow interested in a military solution to every problem. Let me get someone who hasn't had a chance. Yes.

[41]   *Audience*: If the government doesn't harken to the voice of the people against the arms race, then your government does not reflect the interests of your people.

*Phil Donahue*: Yes.

*Audience*: We can all agree with what has just been said, that there is not much of a chance to find out about each other, but then what about films, for example? In the U.S. there are a lot of films in which Soviet people are shown only from the negative side.

*Phil Donahue*: But I think there are a number of films produced in the Soviet Union in which Americans are portrayed in a stereotypic way.
(Commercials)

[42]   *Audience*: I think that even if President Reagan wants to join in the moratorium he will know the fate of President Kennedy, because everything is up to the military industrial complex. It's they who dictate the policy.

*Phil Donahue*: That is a very narrow view of American society. You have just as narrow a vision of us, if you hold that view, as you accuse us of having of you. Please believe that American society is much more complex than what you make it. You had a suggestion. What was your suggestion?

*Audience*: I suggest that to express our goodwill, we should sing together a very well-known song to America and to us, "We Shall Overcome."

*Phil Donahue*: Everyone here know the—

*Audience*: Yes.

*Phil Donahue*: Who is a good singer who can start us? Who is a good singer? I need someone to start. You want to start?

(Audience singing "We Shall Overcome")

*Phil Donahue*: Goodbye, and thank you all very, very much.

## ANALYSIS: THE LIMITS OF PERSUASION

Near the midpoint of his program, Donahue noted that "we have 60,000 nuclear bombs in the world now, and the United States and the Soviet Union own most of them. When is this madness going to stop?" The answer he provided to this rhetorical question was probably Donahue's justification for doing this program. The potential for military confrontation will end, he said, only when "we stop blaming each other and reach across this gap between East and West and start to talk to each other"[23]. Many professional diplomats believe it is naive to think that contacts between ordinary citizens can make much of a political difference, but fortunately for the human race, communication between nations is usually not limited to intergovernmental contacts. Even so, anyone expecting dramatic persuasive inroads to be made as a result of these exchanges would probably be disappointed. The conversion of these youth by Donahue was as unlikely as the transformation of his television viewers into supporters of the Kremlin.

### Learning by Example

From a Western perspective the most hopeful outcome of this hour might be that it was a small but useful step in presenting a pluralist debate for members of a society that in 1987 had seen too little of it. The fact that a popular television host could dissent from the official policies of his government without impugning anyone's political legitimacy offers its own useful political lesson. Donahue questioned not only the motives of the Soviet government[36] but those of the present American administration as well[34, 39, 40]. It may have been instructive for this audience to hear an American represent not only Official Truth (i.e., "the views of my government") but also sympathetic characterizations of competing factions on issues such as arms control and the Vietnam War. Though less novel in the Soviet Union today, the role of a public celebrity as both a defender and critic of his society was still an unusual communication stance when the program was taped.

Perhaps Donahue's American audience learned that the concerns and doubts of these teens—with the exception of their unusually frank atheism—were not all that different from the views of their American counterparts. Other might have also discovered that Americans and Soviets still know very little about each other's culture or history [20, 23, 37]. Recognition of this sea of ignorance was not only acknowledged by several of the participants but was unintentionally demonstrated in a number of the exchanges. It was not so much that members of the audience had no impressions of life in the West but that their perceptions were occasionally so wide off the mark. The suggestion by one that President Reagan would have been assassinated by the "military industrial complex" if he had endorsed the nuclear freeze moratorium was only the most extreme case [42].

## At Home in the Soviet Union

This cross-cultural dialogue—like most—clearly grew out of two very different sets of culture-bound perceptions that even faithful translations could not completely bridge. With some important exceptions,[27] persuasion is possible only after the preliminary acquisition of shared meanings, assumptions, and values. The chance for persuasion arises only when opposing advocates begin to share the same definitions of what a given situation means. American military activity in other nations may be labeled "justified" by one side and "aggression" by the other. Persuasion occurs when such polar opposites are broken down—if ever—through what is usually a process of lengthy give-and-take. In the words of Kenneth Burke's much-quoted axiom, "You persuade a man only insofar as you can talk his language by speech, gesture, tonality, order, image, attitude, idea, identifying your ways with his."[28]

This is an obvious point, but there is an additional dimension to the idea of "shared definitions." What Burke calls the "tonality" of language involves more than what symbols specifically "mean", but how we negatively or positively react to their concrete referents, as well. Consider for a moment the web of cross-cultural attitudes just in the limited realm of sports. An American and European may initiate a conversation about the glories of "football" but very quickly discover that by that single word they mean two very different games. The European game is what Americans call soccer. Yet even after so basic a misunderstanding is cleared up, there often remains a nationalist subtext of values tied to the way cherished local versions of a sport are understood. The conversation might take a relatively benign turn, for example, with one conversant explaining the rules of a game that is not played in another's country. But often the more ego-satisfying response is to engage in at least an implicit comparison of sports from the distinctive national perspectives of each communicator. The manifest content of a discussion might at first appear to be informational and descriptive, but judgments will probably lie very near the surface. British and American sports enthusiasts thus talk about how "similar" the game of rugby is to the American game of football. A sense of tact may leave the merits of the differences unspoken by each conversant but not unfelt. If this hypothetical talk drifts into a comparison of American baseball and the British equivalent of "rounders," the American may only later discover that many British perceive their version as too feminine for adult men to play. Sports, like national politics, is layered with assumptions about the prowess, guile, and motivations of its players. Thus, while foreign visitors may be expected to learn the rules of a domestic sport, natives will often express doubts that they can ever fully understand its place in the culture.

To a significant extent Donahue and his audience were probably caught in a similar cross-cultural trap: at once sharing the hopeful language of conciliation while still remaining captive to the verbal residues of the cold war. Even when we travel, we are linguistically still "at home." Few of the participants should have been expected to escape domestically generated preconceptions. After simultaneous translation everyone in the studio ostensibly communicated with the same words—for example, "ideology," "disarmament," "Vietnam," "business," "demonstrations"—but even this terminology of places and things probably carried a good deal of nationalistic baggage. The obvious goodwill among all concerned could not have been expected to overcome the term-guided judgments subtly acting to maintain rather than diminish national differences. "Afghanistan," "atheism," and "human rights" have built-in anti-Soviet tonalities for Americans, just as "materialism," "crime," and "property" carry negative judgments for many Soviets. For one student, Soviet military involvement in Afghanistan was a matter of "internationalist duty"[29]; for Donahue and his American viewers it was a symbol of Soviet aggression[19, 20].

Part of what was obviously guiding perceptions here were years of public exposure to official views communicated by each country's dominant media. It is "the ideology of our government," asserted one of the Soviet teens, to "tell us everything as it is about your country"[23], but to read this transcript is to sense the effects of decades of political propaganda faithfully communicated to each nation's citizens through the agenda-setting media in each country: Time, "NBC Nightly News," Pravda, Soviet television's "Vremya," and others. Donahue and his audience appeared to be freely exchanging views in the program, but in a real sense their issues were determined for them. In most cases, agenda-setting media will dictate the four or five pivotal issues that will provide the framework for most formal meetings of East and West block citizens.[29] Most of them appeared here, including American concerns about human rights and Soviet military aggression, and Russian questions probing the gap between American poverty and prosperity. Growing out of the cold war, such issues have made most of us the captives of homegrown truths about very distant cultures. As one student revealingly noted after talking with an American, "When we talked about art and science and things like that, we understood each other very well. But as soon as we started talking about politics, it turned out that two different people were talking"[21]. Her observation was revealing. On political issues both were probably acting less as free agents than as faithful carriers of nationalistic news agendas.

## The Gulf of Hidden Assumptions

An important assumption that seems to have been felt by this audience, if never explicitly addressed, is the durable idea that an attack on official doctrine is somehow an attack on the state. As the discussion of Afghanistan especially illustrated [27–34], the symbols of Soviet officialdom can carry enormous political legitimacy. Soviet citizens are more inclined than Americans to submerge their private feelings about policy in favor of more visible sanctioned expressions of support for the state. Although they can be extremely critical of the inefficiencies of ordinary governmental bureaucracies, they tend to step carefully around the sharp line that divides their cynicism from their ritual support for official Soviet policy. The institutional conflicts that are formally preserved in American life—for example, between opposing parties, between the president and Congress, between the mass media and public officials—have no similar legitimacy in Soviet culture. Under the "new openness" the average citizen has become aware that members of the Chamber of Deputies may dissent from the general secretary, but as late as 1987 many citizens still looked hard to find personal vindication in the official actions of their government.

The same can be said for many Americans, but the relationship between the nation and the individual is somewhat different. There is a broader sense of separateness from the state. Governmental symbols ranging from the president to the flag carry the formal authority of honored national institutions. But the romance of American life is enshrined in the very different view that the individual should define his existence more in personal than in national terms. As Europeans sometimes observe, North Americans are better described as patriots rather than as nationalists. Americans generally believe that the genius of their culture resides in acts of private rather than governmental enterprise, a bias reflected well in Thomas Jefferson's assertion that the nation could better do without a government than a free press.[30]

Thus, a deeper meeting of minds would have required a new universe of discourse established, if ever, by long-term direct contacts rather than brief encounters. Even then, it would have been an uphill struggle for Donahue to convince these students of the wisdom of challenging official policy on Afghanistan or for the Soviet audience to persuade American viewers that there is something demeaning about so easily dismissing one's own national culture.

## Donahue as Uncle Sam

Donahue's gift for television lies in his ability to facilitate dialectic. As we have seen, a typical program involves bringing an articulate audience in contact with guests who have often lived through unusual events. By these standards, the Soviet encounter seems to have presented a difficult problem. As it was set up in Moscow, Donahue functioned essentially as his own guest. There was no one else to mediate between. The program lacked the usual discussion-by-triangulation that works so well when he can play guests against audiences or guests against other guests. Donahue has a large repertoire of communication responses, including those of fact finder, advocate, questioner, skeptic, and mediator. He depends on these roles to maintain the television persona of a forceful but undogmatic presence. In Moscow, however, the absence of guests left him restricted. He soon discovered that there were no personal crises or factual biographies to coax out of these youth; hence, there was no place for the therapeutic mediator. Moreover, his ability to function as a skeptic was partially restricted by the necessity to perform for this audience; the youthful—and in some ways vulnerable—extensions of his official hosts. Since sarcastic incredulity and verbal combat would have seemed ungenerous, he was left with the limited options of questioning his audience, listening to their views, and sometimes defending American points of view.

No persuasive encounter is more difficult than when an advocate facing a hostile audience must serve as a surrogate for the interests of a secondary audience. This relationship can be summed up in the question Donahue's American television viewers might have asked themselves as the program unfolded: "How well will he do at defending *our* way of life against *theirs*?" Publicly representing or "fronting" for the interests of one collectivity presents an interesting rhetorical problem. This task comes easy to some, but it is poison for most journalists who cherish an *ethos* of independence. It is no secret that Donahue is better at deflating public relations puffery than producing it. He once threatened to leave his show when its corporate owners refused to allow FCC commissioner and television foe Nicholas Johnson to appear.[31] Few journalists who value their independence want to be put in the position of a spokesperson; it suggests a kind of "flackdom" that is abhorrent to their ideal of editorial independence.

Deprived of his customary format, Donahue was thus forced to walk a thin line that would allow him to retain his reputation as a free agent while still representing American national values. The issue of Soviet troops in Afghanistan, for example, raised questions about American actions in Vietnam. Was Vietnam "a just war or not for the American people?" Donahue was asked. His response was at once a dissent *and* a patriot's affirmation, reflecting his two very different audiences:

My personal opinion, which my country allows me to express, is that the Vietnam War . . . was a mistake. I do not think the United States should have done that. Not everybody in America agrees with me. The Vietnam War split our country very badly. Even today arguments continue about whether or not we should have engaged in it. My point is that many people in the United States are saying at least we can argue about whether or not this particular foreign policy decision is a good idea. They see the Soviet Union as a place where no argument is tolerated.[34]

In the short space of one hour there was probably no pretense of doing more than exchanging very different and often conflicting impressions. Even so, this brief event was successful if it simply nurtured the goodwill necessary to carry on the process of rapprochement at other times and in other places.

## A FINAL THOUGHT

Finally, beyond the limited effects of this one program, it is worth noting that the general form of the information-oriented talk show speaks to a fundamental change in the way issues are framed for the American public. Too often analysts and journalists still proceed on the assumption that policy advocacy is largely the domain of legal or official advocates communicating through the familiar channels of the newspaper and the newscast. Traditional news formulas for policy discussion usually give preference to professional advocates on issues: politicians, industry leaders, academics, and others. What has changed? For the average television viewer, the costs and consequences of public issues—ranging from the use of state funds for religious schools to the virtues of rapprochement with the Soviet Union—are increasingly represented in the responses of guests who appear on programs like "Donahue" as victims or advocates. We are attracted to these populist sources because of their willingness to "witness" in behalf of the traumatic or therapeutic consequences of public policy. These relatively new shows point to the fact that our civil life is bound up in a new hybrid forum that owes as much to teleevangelism as to political journalism.

### NOTES

1. Michael J. Arlen, *The Camera Age: Essays in Television* (New York: Farrar, Straus, and Giroux, 1981), p. 318.

2. "The Talk of Television," *Newsweek* October 29, 1979, p. 76.

3. Brian G. Rose, "The Talk Show," in *TV Genres: A Handbook and Reference Guide*, ed. Brian G. Rose (Westport, Conn.: Greenwood Press, 1985), pp. 330–331.

4. Marvin Kitman, "Keeping Up with America," *The New Leader* June 18, 1979, p. 25.

5. "The Talk of Television," p. 77.

6. Nan Robertson, "Donahue vs. Winfrey: A Clash of Talk Titans," *New York Times* February 1, 1988, p. C30.

7. Phil Donahue, *Donahue: My Own Story* (New York: Simon and Schuster, 1979), pp. 212–213.

8. Ibid., pp. 99–100. This claim might be challenged now, given the intense competition for audience share that exists between syndicated talk programs. Any "snapshot" of program topics presents a mixed picture. For example, a consecutive five-day period between October 16 and October 20, 1989, included the following scheduled "Donahue" titles for New York City's WNBC: "Abortion for Rape and Incest Victims," "Sexual Minorities," "Rules for Marriage," "How Far People Will Go for Entertainment," and "Female Sexual Stereotypes." For the same week and time period, New York's WCBS offered "Geraldo" with these scheduled topics: "Crimes of Madness," "Vigilantes," "Rich Women Addicted to Cocaine," and "Lisa Lisa, Cool Moe Dee, and Paul Anthony." The Tuesday "Geraldo" segment was replaced by a network program. (Source: "Television," *New York Times*, October 15, 1989, sec. 11.)

9. This is a paraphrase of an assertion that Friendly has made many times and is

best documented in his book *Due to Circumstances beyond Our Control* (New York: Random House, 1967).

10. *Newsweek* "The Talk of Television," p. 78.

11. Frank McConnell, "Watching Talk," *Commonweal* April 22, 1983, p. 246.

12. Among the most exotic of the mean-spirited shows was Morton Downey, Jr.'s, before it was canceled in 1989. A nightly exercise in invective and ad hominem attacks, his prime-time program specialized in victimizing "bleeding heart liberals," "communist sympathizers," homosexuals, and intellectuals. In comparison with the polite audiences of "Oprah" or "Donahue," Downey's audiences were predominately white, male, and angry. A common feature of most programs involved the evocation of jingoistic patriotism to flail against alien values at home and hostile forces abroad. Whether or not Downey's working-class angst was genuine, his audiences seemed to enjoy the thrills that come from watching their favorite hulks go through the motions of throwing their weight around. See Randall Rothenberg, "Morton Downey, Jr. Is Taking His Abrasive Style Nationwide," *New York Times* May 16, 1988, p. C15; and Harry F. Waters, "Trash TV," *Newsweek* November 14, 1988, pp. 72–78.

13. Plato, *Theaetetus* in *The Dialogues of Plato, Volume II*, trans. B. Jowett (New York: Random House, 1937), pp. 151–152.

14. "Donahue" broadcast, WPVI, Philadelphia, February 16, 1988.

15. "Donahue" broadcast, WPVI, Philadelphia, February 18, 1988.

16. For more detailed discussions of therapeutic rhetoric, see Carl Rogers, *Client Centered Therapy* (Boston: Houghton Mifflin, 1951); Richard L. Johannesen, *Ethics in Human Communication, Second Edition* (Prospect Heights, Ill.: Waveland, 1983), pp. 45–65; and Wayne Brockriede, "Arguers as Lovers," *Philosophy and Rhetoric*, Winter 1972, pp. 1–11.

17. This is the well-argued central point of Christopher Lasch's *The Culture of Narcissism* (New York: Norton, 1978).

18. Richard Sennett, *The Fall of Public Man* (New York: Vintage, 1978), p. 5.

19. Richard Zoglin, "Stirring Up the Comrades," *Time*, February 16, 1987, p. 79.

20. Hedrick Smith, *The Russians* (New York: Ballantine, 1976), p. 231.

21. David K. Shipler, *Russia: Broken Idols, Solemn Dreams* (New York: Times Books, 1983), pp. 51–93.

22. See, for example, Daniel Ford, "A Reporter at Large: Rebirth of a Nation," *The New Yorker*, March 28, 1988, pp. 61–80.

23. Shipler, *Russia*, p. 128.

24. Zoglin, "Stirring Up the Comrades," p. 79.

25. John Corry, "A Week of Donahue Taped in Soviet Union," *New York Times*, February 12, 1987, p. C30.

26. This transcript of the broadcast was furnished by the "Donahue Show," © 1987 Multimedia Entertainment, Inc. Most of the comments from the audience are translations from Russian. The grammar and syntax of some comments have been slightly edited to improve the readability of the transcript.

27. The primary exception is persuasion by mystification. It has been defined elsewhere as "the use of jargon to imply that the persuader has special authority and expertise to which others should defer." See, for example, Gary C. Woodward and Robert E. Denton, Jr., *Persuasion and Influence in American Life* (Prospect Heights, Ill.: Waveland, 1988), p. 166. The jargon carries power because it seems to represent a special expertise or knowledge that cannot be matched by the persuadee. In this case the ironic effect is that

mystifications depend on the willingness to defer based on the perception that one has little or no understanding of a subject. We sometimes willingly succumb to the evident (if not fully understood) superiority of the expert. For a wide-ranging discussion of mystification, see Hugh Dalziel Duncan, *Communication and Social Order* (New York: Oxford, 1962), pp. 190–237.

28. Kenneth Burke, *A Rhetoric of Motives* (New York: Prentice-Hall, 1953), p. 55.

29. For background on this agenda-setting function of the mass media, see Maxwell McCombs, "The Agenda Setting Approach,"in *Handbook of Political Communication*, ed. Dan D. Nimmo and Keith R. Sanders (Beverly Hills, Calif.: Sage, 1981), pp. 121–140; and Shanto Iyengar and Donald R. Kinder, *News That Matters* (Chicago: University of Chicago, 1987), pp. 1–33.

30. William Rivers, *The Adversaries: Politics and the Press* (Boston: Beacon, 1970), p. 8.

31. Donahue, *Donahue: My Own Story*, pp. 193–197.

# 6

## Thomas Szasz and the War against Coercive Psychiatry

Psychiatrists are, in fact, crypto-priests, and . . . their job is to bless and to damn. Holywater is holy not because of the kind of water it is, but because a priest has blessed it. A schizophrenic patient is schizophrenic not because of the sort of person he is but because a psychiatrist has damned him.[1]

*Thomas Szasz*

As a polemicist, Szasz has no peer. He has succeeded in focusing attention on the loose and easy quality of psychiatric definitions, on the destructive and indelible stigma that often accompanies psychiatric diagnosis, and on the unique and easily corrupted power that psychiatry has been granted. He has spawned an entire movement of anti-psychiatry.[2]

*Charles Krauthammer*

Szasz attains his role as proxy spokesperson for the rights of the mental patient by ignoring, simply, what it is to be a mental patient.[3]

*Peter Sedgwick*

In 1971 a journalist preparing a profile of Thomas Szasz caught in one small moment the essence of this controversial psychiatrist's work. Szasz and twelve students were engaged in a diagnostic interview with a patient at the Upstate Medical Center in Syracuse, New York. The person seeking help was a heavyset woman in her fifties, complaining through periodic bursts of tears of a "pulling in her head." Szasz thoughtfully took notes on his yellow legal pad while his clutch of future therapists listened and looked on. It was a routine interview.

The patient anguished over the course that her life had taken and offered vague descriptions of the physical sensations inside her head. After the session with the troubled woman he queried his students on what they had seen.

"Well, what is your diagnosis?"

"I think that she's in a chronic depression," concluded one intern.

"I think that it's a case of involutional melancholia," ventured another, "but for right now I guess I'd concur in a diagnosis of chronic, severe depression."

"And how would you go about treating this 'condition'?" Szasz asked.

Someone suggested that the woman could be given Elavil, an antidepressant drug.

"So you would treat this sickness with drugs?"

The way Szasz posed the question made it obvious to these wary students that yet another sacred principle of conventional psychiatry was about to be challenged. He urged them to consider two parallel explanations for the patient's condition. "Has she got an illness called depression, or has she got a lot of problems and troubles which make her unhappy?" In the world of institutional psychiatry, there is no safer clinical diagnosis, but it is a world that Szasz has ceaselessly attacked. He was clearly pushing for an alternative explanation. What they observed, he suggested, was not a "sick" person with "depression" but an "unhappy human being." "Tell me, does the psychiatric term say more than the simple descriptive phrase? Does it do anything other than turn a 'person' with problems into a 'patient' with a 'sickness'?"[4] The patient did not need drugs or conventional "therapy." Since her real problem was, as Szasz might say, "in not knowing how to live more successfully," its solution could not be found in the misused and overused metaphor of "illness."

This episode illustrates why Thomas Szasz has angered and frustrated many of his colleagues. For him the very idea of mental illness is a mask, a convenient but misleading label to account for the behavior of others that we do not like or do not understand. "Illness" carries the expectation that medical problems can be found and externally treated—a legitimate objective when pathologies stem from biological and chemical malfunctions. But he has consistently argued that psychiatry has no comparable mandate to treat "problems of adjustment" as if they were diseases.

Even as he approaches seventy, Szasz remains an enigma to the mental health field. He is a professor of psychiatry, and yet he does not believe in many of its major tenets. He maintains a private practice, but he continues to reject many of the fundamental principles of psychotherapy. Well-known labels for emotional and mental disorders such as *paranoia* and *schizophrenia* carry no legitimacy in his work. Using every forum available to him—from *TV Guide* to the most obscure journals, from widely read books to television talk show appearances—Szasz has railed against the conventional wisdom about "mental disease," "drug abuse," and links between crime and insanity. All are "myths," he claims, perpetuated by a mental health movement that has done a better job of giving employment to administrators and therapists than in treating the problems of the "mentally ill."

## SZASZ AND THE PROBLEM OF SERIAL PERSUASION

Szasz's persuasive themes are explored here not only because they challenge so many of the assumptions and principles of modern psychiatry but also because the way they have reached the public is typical of the serial nature of many influential forms of communication. Thus far in this book we have focused largely on single and dramatic confrontations, but the reality of public persuasion is that it is often a continuing process rather than a specific event. Szasz's impact on his colleagues and interested observers has been cumulative, beginning in 1961 with the publication of *The Myth of Mental Illness* and continuing in a steady stream of nearly 400 articles and 15 books.[5] As in the work of so many other advocates of political and social doctrines, there is no single rhetorical moment that can be credited with establishing his activist reputation or his influence. In the mental health field his ideas have been stewing in the caldron of public debate for three decades, imparting their pungent flavor to a wide range of psychiatric and legal issues.

It is obviously very difficult to track the longitudinal persuasion that is common to social movements or lifelong advocates. Most studies of persuaders—including those examined elsewhere in this book—proceed implicitly from psychologically oriented microtheories capable of accounting for how messages have affected specific respondents. In early experimental research on compliance and resistance to messages, subjects exposed to persuasion were never very far from question-naires or other measurement techniques designed to detect small changes in attitudes.[6] But even the most evocative ideas are subject to time-delayed effects, following both visible and subterranean routes through the culture. Sometimes influence is direct and immediate; at other times, an advocate's ideas are carried by others.[7] The differences in these two patterns are summarized in Figure 6.1.

As the model of "simple persuasion" indicates, a base-line expectation for persuasion is that at least small changes in attitude will occur in some audience members after they are exposed to a message. This expectation holds if the message is salient—that is, seems relevant and well argued—and if the available evidence of the audience's reactions supports its saliency. The study of Edward Kennedy's Liberty Baptist speech in Chapter 3 is an example. The well-crafted message and various accounts of public reactions to it provided evidence of its effectiveness. Szasz's style of confrontation, however, has been very different. In serial persuasion hundreds of messages with different emphases filter through society from both primary advocates and their surrogates. Few Americans have probably read Szasz's provocative books and articles, but many have probably had indirect contact with his ideas. His persuasion is the product of a diffusion process involving various advocates and media. Such multistep advocacy is dif-

Figure 6.1
Single versus Serial Persuasion: Idealized Effects of Messages on Prior and New Attitudes

## Single Persuasion

Some persuasion involves a single message directed to a gathering of individuals, i.e.:

Message ------- Audience (individuals A, B, C, D, etc.)

A general attitude can be found and recorded as relative disagreement or agreement. In simple persuasion the net change that occurs because of exposure to a message can be expressed as the difference between prior and new attitudes; for example, in individual "D":

(Prior)        disagree-----+----------agree

(New)          disagree------+---------agree

The marginal change reflects the limited potential of most single events.

## Serial Persuasion

Persuasion often occurs in a series of messages presented by a variety of advocates over longer periods of time. Changes in attitudes are still incremental, but multiple opportunities for access to individuals means that serial persuasion may keep producing new attitudes, for example:

(Attitude change in D)

Message[1] ------- --------+-+--------

Message[2] ------ ------+-+--------

Message[3] --- ----------+-+-------

The pattern renews itself as converts such as D carry their own messages forward to others:

(Attitude change in E)

Message[4] ------- --------+-+---------

Message[5] ----- ----------+-+-------

Message[6] --- ----------+-+-------

etc., etc.

ficult to grasp, but it is the foundation of persuasion ranging from advertising to single-issue political movements.

This chapter is thus not primarily about an individual message given to a specific audience, nor is it exclusively about Szasz the psychiatrist. It focuses instead on a coherent body of rhetoric that is interesting for two reasons. Most clearly, it carries the imprint of professional betrayal; Szasz is ostensibly a part of the field he seeks to indict. In addition, Szasz is also a persuasion theorist. His belief that labels often constitute "treatment" suggests that even ostensibly clinical procedures are bound up in the potent medicine of language. Psychiatry, he argues, is primarily about the power to name.

We begin with a review of several major themes that he has consistently reiterated in his work. These are further illustrated in two brief samples of his argumentation. In the last third of this chapter we explore some of the dimensions of the surprisingly truncated debate that has occurred between Szasz and other mental health professionals, specifically: the probable effects of his polemical style on his own credibility and on public perceptions about mental health. It is obvious that this synoptic treatment must be more suggestive rather than definitive. Even so, his work must be understood for what it is—something close to a one-man crusade against a deeply entrenched establishment. To date, notes Dava Sobel, Szasz has waged nothing less than a "Thirty Years War with organized psychiatry."[8]

## MAJOR THEMES IN SZASZ'S WORK

Szasz is known primarily for his assertion that the concept of mental illness is a myth. This view, elaborated in so many forums, flows from two basic premises repeated many times. One asserts that the medical paradigm for describing "deviant" behavior, with its emphasis on disease and therapy, is inappropriate for characterizing mental problems. The second elaborates a libertarian doctrine—explored at length in more recent works—asserting that wide acceptance of the "therapeutic state" neglects the fact that all persons are free agents, even when their behavior affronts us.

### The Power to Name

The first premise stems from Szasz's observation that psychiatry has incorrectly defined itself as a branch of medical science with its own diagnostic/therapeutic terminology. He has consistently argued that the supposed medical roots of psychiatry are metaphoric, not literal. Whereas medical doctors discover physical anomalies and then give them more or less precise names (i.e., high blood pressure, low blood sugar, etc.), psychiatrists tend to function in the reverse. For them, names become the primary tools for focusing on alleged "illnesses" that usually cannot be understood through biological or chemical phenomena.[9] They repeatedly make the mistake of assigning scientific words to *patterns of personal conduct*: words that implicitly describe behaviors as quasi-medical "conditions." To be sure, Szasz recognizes that some forms of erratic behavior can result from brain disease, but he remains totally skeptical of efforts to find biological roots for common psychiatric disorders.[10]

He goes on to assert that the "medicalization" of unusual behavior is an authoritarian act because it unjustly makes one person the ward of another. Psychiatrists function too often as "classification officers" with the necessary prestige and legal mandate to justify someone's removal from society. "To classify another persons's behavior is usually a means of constraining him. This is particularly true of psychiatric classification, which too often has the effect of legitimizing social controls placed on so-called mental patients."[11] Words like "neurosis," "psychosis," "emotional illness," and "psychoanalytic treatment" represent an "outmoded conceptual framework." Not only do they function more as judgments than factual descriptions of behaviors, but their disease-oriented subtext conceals considerations of personal choice that should surface when a person's behavior is called into question.[12] When behavior is renamed as an "illness," it creates expectations that the patient has an unusual condition that warrants submission to the will of a "mental health"specialist.

For example, Szasz believes that the movement to redefine alcoholism as a "disease" represents a key linguistic mistake. When the problematic behavior of drinking too much carries the label of a "disease," it has the effect of making the sufferer a victim rather than a free agent with moral and social responsibilities. "Excessive drinking is a habit," he notes. "According to the person's values, he may consider it a good or bad habit. If we choose to call bad habits 'diseases,' there is no limit to what we may define as 'disease'—and 'treat' involuntarily."[13] For better or worse, the heavy drinker has made choices that carry consequences.

## Freedom and Choice

Szasz's second major assumption grows out of the first. Underpinning most of his work is the view that all adults have the right to make their own choices, just as they have obligations to observe the choices made by others. Individuals must be free to choose their own life options unfettered by the large hand of the state or by psychiatrists who are given power by the state to inhibit individual freedom. Autonomy is more than a nice democratic ideal; it is the basic measure against which all other human and institutional action should be judged. Individual liberty is a "hard won prize" that is a prerequisite for everything else in society worth having. From his perspective, "personal development" means "individual liberation, in which self-control and self-direction supplant internal anarchy and external constraint."[14] The options people exercise in their lives carry moral implications from which they should not be excused, even under the guise of mental illness. Authorities who seek to restrict individual freedom must bear the burden of proving that they do so only to protect others from harm.

These twin values of autonomy and responsibility have the ironic but significant effect of reframing the origins and practices of psychiatry in the language and assumptions of political philosophy. His political roots reflect the libertarian view that the fewer controls and regulations placed on human action, the better. Sometimes this view has made Szasz appear to be an avid supporter of patient's' rights. At other times his critics have noted that it provides a potent rationale for reducing federal and state assistance to Americans on the fringes of sanity. Either way no ethical assumption so clearly guides the judgments he passes on the work of his peers. This shift from a scientific to a normative vocabulary obviously has enormous consequences for how he views the recent history and current practices of psychiatry.

### Attacks on "Institutional Psychiatry"

At its worst, psychiatry is a "pseudoscience" that legitimizes the removal from society of people who make the rest of us feel uncomfortable. Its widespread acceptance has parallels in the Inquisition of the Middle Ages and in the detention of Soviet dissidents in "psychiatric hospitals." This pseudoscience has fraudulently provided ways to force conformity on individuals who are sometimes guilty of nothing more than being out of step with the dominant ideologies of their times.

For Szasz, the mental patient is usually better understood as "a person who fails, or refuses, to assume a legitimate social role." People with "so-called mental health problems" may engage in socially unacceptable acts, but their deviance is no reason to suspend their fundamental right to make choices. Most never harm anyone. Even so, the fact that they offend others is usually enough to see them "recaptured, first symbolically, by being classified as mentally ill; and then physically, by being brought to the psychiatrist for processing into formal psychiatric identities and for psychiatric detention."[15] "As far as I'm concerned," he noted in 1971, "the concept of illness should be restricted to disorders of the body—things like diabetes, organic brain damage, cancer. Because, as the most simple-minded observations ought to make clear, what is called 'mentally ill' is in fact behavior which is disapproved of by the speaker."[16]

The view that the "mentally ill" person is a "patient" helplessly in the grip of an "illness" that "causes" him to display abnormal behavior is false. Although many so-called mentally ill persons do not deliberately ("consciously") choose their "symptoms" and suffering, their behavior is, nonetheless, conduct. Such persons do not lack the capacity to make moral decisions; on the contrary, they exaggerate the moral dimensions of ordinary acts, displaying a caricature of decision making behavior. "The last thing that can be said of a lunatic," wrote Gilbert K. Chesterton, "is that his actions are causeless. If any human acts may loosely be called causeless, they are the minor acts of a healthy man; whistling as he walks; slashing the grass with a stick; kicking his heels or rubbing his hand . . . .
The madman is not the man who has lost his reason. The madman is the man who has lost everything except his reason."[17]

But what about people who have harmed others? How do we account for the horrible and incomprehensible actions of mass murderers, assassins, and individuals who commit suicide? Szasz's answers are comparatively simple, if not very satisfactory to his critics. He believes that in spite of legal defenses to the contrary, most people who commit even the most bizarre crimes can be held responsible for their actions. If they have harmed others in ways that seem irrational to us, their actions represent bad choices, not "illnesses." If a clear biological or neurological disorder is evident, of course it should be treated if the patient so desires. But a mass murderer should be punished, not excused through the inappropriate application of a medical metaphor. "All criminal behavior should be controlled by means of the criminal law, from the administration of which psychiatrists ought to be excluded."[18] He believes that we mistakenly assume that behavior that makes no sense to us cannot have a rational basis in anyone else's mind. Someone who kills ten other people may receive pleasure from his acts. For that person, the satisfaction of killing may be the logical if unacceptable outcome of what Szasz would view as an "evil" rather than "insane" person. The state, he says, is right to exercise its displeasure by punishing rather than explaining such dark behavior.

As for the suicidal person, just because we are unable to comprehend the reasons of people who attempt to take their own lives, we should not assume that there are none or that they are irrational. The despondency that triggers a suicide may be based in solid reasons that psychiatric jargon masks rather than illuminates. Since freedom carries responsibility, people must relearn the fact that many so-called medical problems such as suicide involve predominantly moral rather than therapeutic issues.

I maintain that suicide is an act, not a disease. It is therefore a moral, not a medical, problem. The fact that suicide results in death does not make it a medical problem any more than the fact that execution in the electric chair results in death makes the death penalty a medical problem. Hence, it is morally absurd—and, in a free society, politically illegitimate to deprive an adult of a drug because he might use it to kill himself. To do so is to treat people as institutional psychiatrists treat so-called psychotics; they not only imprison such persons but take everything away from them . . . until the "patients" lie naked on a mattress in a padded cell, lest they kill themselves. The result is one of the most degrading tyrannizations in the annals of human history.[19]

## Treating "Clients" Rather Than "Patients"

Even this brief overview is enough to raise an obvious question about what a Szaszian psychiatrist does. If mental illness is a myth, if people experiencing "problems in living" are misdiagnosed as "sick," is there any legitimate role for psychotherapy? No review of Szasz's ideas can be complete without noting how he responds to this apparent paradox.

While it is true that Szasz is primarily known for ransacking the house of psychiatry, he has developed in *The Ethics of Psychoanalysis* and elsewhere at least a partial substitute vision of his discipline.[20] In response to the traditional therapeutic goal of making the patient better able to function in society, he substitutes the more modest objective of having a "client" come to grips with life's options. The result is a distinctly noninstitutionalized form of psychiatry.

Although I consider the concept of mental illness to be unserviceable, I believe that psychiatry could be a science. I also believe that psychotherapy is an effective method of helping people—not to recover from an "illness," it is true, but rather to learn about themselves, others, and life.[21]

Szasz sees little benefit in state or legal involvement in psychiatric work. Since the state should not have the power to commit people to its hospitals, it also should not have the authority to declare defendants unfit to stand trial. He believes juries can easily tell if someone is responsible enough to be charged for a crime. Long before court judgments restricting the ability of states to commit patients or force them into treatment,[22] he argued that there is no legal or moral justification for the "warehousing" of the mentally ill in the hundreds of institutions across the country. No psychiatrist should participate in the coerced (but technically "voluntary") commitment of an individual to a hospital. Even behind "the unlocked but well-guarded doors of 'open hospitals,' there are still the involuntary patients, deprived of legal protection and tranquilized into submission."[23] Such institutionalization is a form of political repression, aided by "health professionals" who function as little more than jailers. If some people are actually helped in such hospitals, Szasz notes, it is only because they have been removed from their everyday responsibilities.[24]

Does psychiatry exist to help the individual or society? If the interests of the two are in conflict, as Szasz believes they often are, the psychiatrist can only help one.[25] He comes down firmly on the side of the client's rights over the state, arguing that this is one of the legacies left by the pioneering work of Sigmund Freud. Clients can be helped through a contractual arrangment of "autonomous psychotherapy" paid for by the patient rather than "coercive" institutions of the state, such as the courts. The prime aim of this therapy should be "to give patients constrained by their habitual patterns of action greater freedom in their personal conduct."[26]

As he envisions it, "autonomous psychotherapy" is not predominantly a medical activity. Instead, it is a process of coming to terms with the ethical choices clients face. One specific analytic approach that he describes is the breaking down of verbal traps that unreasonably limit acceptable choices presented to a client. Both clients and therapists, he believes, play "word games." People seeking help from psychotherapy deliberately misname their actions to conceal deeper but unacceptable feelings. Therapists engage in equally deceptive forms of medical naming, especially in the use of terms like "schizophrenia" or "character disorder." The avoidance of these unproductive games involves the creation of "an ideal setting for effecting translation from the language of excuses into the language of responsibility."[27] Thus, in response to a client who claims that "hard as I try, I am unable to love my husband," Szasz suggests that the therapist could help her reach the point where she is able to determine the extent to which

she does not *want* to love her husband . . . and does not *want* to stay marrried . . . . The analyst assumes that, with clearer understanding of her wants, for both continuing and discontinuing the marriage, the patient will be in a better position to decide on the course of action she wishes to pursue.[28]

## Autonomous versus Biological Origins of Behavior

Finally, our brief overview needs to at least touch on an issue that frequently arises as a counterargument to Szasz. Are we not now learning that many behavioral disorders are caused by chemical and biological imbalances that are absent in "normal" people? Is mental health not strongly affected by perhaps poorly understood but nonetheless real biochemical or genetic conditions? Szasz does not rule out the fact that some physical disorders may cause unusual behavior, but he has little faith in the claim that the same kinds of causes can explain common psychiatric categories. "Psychiatrists," he writes, "often claim that mental illnesses have a 'biological basis' and act as if proving this would establish that these so-called illnesses are bona-fide diseases. But being a jockey or basketball player also has biological bases—in the conditions of being short or very tall—but they are nevertheless not diseases."[29] Searching for genetic or biological correlates to traditional psychopathic categories is a vain attempt to make passive "patients" out of active free agents.

Even the increasing attention given to possible genetic and chemical links to schizophrenia leaves Szasz unconvinced.[30] He believes that the well-worn diagnostic category of schizophrenia is little more than a catchall term for people who have failed to understand how to perform workable social roles in their daily lives. Because schizophrenia is defined by behavior, it is best understood as containing discrete acts of volition created by social rather than biological circumstances.

Genetic research on why children of schizophrenic parents are more likely to have schizophrenia than are children of nonschizophrenic parents is like genetic research on why children of French-speaking parents are more likely to speak French than are children of non French-speaking parents.[31]

People allegedly suffering from schizophrenic behavior would benefit more from having a place to live, a job to do, and money to spend than from therapy. "If what we call 'suicide' is a cry for help," Szasz has written, "then what we call 'schizophrenia' is often a cry for housing."[32]

## SZASZ'S ARGUMENTATION: TWO CASES

This overview is sufficient to show how deeply against the grain many of Szasz's key assertions are. It remains to illustrate the distinctly polemical style in which these views have been expressed. As the two following short articles reveal, Szasz's rhetoric is often more assertive than analytic. He is far more likely to define a position by describing how it differs from the norm than how it fits with other accepted ideas. Compared with most exchanges between professionals in the sciences, his attacks on psychiatry sometimes sizzle with indignation. This feature of his work is no small matter; it routinely draws as much attention from his critics as his ideas.

"Back Wards to Back Streets" is a summarizing piece written in 1980 for *TV Guide*. As one of America's most-read magazines, *TV Guide* provides a valuable opportunity to advocates who want to present capsule views of their major themes and arguments. "The Freedom Abusers" first appeared in a 1979 edition of an obscure political journal that has since folded. It offers a uniquely Szaszian analysis of the Reverend Jim Jones, the religious leader who engineered the suicides and mass killings of most of his followers in Jonestown, Guyana, a decade ago. Driven by an intense sense of persecution, the charismatic Jones had convinced many of his followers to leave northern California to establish a religious Eden in the South American jungle. The 1978 visit of a congressman to Jonestown triggered a bizarre bloodbath. Concerned about charges that members of the sect were being held against their will, Representative Leo Ryan's visit triggered the mass suicide and murder of 912 of the camp residents, many of them children. Jones also committed suicide but not before he ordered Ryan and several others in his party also killed.

## "BACK WARDS TO BACK STREETS"[33]

[1]   Like hair styles and popular songs, psychiatric treatments are largely a matter of fashion. In 1938, electric-shock treatment was introduced into psychiatry and was immediately hailed as a cure for schizophrenia. But soon the question was asked, "Does it work?" It was the same story with lobotomy. The doctor who developed it even received the Nobel Prize, in 1949, for his work—the ultimate stamp of approval of our scientific age. But again, the question soon became: "Does it work?" The latest psychiatric fad is "deinstitutionalization"—a professional sounding if grotesque term referring to the policy of transferring patients from mental hospitals to other psychiatrically supervised facilities. This policy, introduced into psychiartry about 15 years ago, has also been hailed as a revolutionary advance. Now people are again asking, "Does it work?"

[2]   As an old saying has it, ask a stupid question and you get a stupid answer. Asking whether electric-shock treatment, lobotomy, or deinstitutionalization work is stupid because such questions assume certain things about mental illness and mental hospitalization that are, quite simply, false.

[3]   To understand the problems that the so-called deinstitutionalization of mental patients was supposed to solve—and the problems it has in turn created—we must first

be clear about why and how people end up in mental hospitals. According to conventional wisdom, "patients" are admitted or committed to mental hospitals because they are mentally ill, are dangerous to themselves or others, and need psychiatric treatment. This is all bunk. Let's examine these ideas, one at a time.

[4]   *Mental Illness.* Aside from the possibility that there may be no such thing (that is, that "mental illnesses" are merely the names we give to certain undesirable patterns of behavior), the presence of mental illness "in" a person does not explain why he or she should be in a hospital any more than the presence of medical illness "in" a person explains why he or she sould be in a regular hospital. Most people suffering from arthritis, diabetes or hypertension are not in hospitals. Why, then, should people suffering from "mental illnesses" be in hospitals?

[5]   *Dangerousness.* It is widely assumed that many so-called mental patients are "dangerous to themselves and others." If by dangerousness we mean that such persons injure themselves or others, then the problems they present are not medical but moral and legal. Injuring oneself—by drinking too much, ingesting toxic drugs, etc.—indeed, result in disease; but the behavior itself is the act of a moral agent, comparable to marrying the wrong man or woman or investing in the wrong stock. Injuring others is, likewise, not a medical problem: It is assault, arson, murder, or some other mischief—for which the only rational remedy is punishing the offender. Just as illness is not a crime, so crime is not an illness.

[6]   *Mental Treatment.* Although the promise of psychiatric treatment is now an acceptable justification for mental hospitalization (both with and without the patient's consent), this is a very feeble justification indeed. In the first place, if there is no mental illness (as I contend), then there can be no such thing as mental treatment (as I also contend). But even if we accept the reality of mental illnesses and treatments, why should mentally ill persons be in mental hospitals to receive mental treatment? The main forms of psychiatric treatment today are conversation ("psychotherapy") and drugs ("chemo-therapy"). Neither method requires hospitalization.

[7]   So the question remains: Why are people in mental hospitals? In my opinion, the correct answer to this question is that they are there either because they have escaped from society or because they have been expelled from it. The former are the voluntary mental patients, the latter the involuntary ones.

[8]   Some persons—because they are fearful, weak, or lazy—want to drop out of society; others—because they are ineffectual, odd, or offensive—are dropped out of it. In the modern world, the mental hospital has become the natural habitat of such persons—where they quickly become even more desocialized.

[9]   In my view, the mental hospital is not a hospital at all; it's only; *called* that. Unlike medical hospitals, mental hospitals are homes for the homeless—asylums for those who have, for a variety of reasons, no place of their own and none where they are welcome. In short, they are orphanages for adults. (They are also prisons for certain lawbreakers, but this function of the mental hospital cannot be considered in this brief space.) In addition, the mental hospital furnishes employment to large numbers of people with no salable skills in a free market. Satisfying the self-defined aspirations, interests and needs of so-called mental patients was never among the aims or functions of the mental hospital system. It still isn't.

[10]   Now we are ready to take a fresh look at the "deinstitutionalizing"—or "dump-ing"—of mental patients. As we say, the problems that this policy was supposed to solve were themselves wholly artificial: If doctors and lawyers—and last but not least, the

relatives of so-called mental patients—had not commited hundreds of thousands of individuals to mental hospitals, there would have been no chronic "institutionalized" patients to discharge.

[11]   About 15 years ago, for a number of complex reasons, psychiatric bureaucrats and politicians decided that mental hospitals were bad places for mental patients. This is a supremely ironic idea, since it is what involuntary mental patients had been asserting for the past 200 years. But that is beside the point here. The point is that, since most people in mental hospitals are more or less socially disabled, they cannot simply be discharged. Moreover, many mental-hospital patients (even if they enter the hospital involuntarily), come to like it in the institution—which provides them not only with room and board but also with an escape from the day-to-day responsibilities of ordinary life. In short, deinstitutionalization is yet just another sham "reform" or "treatment"— and here are the reasons why.

[12]   Like other psychiatric "reforms" and "treatments," deinstitutionalization is supposed to be something that we—psychiatrists, sane people, society—do *for* crazy mental patients. But it's not true. Just as years ago "crazy" people were incarcerated in mental hospitals against their will—now they are evicted from them against their will. Mental-hospital patients are not given a choice between staying in the institutions that have become their homes or moving into broken-down hotels in the slums. In the name of doing something good *for* mental patients, once more something terrible is being done *to* them.

[13]   Psychiatrists, lawyers, and sane people continue to treat deinstitutionalized mental patients as they always have—as crazy, sick, irresponsible. The vicious circle generated by a psychiatry based on "mental illness" and "mental treatment" remains unbroken: the "patients" are psychiatrically supervised and medicated (whether they like it or not); are stigmatized as crazy; and are not punished when they commit crimes (after all, they are "mentally ill" and hence not responsible for their actions).

[14]   So, of course, deinstitutionalization will not "work" either. Why should it? It's another smoke screen, another evasion—by the medical and legal professions as well as by the public—of the brutal facts of the human destiny; namely, that not everyone can "make it" in life; that those who cannot are not sick; and that a free society cannot afford to regard as "insane" or "irresponsible" either those who wish to escape from their responsibilities because they find society too demanding or those whom society wishes to expel because it finds them too demanding.

[15]   Institutionalizing human beings in the name of psychiatric care was, as now nearly everyone admits, a shame. Deinstitutionalizing them in the name of psychiatric progress is a sham.

[16]   I am frequently asked: What *should* be done, then, about those we call "mentally ill"? I have addressed the implications of that deceptively simple question in some 15 books and scores of articles; it cannot be answered here in a few lines. Drugs and talk can help. But there is, in my opinion, no medical, moral, or legal justification for involuntary psychiatric interventions. Thus, "mentally ill" persons residing in hospitals should not be forcibly evicted; nor should those residing in the community be forcibly hospitalized.

[17]   Life is at once an intolerable burden and an immeasurable treasure. Our task, I believe, should be to devise fresh, more civilized ways of looking and dealing with those who shirk their burdens—a task we cannot even begin to address so long as we insist, in

the name of mental health, on lifting the burden from the shoulders of those who carry it in ways that disturb us.

## "THE FREEDOM ABUSERS"[34]

[18]   Since the death of the Reverend Jim Jones, the diagnosis of paranoia has been falling on his memory like snowflakes in a winter storm in Syracuse. I suggest that we take another look at some of the facts reported about this Marxist-Christian minister before the sordid truths about his behavior and that of his followers are completely buried beneath a blanket of psychiatric speculations and diagnoses.

[19]   Virtually everyone who knew Jones—among them some prominent and presumably perceptive and intelligent men and women—regarded him as perfectly healthy mentally. For instance, during the 1976 Carter presidential campaign, Rosalynn Carter and Jim Jones dined together in San Francisco. Mrs. Carter, who is, as we know, one of America's foremost experts on mental health, found no sign of mental illness in Jones—on the contrary: In March 1977, she wrote him a letter praising his proposal to give medical aid to Cuba, and after the election she invited him to attend the inauguration, which he did.

[20]   That Jones was accepted as at least "normal" in California liberal political circles has by now become notorious. That he was still widely regarded as both mentally healthy and morally admirable during the weeks and days immediately preceding the massacre is evident from the fact that a gala, $25-a-plate dinner benefit from the People's Temple was planned in San Francisco for December 2, 1978. Called "A Struggle against Oppression," the affair was to feature Dick Gregory and the Temple's two lawyers, Mark Lane and Charles Garry, as speakers. It was endorsed by 75 prominent city leaders and politicians. It was cancelled after the massacre.

[21]   Actually, in view of Jones' impressive record of good "psychotherapeutic" works, the enthusiasm of evangelistic mental healthers for him should come as no surprise. Jones "cured drug addicts." He "rehabilitated" aimless Americans and put them on the road to a communitarian salvation. He was, officially at least, even against suicide—when it was a course chosen on one's own. On Memorial Day in 1977 (only 18 months before the Jonestown massacre), Jones led a delegation of People's Temple members on a march on the Golden Gate Bridge in San Francisco, demanding that the city build a suicide barrier on the bridge.

[22]   In addition to these testimonials to Jones' good mental health and commendable character, we have the word of Jones' personal physicians that the minister was both psychiatrically normal and morally admirable. Dr. Carlton Goodlett, identified as a "prominent black doctor" in San Francisco who had also attended Jones in Guyana, told the *New York Times*: "I was convinced that Jones was involved in a brilliant experiment in Guyana that actually put people in better shape down there than they had been in San Francisco." Even after the massacre Dr. Goodlett offered this psychiatric opinion—not about Jones, but about his disenchanted followers: "The deserters from the church had come to me, but they were just a neurotic fringe."

[23]   To say that Jim Jones was widely regarded as mentally healthy is indeed an understatement: He was regarded as a brilliant healer of minds, a great "therapist." Many of his followers were former drug users. Two survived the massacre. One of them, Tim Carter, told the *Times* he had been "heavily involved in drugs in California" and was

cured by Jones. Tim's father, Francis Carter (both of whose sons were on "drugs"), praised Jones' treatment of drug abuse to a *Times* reporter: After joining the Temple "they gave up drugs, became rehabilitated, and got better." Odel Rhodes, another survivor, "had been a heroin addict from the Detroit ghetto. [W]ith the help of Jim Jones' power he had beat heroin, he said. He felt he needed his mentor to keep him straight."

[24]   After the butchery in Guyana, Jones' followers and friends were eager to dismiss him as "paranoid." Steven Jones lost no time diagnosing his father as psychotic, an opinion he kept carefully to himself unitl "dad" was dead. Why did Steven Jones think his father was mad? Because he destroyed the concentration camp that young Jones evidently loved dearly. "He has destroyed everyting I've worked for," said Steven Jones.

[25]   One of Jones' lawyers, Charles Garry, characterized the commune as "a beautiful jewel. There is no racism, no sexism, no ageism, no elitism [sic], no hunger." After the massacre, Garry declared: "I am convinced this guy was stark raving mad." If Garry believed this before November 18, 1978, he violated his professional responsibilities as a lawyer and his moral responsibilities as a human being; and if he concluded it only because Jones finally carried out his oft-repeated threat of mass murder and suicide, then Garry is asserting a platitude in declaring his safely deceased client "mad."

[26]   Mark Lane, Jones' other lawyer and a renowned expert on conspiracy and paranoia, described his former client to the *Times* as "a paranoid murderer who, after four weeks of drug injections, gave the orders that resulted last weekend in the deaths of Representative Leo Ryan . . . ." The great conspiracy-hunter thus sought to exonerate Jones by attributing the mass murder and suicide not only to "paranoia" but also to "drugs." But the fact is that Lane accepted Jones as a client and continued to represent him, up to the very moment of the debacle.

[27]   I cite all this as presumptive evidence that, before the final moment, those closest to Jones did not believe that he was psychotic. Their subsequent conclusion that Jones was paranoid is intellectually empty and patently self-serving. (Today everyone who reads newspapers and watches television has been taught that mass murderers are mad.) While Jones was alive his friends and followers did not regard him as paranoid, quite simply because they liked what he was doing. For the bottom line is a moral judgment: Jones' supporters think that he was a good man who suddenly became mad; I think he was an evil man—and not just on the day of the massacre.

[28]   Whether or not Jones had been "crazy" long before the massacre depends on the meaning one wishes to attach to that word. However, it is now clear that for a long time Jones' behavior had been sordid and evil. It is also clear that when his followers were faced with certain facts, they deliberately looked the other way. Consider the following reports of Jones' behavior during the period when his followers and those "outside" regarded Jones as not merely "normal" but "superior":

> —Jones insisted that everyone call him "dad" or "father." When there was a disagreement in the commune, the members would tranquilize one another and themselves by repeating the incantation "Dad knows best. Just do as Dad tells you."
> —Jones had a wife, several mistresses, and "had sex" with many of the women and several of the men in the commune. "He told their husbands [according to Tim Carter, and aide] that he only did it to help the women."
> —Jones claimed that he was Jesus and could cure cancer.

—According to Jerry Parks, another cult member, "Everyone had to admit that they were homosexual, even the women. He was the only heterosexual."

—Several times before the final butchery, Jones conducted rehearsals of the communal carnage.

—Members of the commune had to turn their possessions over to Jones, had to work like slaves, were starved and were kept from sleeping, and could not leave the commune.

[29]  Despite these unsavory facts (and many others not catalogued here), I cannot recall, in the thousands of words I read about the Jonestown affair, a single commentator—journalist, politician, psychiatrist, anyone—characterizing the Reverend Jim Jones as an evil man. Mad, insane, crazy, paranoid, and variations on that theme—that is the consensus. James Reston's judgment of Jones was sadly typical. After quoting the opinion of "one of the most prominent members of the Carter Administration," according to whom the Jonestown massacre was a symptom of "mass lunacy in the age of emptiness," Reston delivered the craven diagnosis that liberal intellectuals, when faced with evil, instinctively issue. The Reverend Jones, declared Reston, was an "obviously demented man."

[30]  The most imaginative diagnosis was offered, not surprisingly, by a psychiatrist. Explained Dr. Thomas Ungerleider, professor of psychiatry at the University of California at Los Angeles: "I believe it was the jungle. The members got no feedback from the outside world. They did not read *Time* magazine or watch the news at night . . ." Dr. Alvin Poussaint, professor of psychiatry at Harvard and one of the leading black psychiatrists in America, offered this shameful and revealing diagnosis: "We cannot in good conscience fault the mission of the rank-and-file because of the acute psychosis of their leader . . . .The humanitarian experiment itself was not a failure, the Reverend Jones was."

[31]  I think we can do better than that. The evidence—despite Reston and the anonymous high Carter administration official—suggests that Jones was depraved, not "demented," and that what his congregation displayed was mass cruelty and cowardliness, not "mass lunacy." I believe that plain English words such as "evil," "depraved," "cruel," and "cowardly" furnish a better description of what happened at Jonestown than does the lexicon of lunacy in which those despicable and pathetic deeds have been couched.

[32]  This instant metamorphosis of Jones from prophet to psychotic now conceals—as did previously the deliberate denial of the significance of his everyday behavior by those who knew him—the self-evident evil that animated this bestial tyrant long before his supposed "degeneration into paranoia." That is the phrase used by *Time* magazine, where Jones is described as an "Indiana-born humanitarian who degenerated into egomania and paranoia." *Newsweek* confirms the diagnosis: Jones' "mind," we are informed, "deteriorated into paranoia."

[33]  I object. It is fundamentally false and distorting to view every gesture to help the poor—regardless of motives, methods, and consequences—as "humanitarian." What tryant has not claimed to be motivated by a desire to help the helpless? We know only too well that to those hungry for power, the prospect of "helping" life's victims presents a great temptation; one that complements the temptation that the prospect of oblivion through alcohol or drugs presents to those hungry for a simple solution to life's problems. That is why these two types of persons are drawn to each other so powerfully, and why each regards the competent, self-reliant person as his enemy. So much for Jones' "humanitarianism."

[34]   As for Jones' "paranoia," we accept the proverbial wisdom that one man's meat is another man's poison. Similarly, we should accept that one man's prophet is another man's paranoid. It is simply not true that Jones "degenerated into paranoia." Jones was the same person on November 18, 1978 (the date of the mass murder and suicide) that he was the day before, the month before, the year before. Jones did not suddenly change. What did change suddenly was the opinion certain people entertained and expressed about him.

[35]   What we need, then, is not so much an explanation of what happened in Jonestown, which is clear enough, but rather an explanation of the explanations of the carnage that the purveyors of conventional wisdom have offered us. Briefly put, such a metaexplanation might state that paranoia in a dead and dishonored "cult" leader is caused by the sudden realization of his followers and others that they have been duped, which instantly transforms them from sycophants (and sympathizers) into psychodiagnosticians.

[36]   Much could be, and should be, made of the carnage of Jonestown. What I want to make out of it here is, briefly, this: Access to drugs entails what is now smugly called "drug abuse." How, indeed, could it be otherwise? Why, the, the shocked surprise that access to freedom entails "freedom abuse"? Assuredly the abuse of freedom—like the abuse of alcohol, drugs, and food, or any other good that nature or human ingenuity provides us—is a small price to pay for the boundless benefits of freedom. That the abuse of freedom entails risks to innocent persons is one of the tragic facts of life. The children murdered at Jonestown are a somber reminder of the awesome power parents have over their children—a power that, as Jonestown and other communal experiments have shown, the collectivization of the family can only amplify.

[37]   The ultimate ugly and undeniable facts are that of the 909 bodies at Jonestown, 260 were those of children, butchered by the peaceloving "humanitarian" followers of the Reverend Jones; and that, like their leader, these butchers hated the open society and "fled" their homeland to settle in a socialist country. The men and women of Jonestown rejected liberty. It is as if they had turned Patrick Henry's maxim; "Give me Liberty or give me death!" on its head, and had sworn allegiance to the maxim, "Give me death rather than liberty!"

## THE APPEAL AND VALUE OF THE POLEMICAL STYLE

In these articles, as in many others, it is evident that Szasz hopes to reach two audiences. Psychiatrists, mental health policymakers, and lawyers are obviously important to his general goal of changing basic psychiatric conventions. But it is also apparent that his vast rhetorical output has been designed to reshape expectations in the general public as well. To reach these larger audiences, Szasz often forsakes the technical style of the clinician, with its emphasis on experimental research, the precedents established by major theorists, and nonevocative forms of relatively dry prose. Although some of his books have the features of this standard "scientific" expository style—notably in *The Ethics of Psychoanalysis* and *The Myth of Mental Illness*—his work is characteristically polemical. As in both of the short pieces above, what the reader remembers are his dramatic, unqualified, and judgmental assertions rather than his use of evidence or the analysis of subtle distinctions.

This polemic style is largely from another era, when fierce vehemence was a measure of commitment rather than zealotry. What was a virtue of nineteenth-century reformers is now largely seen as a twentieth-century vice. It arose from the valuable impulse to reexamine conventional values and the inertia against change that they often represented. Like Wendell Phillips cited in Chapter 1, social activists in particular were expected to display their passion in a rhetoric that would *declare* as much as it argued. Polemical discourse attracts attention by overt confrontation, then maintains it with the use of examples that have an immediate visceral impact. Its users often delight in cutting through the gloss of superficial similarities that we routinely use in everyday conversation to keep our differences from surfacing. They are typically challengers and questioners. Their irreverence is similar to the kind that Saul Alinsky praised in his book *Rules for Radicals.*

To the questioner nothing is sacred. He detests dogma, defies any finite definition of morality, rebels against any repression of a free open search for ideas no matter where they may lead. He is challenging, insulting, agitating, discrediting. He stirs unrest.[35]

Most medical and mental health professionals writing for *TV Guide* would probably need considerable editorial help to adapt to its condensed mode. But Szasz develops his ideas like MGM developed color in its 1940s films: his assertions appear as vivid images against an artificially simplified background. His argumentative style is combative, with a tendency of presenting observations and alternatives that leave little room for competing explanations or troublesome exceptions. Jim Jones, for example, was a "tyrant," and his followers were "helpless"[33]. In the first article, even the suggestion that some patients might be better treated in mental hospitals because they are ill or "dangerous to themselves or others" is dismissed as "bunk"[3].

Unqualified declarations and razor-sharp definitions are two of Szasz's trademarks. His 1976 book *Heresies* is written in a style of pure assertion that reads like a political tract. Broken down into sections on the "Family," "Marriage," "Law," and other topics, it is a compilation of aphorisms and declarations unencumbered by evidence or exposition. As excerpts from a section titled "Personal Conduct" show *Heresies* provides its readers easy access to ideas reduced to one-sentence observations and single-paragraph arguments.

There are no universal geniuses; there are only universal fools.

Usually it is painful to be wrong; sometimes it is fatal to be right.

There is no good digestion without hydrochloric acid; and no good thinking without adrenaline.

As the price of liberty is vigilance—so the price of independence is self-determination, the price of dignity is self-assertion, and the price of respect is self-respect.[36]

In a more recent 1987 book, *Insanity,* Szasz employs the same kind of simple language to define what it is that most psychiatrists actually *do.* The descriptions are both vivid and devastating: some are "in the business of drugging"; others are "in the business of conversation and moral guidance"; and one group is "in the business of producing brain damage." This latter group of colleagues, he notes, is made up of

1. The lobotomists: dealers in amputating the frontal lobes.
2. The electroshockers: dealers in delivering artificial epilepsy.
3. The insulin-coma producers: dealers in insulin overdosage.[37]

Social scientists have frequently been criticized for writing about human behavior in Latinate "scientistic" terms that conceal "hidden" judgments and "smuggled" assumptions.[38] But such a charge cannot be made against Szasz. There is a wonderful directness in his arguments. Their artificial simplicity focuses attention on the working assumptions and day-to-day processes of psychiatric care. They clarify rather than conceal their subjects. Whatever the shortcomings of his professional rhetoric—and his critics cite many—Szasz cannot be accused of obfuscating his message. He resolutely refuses to "pull rank" on his readers by evoking a language of special expertise. He generally will not yield mental health issues to arbitration by evidence that could be grounded in biological and sociological "facts." His detractors constantly criticize the logic he uses to assert that mental illness is a faulty metaphor rather than a viable category designating real dysfunctions.[39] Against most of his peers, he holds that the only legitimate measure of psychiatric legitimacy is in a moral rather than scientific rationale. The thesis of the "myth of mental illness," notes Washington psychiatrist Charles Krauthammer, is "incomprehensible on scientific grounds," but it "becomes understandable when seen as a product of a political ideology."[40] By persistently framing his vision of psychiatry in moral terms, in "good" and "bad" choices, his doctrine maintains a rationale that is accessible. In his world, clinical explanations of behavior are subordinate to issues of moral choice. With many Americans he believes that disruptive and unacceptable behavior may be less "treatable" than punishable.

This explains part of Szasz's appeal. His conclusions are not only clear, but they touch on deep ideological roots that support the views of political conservatives and social Darwinists opposed to state funding of diverse social services. He also taps a strong American suspicion of the state's reliance on psychiatric experts to short-circuit the process of legal accountability—what Krauthammer calls "psychiatry's power to commit and acquit."[41] Not only is there an anti-collectivist/anti-Soviet angle to this view, given past reports about the use of Soviet psychiatry to suppress troublesome dissidents, but it also affirms common views about the futility of psychiatric "treatment." For example, even while Americans generally endorse the abstract idea of mental illness, popular films ranging from *One Flew Over the Cuckoo's Nest* to the more recent *Nuts* testify to continuing suspicions about psychiatric categories and methods. The first film was based on Ken Kesey's best-selling novel about the resourceful R. P.

McMurphy—played by Jack Nicholson—who falls victim to a psychiatric gulag that relentlessly drains away his humanity. Like Barbara Streisand's prostitute fighting an insanity verdict in the 1987 film *Nuts*, McMurphy is the embodiment of Szasz's description of the colorful character who is denied the freedom to make his own life. These films have enacted in one arena what Szasz's writing has dramatized in another. The specter of the impersonal state as the destroyer of fragile human rights [13] draws its power from widespread doubts about the psychiatric establishment. Not so incidentally, these suspicions also make Szasz's work less attractive than it might have been for his critics. Not only are they in step with many Americans' beliefs, but his view that individuals are free agents also helps him occupy high ground that is difficult to attack. In American life both positions carry a prima facie credibility that cannot be easily displaced.

## WEAKNESSES OF THE POLEMICAL STYLE

As evocative as it is, much of Szasz's rhetoric carries the liabilities common to most polemics. His arguments can be carelessly constructed, sometimes ungenerous toward those who positions he opposes, and blind to the grays that exist between heightened evocations of black and white. The article on the People's Temple illustrates several of these patterns. The central idea of the piece is that no diagnostic language should obscure the judgment that Jones was an "evil" man and his followers were "cowardly" in relinquishing their freedom [34–35]. He takes issue with the "shameful" use of diagnostic terms that were employed to account for the mental conditions of Jones and his followers [27, 30, 32]. While there can be little doubt that terms like "psychotic" and "paranoid" were used in nearly meaningless ways by Jones's friends and explainers, Szasz probably does little to further our understanding by labeling Jones's victims "cruel" and "cowardly." As Szasz himself notes, the misused language of mental derangement is neither precise nor very helpful at coming to terms about the motives and actions of the residents at Jonestown. But neither is his substitution of simple pejorative terms, among them "bestial tyrant" [32] and "depraved" [31]. With hindsight, moral judgments of Jim Jones are easy to make. Explaining his actions in a way that increases our understanding of his kind of cult should be within the reach of modern psychiatry.

Szasz can also push very hard to transform interesting facts of dubious relevance into ironies with questionable meanings. A piece of evidence that is supposed to demonstrate a revealing irony sometimes falls short of showing anything. In paragraph 19, for example, he notes that Rosalynn Carter ("one of America's foremost experts on mental health") ate dinner with Jones during the campaign and corresponded with him. Much is made of the point that Jones was considered "normal" in "liberal political circles" and viewed as "morally admirable"[20]. Part of Szasz's implication is apparently that the charismatic preacher was well entrenched in the political mainstream: a figure whose crimes were conveniently ignored by his political contacts. But there is actually less than is implied in

Szasz's inference that "liberal intellectuals"[29], including the president's wife, overlooked the evil in Jim Jones. In actual fact the San Francisco activist was not an intimate of the Carters. His position in the community made him a *potential* but not an actual political organizer for the Carter campaign. His advocacy of causes in behalf of the poor gave him access to Democratic politics in San Francisco, in which he played no more than a nominal role. He met Mrs. Carter only briefly, long enough to merit the courtesy of a pro- forma but noncommittal reply from her.[42] Given the thousands of yearly contacts made by any president and his wife, it is a shaky logic that places Mrs. Carter and "liberals" with various "sycophants" who knew Jones[35]. Szasz's language is as vague and judgmental in this instance as the psychiatric language he attacks in the article.

Another feature of Szasz's writing is his tendency to define a position by focusing on contrasting extremes. His positions and those of his opponents tend to be defined in opposites, with much of the middle ground overlooked. Revealingly, Szasz rarely exercises the rhetorical option of aligning himself with the views of another colleague. He much more frequently argues from a rhetoric of contrasts. In the first article, for example, the reasonable point that most "mental patients" are usually harmless is *not* particularly helped by a semantic reversal that sounds more logical and forceful than it really is. "Just as illness is not a crime," he notes, "so crime is not an illness"[5]. But the point, of course, cannot be so easily characterized. The more urgent question is probably not whether "crime" in all its forms represents "illness" but whether *some* criminal behavior is the outgrowth of mental problems beyond the control of the "criminal." Similarly, in the second article the urge to keep his argument understandable within a framework of a two-tailed system leads Szasz to the conclusion that Jones's personality could not have changed over time[34]. But it seems an odd all-or-nothing position that makes the once-respected preacher "the same person on November 18 . . . that he was the day before, the month before, the year before"[34]. Such a statement has a superficial cachet. But implying that an individual's psyche is constant seems to be an unusually static view of human behavior for a psychiatrist. It is nearly a universal assumption in the behavioral sciences that human nature is dynamic and variable. The short-term advantage for making the opposite case is in the implicit claim that Jones was always an "evil" misfit. What this position gains in certainty it loses in overlooking the strong possibility that Jones functioned successfully in some environments and disastrously in others. As one of his critics has argued, Szasz's rhetoric has the "power to demolish more eclectic, more qualified positions; but its absolutism renders it impotent to calculate the complex relations between means and ends, risks and benefits which hold in real life."[43] It seems plausible that Jones was— as Szasz quotes *Time*—at different times a "humanitarian" and a paranoid [32].

## THE STRIDENT PERSONA

In ways in which we are not fully aware, a persuader's verbal style often functions as a window into his or her personality. "Discourses contain tokens of their authors," notes Edwin Black. They are taken by listeners and readers as "external signs of internal states."[44] In the case of seminal thinkers like Szasz who depend almost completely on the printed page, it would be difficult to overestimate the importance of inferences of character that come between the lines. Authors can easily become whatever their rhetorical habits imply—a fact that probably works both for and against the Syracuse psychiatrist. Typically described *through cues in his style* as "caustic,"[45] "intemperate,"[46] "devoid of compassion,"[47] and "intransigent,"[48] Szasz projects a hard-edged cynicism that belies his therapeutic profession. It is the professional iconoclast in him who repeatedly operates on the blunt premise that "it's absolutely essential that we look not at what psychiatrists *say* they do, but at what they actually do." [49]

This corrosive rhetorical persona probably plays on his audiences in two very different ways. At one level Szasz's rhetoric seems fundamentally out of character with the "nurturing" persona of the traditional therapist. However penetrating his criticism of his field is, some of his colleagues have wondered if he has the requisite compassion to treat patients who—in his scheme—are usually accomplices to their own confusion and pain. The character of his accusatory rhetoric can be interpreted as evidence that he is, by predisposition, outside the therapeutic canon of a "helping profession." Patients are sometimes identified as people who cannot succeed in a competitive world, people "who shirk their burdens"[17]. Hospitals similarly furnish employment to "people with no salable skills in a free market."[9] Noting views like these, some of his detractors argue that he has contributed more to the deconstruction—rather than the reconstruction—of the field, forsaking constructive change in favor of colorful broadsides aimed at the weakest segments of the psychiatric establishment.[50] They often focus on his apparent rhetorical excess, a fact that makes it easier to ignore the substantive challenges he raises. As one of his colleagues noted:

Tom is far more reasonable in person than in print. I think he does himself a disservice writing in the antagonistic, inflammatory way that he does. When he starts calling psychiatrists "jailers" and involuntary therapies "tortures"—well, people just stop listening. And that's a shame, because he's making important points.[51]

At another level, if his stridency alienates some of his colleagues, his status as an insider carries its own special credibility for nonprofessional readers. The relevant principle here sometimes falls under the heading of "reluctant testimony," which gives the "insider" more believeability precisely because of the price he may pay for his dissent.[52] Criticism that arises internally is usually thought to have greater authority; we expect the insiders' sense of professional loyalty to silence most private doubts before they can become public. This explains why Szasz is sometimes seen as a valuable interpreter of a field that is usually closed to outsiders. Reviewers of his works often cite his courageous willingness to identify the rhetorical games and occupational blind spots of traditional psychiatry.[53] It is no surpise that his books have been more favorably received by nonmedical readers than by members of the mental health establishment. For them, Szasz has reclaimed mental health issues for public discussion in ways that nonexperts could not.

Two of his defenders, for example, include communications theorist Richard Vatz and law professor Lee Weinberg. Among the features they find especially attractive in his work include his rhetorical sensitivity to psychiatric terminology, especially his descriptions of professional judgments concealed in "pseudo-scientific" terms.

Unlike religious and democratic political persuaders who claim no false identity and implicitly recognize man's autonomy, psychiatrists present themselves as scientists and explicitly deny the right of autonomy to those whom they choose to define and control.[54]

It certainly comes as no surprise to us that psychiatrists, and especially institutional psychiatrists, those most threatened by the implications of Szasz's theory, would vociferously denounce him and defend their continued ability to practice a lucrative, high status trade.[55]

Szasz's criticism thus carries a special legitimacy. It performs the valuable function of contributing to the destabilization and reexamination of a variety of psychiatric norms. To some extent—though in ways less dramatic than Szasz probably would like—his output has forced institutional psychiatry into a prolonged (if muted) public debate about its basic goals.

## ESTIMATING EFFECTS: SUBDUED RESPONSES AND MESSAGE SALIENCE

If Szasz seems to write as if he were engaged in a taut battle for the future of psychiatry, it is a battle with a very reluctant opposition. To some extent his work has gone unanswered—but not ignored—by professionals in the disciplines that he has consistently attacked. Tracking the effects of a thinker's output over a number of years is necessarily impressionistic, but it is apparent that Szasz has not created the kind of noisy public debate that his strongly worded tracts might have been expected to trigger. Even his basic manifesto, *The Myth of Mental Illness,* languished in relative obscurity for several years after its publication in 1961. Its radical challenges to the major paradigms of psychiatry were not widely reviewed in either professional or general-interest periodicals. Other books fared somewhat better, gaining limited attention in the review pages of psychiatric journals and limited-circulation magazines such as *The New Republic* and *National Review.* What science writer Maggie Scarf noted in 1971 is still true: Szasz's assertions usually "fall into a well of official silence. No professional colleague has mounted a serious counterattack against Szasz's accusations."[56]

To be sure, there are isolated exchanges with some critics and an occasional systematic analysis of the implications of Szasz's views.[57] But given the extent to which his work has been made availavble to both specialized and general audiences, the absence of sustained counterarguments to his contentions is surprising.

This lack of response may indicate that his work has not been taken seriously, or—more likely—it may signify a grudging respect that results in the internalization of key ideas rather than their public denial. The truth is probably a combination of both. As Scarf wrote, "Either he is simply ignored or—and this is coming to be far more common—he is conceded privately to be raising some important points."[38] This last point cannot be overstated; persuasion theorists must contend with the fact that people rarely leave markers that can be easily followed to reveal subtle changes in the direction of their thinking. What accommodations consumers of persuasion make to new ideas usually occur beyond the detection of even careful observers.

## Rationalization

To the extent he has been ignored, some of the predictions flowing from dissonance theory seem especially relevant. As we noted in Chapter 2, dissonance theory predicts that strong counterarguments that are fundamentally at odds with a receiver's existing beliefs will create the need to adjust those beliefs. The motivation to relieve the inconsistency created by the logical conflict of old and new ideas is thought to pull the receiver in the direction of the new ideas. In this model, Szasz's pejorative characterizations of conventional psychiatry would be expected to motivate *some* practitioners to reconsider their present assumptions and methods. But his relative neglect points to what is sometimes underrepresented in dissonance theory, namely; that the human psyche is very resourceful and selective in the way it processes information. Potential persuadees can easily escape from the apparent need to alter their world in light of new facts or judgments. Our defense mechanisms against new and unwanted information can be formidable. Using the same kinds of devices employed by cigarette smokers in the face of evidence about negative health effects, most people develop a repertoire of defensive mental maneuvers that can overcome dissonant communication. When backed into the corner of a logical inconsistency, we can muster the skill to ignore, compartmentalize, and deny. It is easy to find ways to partition our mental life so that the need for its restructuring is never really felt. In the case of Szasz's indictments, the use of these evasions may be especially easy because his arguments lack the kinds of narrow factualness that are best able to produce dissonance.

## Theories of Diffuse Influence and Pairing

It is also highly likely that Szasz's work *has* been accommodated by large numbers of practitioners and interested observers but in more subtle ways. Several reasons argue for less dramatic but very real message effects. First, it is probably too simplistic to assign to any one person the responsibility for carrying the burden of innovation in any one area of organizational or scientific life. This seems especially true in a field as diverse and splintered as psychiatry. It is far more apparent that—along with R. D. Laing, Michel Foucault, David Cooper, and others—Szasz has provoked a partially hidden but very real crisis of legitimacy in the way psychiatry is viewed in legal and institutional settings.[59] The slow incrementalism of this change has concealed its drama, but arguably no other field aspiring to the status of a serious science has had its basic assumptions and working vocabulary so seriously challenged in the last several decades. The deinstitutionalization of thousands of former mental patients, scores of court cases upholding the rights of patients to refuse treatment, and increased skepticism over the use of the insanity defense are only the most obvious changes that have found their justifications in the words of these different reformers and "anti-psychiatrists."

In addition, there is also a process-oriented reason—defined here as "pairing"—for expecting that attitudes will change slowly and with little dramatic external evidence. Persuasion is usually conceptualized as some form of observable attitude change. In everyday terms, a message or series of messages leads us to change our minds. But somewhere between attitude change and its opposite of outright rejection lies a vast middle ground where ideas make their mark first by slowly becoming salient to many listeners and readers. Salience is a process that starts with an idea's availability and sometimes ends with its acceptance. Only after novel ideas gain sufficient exposure to be noticed do they set up the conditions for attitude change. For them to be truly owned, another event must then take place. Their adoption will likely occur only after they are paired with specific events, events they successfully account for. The pairing of the event with a dormant idea serves to trigger a new perspective that meets a need; *the idea gains acceptance because of its availability as a good explanation.* For example, many of his strongest supporters probably "found" Szasz not just in reading one of his tracts but in pairing one of his major themes with a specific news event. A news reader who learns of a questionable insanity plea or commitment hearing, or who doubts a journalist's description of "pathological gambling," might be moved to transform what had been latent knowledge of Szasz's key themes into manifest endorsement of them. Such a process of using the latent knowledge of an advocate's ideas to explain novel occurrences is likely to contain no obvious benchmarks, but it is no less important for its subtleness.

Finally, any neglect of Szasz by his own field probably resides less in anything that he has done than in the nature of innovation in most of the sciences. As science historian Thomas Kuhn has written in a widely celebrated book, normal science yields very slowly to new insights.[60] He notes that basic "paradigms" in any one field are rarely reversed by dramatic discoveries or radical new theories. Those engaged in the practice of routine science are almost as tradition bound as believers from various walks of life who depend more on faith than fact. Kuhn points out what casual accounts of new scientific breakthroughs tend to simplify: that discoveries usually include long periods of "assimilation" prior to general acceptance. When placed in their historical contexts, new findings are rarely as dramatic as the artificially compressed time of history makes them seem. Even such monumental developments as the discovery of oxygen in the late 1700s and X rays in the late 1800s came about incrementally, after a considerable period when these physical phenomena were alternately discounted and considered. It took nearly a decade for the discovery of X rays to reshape fully older paradigms about electromagnetic theory. One reason change is slow even in science has less to do with the processes of establishing certain proofs and more to do with the psychology of organizations. Few formally structured disciplines are able to handle the unexpected conclusion or the novel result very well. The "professionalization" of science into camps of people subdivided into disciplines has always led "to an immense restriction of the scientist's vision and to a considerable resistance to paradigm change."[61]

## SZASZ'S PLACE

Taking Kuhn's long view, in addition to what we noted earlier in this chapter about the "serial" nature of persuasion, it is possible to project a pattern of limited but significant effects. Without a doubt, Szasz's libertarian polemics and all-or-nothing arguments have given his critics reasons to ignore him. But the consistency of his attacks on eminently questionable practices, such as his field's reliance on the disease metaphor, has also had an impact on American psychiatry. If his critics are reluctant to concede that he has been right, most of them at least acknowledge that he has raised important ethical issues to a higher level of visibility. Unlike few others in his field, Szasz has pressed psychiatric and legal professionals to defend their orientations to both the patient and the "public good." He has also provided the valuable service of demystifying his field in a way that has led to the empowerment of its clients and critics. In the hundreds of tracts he has published—and in ways we will never be ble to trace fully—he has reclaimed issues of mental health ethics as topics for general public discussion.

## NOTES

1. Thomas S. Szasz, "The Concept of Mental Illness: Explanation or Justification," in *Concepts of Health and Disease*, ed. Arthur L. Caplan, H. Tristram Engelhardt, Jr., and James J. McCartney (Reading, Mass.: Addison-Wesley, 1981), p. 466.

2. Charles Krauthammer, "The Myth of Thomas Szasz," *The New Republic* December 22, 1979, p. 13.

3. Peter Sedgwick, *Psycho Politics: Laing, Foucault, Goffman, Szasz, and the Future of Mass Psychiatry* (New York: Harper & Row, 1982), p.158.

4. Maggie Scarf, "Normality Is a Square Circle or a Four-Sided Triangle," *New York Times Magazine* October 3, 1971, p. 16.

5. Thomas S. Szasz, *The Myth of Mental Illness* (New York: Hoeber-Harper, 1961). A shorter version of the book's argument is presented in idem, "The Myth of Mental Illness," *American Psychologist*, February 1960, pp. 113–118.

6. See, for example, Carl I. Hovland, Irving L. Janis, and Harold H. Kelly, *Communication and Persuasion* (New Haven: Yale University, 1953), pp. 157–165.

7. What have not emerged are equally viable macrotheories that can account for the movement of these ideas through society. We do not yet have a reliable perspective and corresponding vocabulary to account for the problems and possibilities that arise from a lifetime of consistent advocacy. For a useful sample of work in this direction, see Elihu Katz and P. F. Lazarfield, *Personal Influence: The Part Played by People in the Flow of Mass Communications* (Glencoe, Ill.: Free Press, 1955).

8. Dava Sobel, "Raskolnikov Could Cop a Plea," *New York Times Book Review*, March 15, 1987, p. 22.

9. Szasz, "The Myth of Mental Illness," p. 114.

10. See, for example, Thomas Szasz, *Insanity: The Idea and Its Consequences* (New York: John Wiley, 1987), pp. 70–78; and idem, "What Counts as a Disease?" *Canadian Medical Association Journal* October 15, 1986, pp. 859–860.

11. Thomas S. Szasz, *Ideology and Insanity: Essays on the Psychiatric Dehumanization of Man* (New York: Anchor, 1970), p. 213.

12. Szasz, *The Myth of Mental Illness*, p. 4.

13. Thomas S. Szasz, *The Therapeutic State: Psychiatry in the Mirror of Current Events* (Buffalo, N.Y.: Prometheus, 1984), p.241.

14. Szasz, *Ideology and Insanity*, p. 2.

15. Ibid., p. 210.

16. Scarf, "Normality Is a Square Circle," p. 40.

17. Szasz, *The Therapeutic State*, p. 31.

18. Ibid.

19. Ibid., p. 269.

20. See Thomas S. Szasz, *The Ethics of Psychoanalysis: The Theory and Method of Autonomous Psychotherapy* (New York: Basic, 1965); and idem, *The Myth of Mental Illness*.

21. Szasz, *The Myth of Mental Illness* p. xi.

22. See, for example, Phil Brown, *The Transfer of Care: Psychiatric Deinstitutionalization and Its Aftermath* (London: Routledge and Kegan Paul, 1985), pp. 172–179.

23. Szasz, *The Ethics of Psychoanalysis*, p. 28.

24. Szasz, *Ideology and Insanity*, pp. 85–86.

25. Szasz, *The Ethics of Psychoanalysis*, pp. 12–21.

26. Ibid., p. 18.

27. Ibid., p. 202.

28. Ibid., p. 203.

29. Thomas Szasz, *Heresies* (New York: Anchor, 1976), p. 161; idem, *Insanity*, pp. 70–78.

30. See, for example, Joseph Alpher, "Biology and Mental Illness," *The Atlantic*, December 1983, pp. 70–76.

31. Szasz, *Heresies* p. 161.

32. Ibid.

33. Thomas Szasz, "Back Wards to Back Streets," *TV Guide*, May 17–23, 1980, pp. 32–36. Reprinted by permission.

34. Thomas Szasz, "The Freedom Abusers." Reprinted by permission. This manuscript also appears in Szasz, *The Therapeutic State*, pp. 182–186.

35. Saul D. Alinsky, *Rules for Radicals* (New York: Random House, 1971), p. 73.

36. Szasz, *Heresies*, pp. 61–62.

37. Szasz, *Insanity*, p. 125.

38. Samples of this criticism, from both the political Right and Left, can be found in Harold J. Laski, "The Limitations of the Expert," *Harper's Monthly*, December 1930, pp. 101–110; Andrew Weigert, "The Immoral Rhetoric of Scientific Sociology," *American Sociologist*, May 1970, pp. 111–119, and Richard Weaver, *The Ethics of Rhetoric* (Chicago: Henry Regnery, 1953), pp. 186–210.

39. See Krauthammer, "The Myth of Thomas Szasz," pp. 13–14; and Baruch Brody, "Szasz on Mental Illness," in Caplan, Engelhardt, Jr., and McCartney, *Concepts of Health and Disease*, pp. 478–480.

40. Krauthammer, "The Myth of Thomas Szasz," p. 16.

41. Ibid., p. 15.

42. Steven V. Roberts, "Letters Extolling Jones Typify Common Washington Practice," *New York Times*, November 22, 1978, p. A12.

43. Sedgwick, *Psycho Politics*, p. 154.

44. Edwin Black, "The Second Persona," *Quarterly Journal of Speech*, April 1970, p. 110.

45. Scarf, "Normality Is a Square Circle," p. 40.

46. Lawrence Zelic Freedman, Review of *Psychiatric Justice* by Thomas Szasz, *Political Science Quarterly*, September 1966, p. 512.

47. Mark Hendrickson, Review of *The Therapeutic State* by Thomas Szasz, *Christian Science Monitor*, October 3, 1984, p. 22.

48. Paul Chodoff and Roger Peele, "The Psychiatric Will of Dr. Szasz," *Hastings Center Report*, April 1983, p. 11.

49. Scarf, "Normality Is a Square Circle," p. 40.

50. See especially Sedgwick, *Psycho Politics*, pp. 149–184.

51. Scarf, "Normality Is a Square Circle," p. 40.

52. Robert P. Newman and Dale R. Newman, *Evidence* (Boston: Houghton Mifflin, 1969), p. 79.

53. See, for example, Peter Lomas, "Are Psychiatrists Human? All Too," *New York Times Book Review*, May 10, 1970, pp. 3, 35.

54. Richard E. Vatz and Lee S. Weinberg, *Thomas Szasz: Primary Values and Major Contentions* (Buffalo, N.Y.: Prometheus, 1983), p. 14.

55. Ibid., p. 215.

56. Scarf, "Normality Is a Square Circle," p. 42.

57. One representative exchange took place in early 1982. Szasz published an article in the *American Psychologist* ("The Psychiatric Will—A New Mechanism for Protecting Persons against Psychosis," July 1982, pp. 767–770) advocating that ordinary people should be allowed to decide in advance if they want possible commitment or treatment if they become mentally incompetent. Szasz's version of the medical "living will" that allows people to determine certain parameters of medical treatment was refuted by two authors the following year in an issue of *The Hastings Center Report* (Chodoff and Peele, "The Psychiatric Will of Dr. Szasz," pp. 11–13). Shortly afterward, new defenses of Szasz's proposal came from Richard Vatz and Lee Weinberg in a letter published in the *Hastings Center Report* and a 1984 article entitled "The Psychiatric Will" in the *Journal of Psychiatry and Law*. On this issue, Szasz initiated a proposal that was debated largely by others. For other sample exchanges, see Michael S. Moore, "Some Myths about Mental Illness," in Vatz and Weinberg, *Thomas Szasz*, pp. 181–192; idem, *Law*

*and Psychiatry: Rethinking the Relationship* (New York: Cambridge University, 1984), pp. 155–162; "The Concept of Mental Illness" pp. 459–474; and Brody, "Szasz on Mental Illness," pp. 475–481.

58. Scarf, "Normality Is a Square Circle," p. 42.

59. For overviews of these theorists, see Sedgwick, *Psycho Politics*; and Brown, *The Transfer of Care*, pp. 167–205.

60. Thomas S. Kuhn, *The Structure of Scientific Revolutions, Second Edition* (Chicago: University of Chicago, 1970), pp. 52–65.

61. Ibid., p. 64.

# 7

# "How Am I Doing?": Gorilla Politics in the Town Meetings of Ed Koch

A [Greenwich] Villager is a special kind of New Yorker. Anyone who chooses to live in the Village opts for the extremes of city life—squalor and elegance; beauty and danger; stoop ball and art show. He also indicates that he enjoys the anarchy of city life—an idea that appeals to more than dare admit it.[1]

*Roger Rosenblatt*

There are hundreds of tales about Ed Koch that have become part of the political folklore of New York City. Among the most-told tales is a simple story from the campaign trail, when Koch was seeking reelection as one of Manhattan's representatives in Congress. He had decided to take a walking tour with his friend Robert Morganthau, who was then running for district attorney. A reserved man, Morganthau had little experience as a campaigner and no taste for appealing to strangers for their support. He disliked bothering people for anything, including requests for their votes. No such reserve bothered Koch, who was only too happy to bring him along on a campaign trek that eventually ended up on a busy sidewalk near Bloomingdale's. Suddenly three young men from the Progressive Labor party appeared, clutching megaphones and shadowing the campaigners as they crossed Fifty-ninth Street in front of the store. "Here they come," they trumpeted to anyone who would listen, "the two war criminals." For reasons perhaps known only to themselves, these activists had identified Koch and Morganthau as part of a sinister plot against humanity. With his reluctant colleague in tow, Koch continued to ask for votes and greet supporters. "Me it doesn't bother," he later recalled. "Morganthau, if he could, would have jumped into a cab and gone across town—anything to avoid the embarrassment . . . I said, 'No, you can't let them drive you off the block.' " Finally, "one of these guys sticks the megaphone next to my ear and he yells, 'War criminal! War criminal!' I say to him, 'Fuck off!' And he really is very upset and very shocked at this. He says to me, 'Can I repeat that?' I say, 'Sure.' " About to set his own trap, the protester turned to the gathering crowd and triumphantly reported that "Congressman Koch just told me to Fuck off." Cheers and applause broke out among the several hundred people who had gathered around.[2]

At the beginning of the 1980s any listing of the most popular leaders in the United States would have undoubtedly included President Ronald Reagan and New York mayor Edward I. Koch. But no two figures could be more different. The ever-polite and politically conservative Californian was hardly from the same mold as the far more confrontational activist from Brooklyn. Reagan was the product of a small midwestern town and made the most of a photogenic face and sympathetic demeanor. Koch was the survivor of the battles of Greenwich Village politics and seemingly lacked the face and finesse to be a modern political icon. Yet when he ran for his second term in 1981, he pulled off the electoral miracle of winning the endorsements of both parties, along with 75 percent of all the votes cast in the election.

In a cover story in the same year, *Time* magazine marveled at this ability to win over New Yorkers with a no-nonsense political style peppered with irreverent barbs and one-liners.[3] He had neither the head for numbers that characterized his immediate predecessor, Abraham Beame nor the good looks and access to the wealthy of John Lindsay. Bald and round faced, Koch was sometimes mistaken for chicken tycoon Frank Purdue. Moreover, with his fondness for the Yiddish expressions of his Polish ancestors and the exaggerated inflections of a leprechaun, he hardly conformed to the no-ruffled-feathers ideal of the modern television politician. No matter. The rest of the country might like their politics declaimed by leaders with flat resonances and an overriding instinct to please. Koch would give them something better suited to the daily indignities of life in the city: passion on key issues, candor about the region's problems, and a gift for quotable one-liners that could sting opponents. He would embody what many inhabitants of Gotham liked to think about themselves: that they could take the truth unvarnished and that the nation's greatest city flourished in the ferment of economic and political conflict. With Ronald Reagan, he also had discovered that criticism of big government and wasteful bureaucracies hit a responsive chord.[4] Reagan would play his own melancholy version of this theme, rhapsodizing about how American resourcefulness could overcome errant governmental activism. Koch learned to add his own variations and considerably raised the decibel level by attacking his city hall predecessors, the municipal unions, and members of city council.

This approach worked for almost twelve years, especially with his white middle-class constituents. Koch's surprising defeat after his third term pointed out that many of his potent rhetorical strengths had also become his liabilities. A racially polarized city decided in 1989 that it wanted the less confrontational style of former Manhattan borough president David Dinkins.

## THE UNLIKELY RISE OF ED KOCH

Koch's political career began in 1956, when he organized a reform Democratic club in the crowded low-rise neighborhoods that make up Greenwich Village. Then, as now, residents living in the old five-story walk-ups and lofts considered themselves different from their counterparts in other parts of the city. Villagers nurtured their reputations as Bohemians. Like those who frequented the art galleries, experimental theaters, and universities in their neighborhoods, they liked to be known as individualists who were more likely to question the city's traditional institutions than to work for them. The Village was like its counterparts in San Francisco, Pittsburgh, or Los Angeles: the preferred address if you wanted to spend time exploring the fringes of the culture before joining its mainstream.

After completing his law degree at New York University in the northern edge of the Village, Koch soon discovered that the routine of practicing law bored him, especially in comparison with the much more flamboyant nature of municipal politics. He shared an apartment on Bedford Street and became active as a participant in local forums and debates that sprang up in the area. The minister of one church recalled that some of the participants in these meetings were "crazies," but Koch was a good moderator and—if not exactly in the mold of a 1960s "free spirit"—a man who genuinely loved the clash of ideas.[5] With the support of the reform-minded *Village Voice*, he went on to challenge the entrenched and effective political machine of longtime Village patriarch Carmine DeSapio, emerging in 1963 as the leader of the Village Independent Democrats. He was part of the influx of new and largely young and mostly single residents— many of them artists and musicians from all over the country—who displaced the families and small businesses in what had been a predominantly Italian area.

Among the happiest memories Koch remembers from this time was standing on a street corner attempting to win votes for himself or for a cause like the election of Adlai Stevenson. "I *loved* those street corner debates," he later recalled. "I found that I'm very good at it. Any time you get a heckler, it enhances your ability to move a crowd, and I delighted in those exchanges, just loved 'em."[6] Hostile listeners did not intimidate him. Even a vacation stint in 1964 as a volunteer civil rights lawyer in Mississippi was more of an adventure into an unknown territory than a burdensome task.

After serving for two years on city council, Koch decided to run for Congress from Manhattan's Seventeenth District. Few thought he could win it. The conventional wisdom was that he was wrong for a district that included a large chunk of the city's wealthiest Upper East Side neighborhoods. In a town dominated by issues of race and class, political handicappers considered him "too bald, too poor, [and] too—well, Jewish."[7] In the face of these odds, he successfully carried the district in 1969 and used his seat to continue his support for the reform wing of the Democratic party. Koch opposed the Vietnam War, supported amnesty for resisters who refused to serve, and worked for greater federal aid for housing and the aged.

In spite of his considerable successes in Congress, it was not the ideal milieu for a constituent-based politician. Koch was frustrated by the obvious disadvantages of having to compete for power with 500 other members and learning to cope with the glacial pace of congressional action. In addition, life in Washington forced him to be physically separated from his constituents much of the time— a blessing for many members but not the ideal arrangement for a man who cherished his maverick image and enjoyed the center of attention.

His dilemma was evident in a controversy that he willingly entered over the planned construction of a new public housing project. Plans had been announced for low-cost apartments to be built in the middle-class Forest Hills section of Queens. The issue touched on the sensitive turf question, raising fears—some more genuine than others—that the entire area would be negatively affected. Congressman Koch opposed the proposal, even though it was not within his own district. He noted that the residents of a successful neighborhood should not be required to deal with the influx of thousands of poor welfare recipients. On this issue, at least, his support for a policy of building better housing for the poor was tempered by different objectives. Whether his position was taken only for altruistic reasons, or with an eye on a run for city hall, his support for the local residents in their fight against the city had the unmistakable stamp of constituency politics. Members of Congress tend to define all but the most local issues in terms of their underlying principles. Yet even in Washington, Koch was eager to speak for the fears and resentments of the city's middle class. It was his rubicon, he later noted.[8] The fight over the Forest Hills housing plan won him thousands of supporters well beyond the limited borders of the Village and Manhattan's East Side. It became an object lesson in how a "liberal who has been mugged by reality"[9] could tap into deep resentments to win control of the largest municipal government in the Western world.

## NEW YORK AND ITS RHETORICAL MAYOR

The city that Ed Koch inherited in 1977 arguably defied anyone's control. It not only continued to have its chronic problems of crime and inadequate city services, but for several years before his election, it teetered on the edge of financial default. Brokers would not handle the city's bonds, which slowly took on ratings more appropriate to a Third World nation than an American metropolis. New York was spending far more for services than it was receiving from taxes and federal and state grants. Two years before Koch took over, Mayor Abraham Beame had no choice but to find ways to cut expenses out of the city's multibillion-dollar budget and secure much-needed loans. Some 20,000 city employees were fired. Unions agreed to some salary concessions and alterations in work rules. Governor Hugh Carey established the Emergency Financial Control Board, which began to audit city finances regularly. And appeals were made to President Gerald Ford for federal help. Few New Yorkers will forget the desperate straits of the city reflected in the rebuke carried in a *Daily News* headline: "Ford to City: Drop Dead." Eventually the federal government relented and agreed to a loan of over $2 billion, but all these measures came at a painfully high cost. By the time Ed Koch was sworn in on the steps of city hall, many of the decisions that normally would have been made in the mayor's corner office had already been decided in Albany and Washington.

To judge by the early headlines and press reports, the new mayor hardly gave in to the reality of a city on its knees. If he could do little but preside over an austerity budget that limited expensive initiatives, there was nothing to keep him from some important symbolic gestures and a barrage of rhetorical assaults on the city's doubters and enemies. Koch started by making it clear that he would keep his three-bedroom rent-controlled apartment in the Village, using the traditionally mayor's residence by the East River only part-time. He soon followed up with what was increasingly to be his trademark: winning supporters by subjecting their enemies to well-placed barbs. For example, he gained continuous notoriety from his first days in office until his last by giving his city its very own foreign policy. City hall reporters joked about whether they should be given the expense accounts that come with being "foreign correspondents," but such jibes did not deter the mayor. A strong supporter of Israel and mindful of a large Jewish constituency, he attacked nations like Austria that gave official recognition to the Palestine Liberation Front. "Austria has come full circle," he once noted. "Hitler was born there, and now the PLO receives support from the Austrian government."[10] He disliked a joint resolution arranged between the Soviet Union and the United States urging the end of hostilities in the Middle East, using a public ceremony with an angry Jimmy Carter to pass on a letter with that message.[11] On other occasions, he described some members of the United Nations as "gangsters, cutthroats and piranhas." And to a group of Soviet schoolchildren who visited city hall he characterized their government as "the pits."[12]

Koch's arrows were not just shot in the direction of foreigners but at domestic targets as well. Barely into his first term he made the conscious decision to use a gathering of leaders in business, the media, and labor to emphasize what had been done wrong in the past. With two former mayors present, he noted that he intended to make every decision purely "on the merits. And that hasn't been done for a long time."[13] Other judgments soon followed. Richard Nixon was a "phony," and his vice president was "spittle" and "beneath contempt."[14] President Carter's sometimes outspoken brother was a "wacko"; and city council president Carol Bellamy was a "pain in the ass."[15] To a *Playboy* interviewer he described what he considered to be the barren existence of anyone who lives beyond the borders of a city, especially the unfortunate people of rural America who were "wasting time in a pickup truck" or forced to "drive 20 miles to buy a gingham dress or a Sears Roebuck suit."[16] As for living in the suburbs? "It's nothing, it's wasting your life. And people do not wish to waste their lives once they've seen New York."[17]

After years of hearing outsiders tell them how they were living beyond the city's means, many New Yorkers liked these mayoral broadsides. If Koch had his way, they reasoned, the city would not only survive, but it would again prosper as the mecca for business, education, and the arts as well. He gave back the city's morale, noted Senator Daniel Moynihan. "Seizing the soul of the city, holding on to it, asserting it and marching up Fifth Avenue with thumbs up, it is a huge, intensely personal achievement."[18]

## Managing the City

Over New York City's 365 square miles are spread five boroughs, each retaining it own identity. The southern two thirds of Manhattan represents the familiar post-card impression, with its twin-peaked skyline towering over the downtown and midtown areas and it expensive stores, apartments, and theaters. But these twenty square miles are perhaps the least representative of the entire region. To the north, above the upper reaches of Central Park, Harlem, which is home to many of the city's black residents, stretches out in regular grids of aging row houses and apartment blocks. Immediately across the Harlem River are the remains of the burned-out neighborhoods in the southern end of the Bronx, national symbols of the complete disintegration of urban life. A traveler heading back into Manhattan toward its southern tip passes through midtown and the Village and eventually to the downtown banks and brokerage houses that tower over the New York Stock Exchange. From this narrow point of Manhattan one can see across the ten miles of New York Bay, past the Statue of Liberty to what is still more of the city. The distant shore of green visible across the water is the northern edge of Staten Island, with its spacious suburban homes and still-to-be-developed land. But most of the residents of the city live in the huge boroughs of Queens and Brooklyn, their old ports sprawling along the length of the East River opposite Manhattan. With over 4 million inhabitants between them, they surpass in size and duplicate in many ways the older neighborhoods that ring most of America's urban centers. These boroughs are filled with blocks of aging warehouses, plain red brick apartments, corner groceries, and auto repair shops. On the eastern ends of these cities-within-cities, attached three-story row homes and individual bungalows spread out beyond the inner-city core. If there is only one Manhattan, the vast reaches of Queens and Brooklyn could easily stand in for Cleveland, Baltimore, or St. Louis, with their concentric circles of industrial and residential neighborhoods connected by the spokes of business thoroughfares.

In the endless expanses of the boroughs beyond Manhattan, the spectacular excesses of the tourist's New York yield to the familiar routines of urban life elsewhere. Whatever differences there exist are more a function of size rather than type. The most durable of all clichés about New York is not that its problems are so usual but that its scale makes it nearly ungovernable. Its 7.5 million people occupy only a few slivers of land, but their numbers are greater than the combined inhabitants in the vast spaces covered by Colorado, Wyoming, and Montana. Nearly a quarter of them live below the federally defined poverty level, and 60,000 are estimated to be homeless.[19] In 1981 the city itself was the landlord of last resort for 400,000 citizens, many of whom must subsist in squalid apartments abandoned by their owners and reluctantly taken over by underfunded municipal agencies. Among the essential services citizens expect are schools— over 1,000 of them—for 936,000 students,[20] subways for one 1 billion annual riders, and roads for the nearly 800,000 cars that enter just Manhattan on a typical day.[21]

New Yorkers know, too, that even the 27,000 uniformed police working in the city cannot prevent crime. Although a few other urban areas have greater rates of crime per capita, the sheer number of cases is stunning. In 1988, for example, the city's Child Welfare Administration received over 59,000 reports of neglected or abused children and predicted that it would have to find foster homes for over 50,000 of them.[22] In the same year the police had to deal with over 1,800 murders and confiscated 16,000 illegally owned guns.[23] With statistics like these it is hardly surprising that the resources that are allocated to the criminal justice system are never enough to process efficiently the thousands of arrests and convictions involving serious thefts and assaults. Legal aide attorneys assigned to the poorest of those prosecuted are routinely overloaded with clients, forcing many of them to negotiate pleas in order to cut down on time-consuming trials. Prisons are similarly overtaxed, largely because residents of the city resist spending funds on new facilities, but also because opposition is intense when plans are made to locate correctional facilities in specific neighborhoods.[24]

As for the quality of life in the city, perhaps the most common perception among vistors and residents during the Koch years was that most of the city's pleasures were still intact, if not as accessible as they once were. It remains true that no other urban region in the United States can offer the rich cultural splendors available in New York. Baseball's Mets and Yankees still play their home games within several miles of each other and within the distance of an easy subway ride. A half dozen major concert halls, nearly 500 mainstream and showcase theaters, a massive city university system, and scores of museums are only the most obvious cultural landmarks. They are augmented by countless activities organized in the city's parks and by educational and arts-oriented programs sponsored by nearly every church and synagogue in the city. Few Americans have the luxury of choosing from the offerings of over 100 film theaters or from the estimated 30,000 restaurants in New York. And few children have what is at least the theoretical possibility to grow up with so much cultural diversity just beyond their front doors.

But if New York's wonderful opportunities are still available, taking advantage of them is not as easy as it once was. The cost of living and working in good neighborhoods continued to spiral through the Koch years. A Manhattan store that leased for $800 a month in 1977 commanded $15,000 in 1988.[25] Over the same period a ticket to a Broadway play went from an average of $17 to over $50. And like many cities in the 1980s, New York saw a net loss in well-paying manufacturing and white-collar positions to other parts of the country. In many cases these were only partially replaced by lower-paying jobs in service industries. Corporations that housed most of their management and support staffs in their Manhattan headquarters began to shift some departments to cheaper offices elsewhere and increasingly found that top executives declined to accept transfer to the city. Concerns over high-cost housing and the quality of the schools ranked high on the list of reasons and contributed to the migration of many companies and employees to the suburbs of Connecticut and New Jersey. The working-class families that have stayed behind in Queens, Brooklyn, and the Bronx must continue to struggle with the irony that while the city has all but given up on some neighborhoods, housing costs in adjacent blocks still remain largely out of reach. As a truck driver from Queens noted in 1989, "The American dream of owning a home—in the city, is dead."[26]

## A Mayor's Job: Administering City Service

Urban life requires a vast range of support services. Garbage collection, sewer and water systems, transportation facilities, and police protection are not only used by residents but by commuters as well. In addition, a city must provide schools, hospitals, and amenities such as parks that make life in densely populated areas tolerable. Mayors live or die by their abilities to oversee the administration of these services. Members of a state legislature or a city council are more insulated from the expectation of performance in dealing with these needs. Their job is to legislate; a mayor's job is to administer. Even if he or she is denied the resources to do the job, a mayor cannot easily duck responsibility for garbage that was not removed from the street or a city hospital that refused to treat a mortally wounded patient.

In theory, at least, municipal services ought to be easier to provide to people in compact work and living spaces than their counterparts spread over less densely populated areas. The task of providing water and sewer service to fifty apartments in one building, for example, is simpler than providing the same facilities to fifty single-family homes in a suburb. But theories do not always account for the messier realities of ordinary life. The services of American cities are under strain for a variety of reasons, not the least of which is the fact that normal economies of scale can no longer offset demands for extended services that smaller municipalities often do not attempt to provide. Tenants in city-managed or privately owned apartments, for example, cannot easily get to their front doors without elevators. An elevator is but one small part of the urban infrastructure that must be maintained. Easy access to one's front door is something that less urbanized Americans take for granted, but in a high-rise city it requires a municipal bureaucracy: building inspectors to enforce housing codes on private landlords, or municipal workers to contract for maintenance in city-owned buildings.

In addition, services that more affluent suburban Americans sometimes provide for themselves have become the obligations of strained agencies with thousands of central city constituents caught in their own webs of personal crises. Because their numbers are large and concentrated in one area, city residents in distress have come to represent the depth of a nation's compassion. There is an ethical imperative that demands that impoverished patients with acquired immune deficiency syndrome (AIDS) must be treated; that single children having their own children must be housed; that the homeless should be sheltered; and that drug dependents should be given the chance to enter detoxification programs. Many of the people facing these problems are rightly seen as victims of decades of discrimination and poverty. In other cases people seeking these services are victims of a different sort, falling into patterns of dependency that have made them liabilities rather than assets to their city. For Koch and other mayors in the 1980s, many of these goals and others like them were laudable but financially unobtainable.[27]

The rhetorical dilemma that emerged in Koch's first term and remained throughout was how to deal with these structural problems. Like most other big-city mayors, he recognized the plight of the city's growing and dependent underclass but sought to portray them in ways that would not alienate the middle class. He did not subscribe to the view of some urban analysts that middle-income residents had their own access to municipal perks in the from of heavy state and local subsidies for transportation and rent control. More than most of his counterparts, Koch was determined to talk about the virtues of the middle class in maintaining the livability of the city. For example, in response to criticism he received for closing of a city hospital in Harlem, Koch defended his actions with a rationale he would use again and again. In a meeting with residents he argued that blacks were not being singled out in budget cuts; those who argued such a racist case were unfair.

We spent in the city of New York, four billion four hundred million dollars on Medicaid and welfare. Can you imagine that? Four billion four hundred million dollars. And of that, one billion one hundred million comes right out of local tax levy dollars, out of our budget, and that goes overwhelmingly to nonwhite people. That's a fact. . . .

Now, it makes no difference to us what the race or religion is; we serve people irrespective of their color. We have a Department of Employment that spends five hundred million dollars that the Federal Government gives us. Overwhelmingly that goes to nonwhite people, because they are overwhelmingly the people who fit the financial requirements that the Federal government sets for getting those jobs. . . .

. . . We've got to provide for the poorest of the poor, and we're going to, but I want to tell you what you have to know is: there are demagogues and ideologues who don't give a damn about the middle class. I speak out for the middle class. You know why?

Because they pay the taxes; they provide the jobs for the poor people, and we're not able to do as much for them economically as I would like.[28]

## KOCH MEETS HIS CONSTITUENTS

More than most politicians, Koch enjoyed contacts with constituents in casual encounters or monthly "town meetings." He nurtured the image of a man who enjoyed the verbal sparring that often comes with question-and-answer sessions with constituents. "I have never feared speaking to any group, whether they were for me or against me," he noted in his 1985 book *Politics.* "I love the combat of the street in politics."[29]

### A Wounded Mayor

One of the nearly 130 meetings that he held occurred in May 1988 at a church on the east side of Manhattan. If the gathering of 300 people in the meeting hall at St. Vartan's Armenian Church was any different, it was probably that many were troubled by Koch's controversial role in the previous month's presidential primary. A large field of Democrats anxious to regain the White House had geared up to compete for New York State's delegates who would vote on a nominee at the summer convention. Among the contenders was Jesse Jackson, and Koch took little time to make it clear that Jewish New Yorkers would "have to be crazy" to support him. In 1984 a journalist had overheard Jackson refer to the city as "hymietown"—a slur that probably figured in the mayor's animosity. Koch surprised most party members by backing Tennessee senator Albert Gore, a relative newcomer to national politics who had little prospect of actually gaining the nomination. In several appearances around the city with Gore, he went beyond praise for the senator to attack repeatedly Jackson as a liar, a coward, and an opponent of Israel.

Democrats gearing up to regain the White House winced at the specter of the outspoken mayor taking on the popular Jackson, especially in a city that was already burdened with years of racial suspicion. Koch's vocal dislike for the leader of the "Rainbow Coalition" was an uncomfortable reminder of the growing rift in New York City between whites and blacks, a rift that occasionally surfaced in open racial warfare. Some local black leaders had long felt that Koch's interest in keeping the middle class from fleeing the city was essentially a message in code, implying that poor and largely nonwhite residents were to be neglected. Recent murders of blacks in largely white enclaves of Brooklyn and Queens added to their feeling that the mayor shared responsibility for hardening racial attitudes. In addition, early in his administration Koch made the questionable political judgment of talking quite frankly about race and bigotry. To his regret, he allowed journalist Ken Auletta to hear an oral history interview intended for posterity but full of sharply worded observations about racial attitudes in the city. Auletta cited Koch's opinion that blacks were prejudiced against Jews in a resulting *New Yorker* profile. "My experience with blacks is that they're basically anti-Semitic," Koch stated. He was careful to add that whites are also antiblack. But only in the latter case, he believed, was racial prejudice "recognized as morally reprehensible, something you have to control."[30] All these factors had a cumulative effect, adding more weight to the claim that Koch had contributed to New York's reputation as a city of polarized neighborhoods.

For his part, the mayor responded to these criticisms by explaining that this constituents were realistic enough to accept honest candor about real attitudes on the street. He frequently pointed out to visitors that it was not his style "to employ duplicity or artifice."[31] He also reminded them that over half of the city's budget was spent on programs for the poor, many of them minorities, and that no administration had so thoroughly recruited blacks and Hispanics into the police and higher managerial ranks.[32]

Placed in the middle of these simmering racial frictions, Gore received a scant 10 percent of the statewide vote. Jackson finished a much stronger second, only slightly behind the eventual party nominee, Michael Dukakis. Moreover, signs that Koch's confrontational style was counterproductive could be found in the fact that Jackson actually won the mayor's city by 6,000 votes.[33] For many members of his party, Koch's racial politics had become the kiss of death. His statements "only reinforced their impression," noted *The New Yorker's* Andy Logan, "that this city is full of loudmouths constantly at each other's throats over racial issues."[34]

Koch paid a high price for not endorsing Dukakis and for alienating Jackson's supporters. Not only did the party decline to issue an invitation to the mayor of the nation's most Democratic city to attend its national convention, but the Jackson episode probably contributed to Koch's own defeat in his bid for a fourth term sixteen months later. Combined with a series of damaging revelations about bribes and influence peddling by various city commissioners, the timing of the coming mayoral primary made it easy for many New Yorkers to vote for new leadership.[35] As the *New York Times* editorialized after he lost the primary to David Dinkins, the mayor "exhausted his beloved city. New Yorkers wanted a change, a respite from his entertaining, often irritating presence."[36]

## The Meeting

If Koch had scars from these recent experiences, he kept them hidden as he entered the church meeting hall to begin his town meeting.[37] As the next hour and one half would demonstrate, his combative style was undiminished. He took his place at the front of the room with an assortment of commissioners and deputies representing the police, planning agencies, public transportation, and sanitation. Like most other meetings, this one would focus on issues of concern to residents within one segment of the city: in this case, the forty-six blocks that make up the boundaries of Community Board District 6. Fifty-nine such districts are spread out over the five boroughs of the city, each with elected representatives who submit recommendations to officials on the full range of services that are provided to them. District 6 is made up of mostly white and middle-class apartment dwellers living in a rectangle along the East River. The northern end of the district nearest its Fifty-ninth Street border includes the midtown headquarters of a number of major corporations, in addition to the luxurious hotels and apartments that surround the United Nations. But most of the district's residents live near the sometimes dangerous streets of its southern edge, especially in the huge Cooper Village and Stuyvesant Town apartments. Thousands live within the anonymous red brick buildings of this massive complex, their twelve-story slabs arranged over six city blocks like a collection of giant dominos.

The concerns that residents would raise on this rainy evening were similar to those that citizens in other parts of the city had expressed. They would include questions about street crime, the fate of children and homeless mothers housed in shabby welfare hotels, the low quality of city services ranging from libraries to garbage collection, and municipal regulation of rents. More unique to the district were questions about a plan to build a massive housing project along the river. A proposed development known as Riverwalk was to reclaim twenty-eight acres from the river to hold five thirty-five to forty-seven story apartment buildings. Not only would cherished views be lost to this new wall of buildings, but many residents feared that more high-rise apartments would further reduce the services and fragile civility on the streets below.[38] Others nearer the portion of the district that runs near the seedy northern edge of Greenwich Village would ask if more could be done to control drug pushers and to put more police back on the streets. And at least a handful came to express concern about the district's massive Bellevue Hospital. For many residents Bellevue was a symbol of a city overwhelmed by its responsibility to be the last option for improverished citizens who had succumbed to the terrors of alcoholism, drug addiction, and AIDS. The hospital's psychiatric wing was also an infamous gulag, the last temporary refuge for thousands of the mentally ill before they moved on to permanent occupancy of the city's streets and subways.

Koch began by issuing a warning concealed in a compliment, noting that he has always learned something from these exchanges that he did not know and assumed that the same should also be true of his audiences. "It doesn't always mean—in the course of discussion—that we'll be in accord, but you'll get an honest answer." He then defined the ground rules for the meeting. "You have a question, you can stand there and you get a followup question . . . .And then, even if you don't like the answer that's it." On this night Koch honored this format but would meander through very long answers that left time for only a little more than a dozen queries. At one point in the evening when he offered to give a civics lesson on how the local community boards functioned, the audience—visibly frustrated at what they saw as a time-consuming filibuster—booed and shouted, "No!"

The tone of the evening was set by the chair of the community board who introduced Koch with a question.

Mr. Mayor, the key question that I think will be reflected over and over to you is why is it that when the city does anything—when there is development, when there is "progress" in quotation marks, there is a decline in services—why is it necessary whenever you have an objective to achieve on a city wide basis, that the local residents end up on the short end of the stick? Why is it that we have to have confrontations with you? Why do we have to scream and shout in order to get the basic things that one can expect in the civility and quality of life that exists in New York City?

Koch responded with a familiar lament. He reminded the group that neighborhoods tend to argue against anything that calls for sharing the burden of the city's problems. Housing for the homeless and halfway houses for drug users are fought by most citizens under the familiar logic of "not in my backyard." So, Koch noted, when people ask him why he does not always agree with the recommendations of local community boards, "If I did, nothing would ever be built in this city that has any adverse impact. Nothing."

The first major issue to surface in the meeting grew out of questions about city-sponsored efforts to keep large corporations in the city. Two common incentives that were familiar to most New Yorkers included giving tax breaks to companies who promised not to leave and arranging financing and tax deferments for developers who sought to construct commercial or residential complexes. The practice of waiving payment of millions of dollars of property taxes has been a carrot that many local governments have used to induce major companies to remain. But it has understandably grated on corporate and private taxpayers who wonder why they are not given the same attractive terms. When this issue rose again, Koch addressed it by pointing out why it was important to keep companies like the National Broadcasting Company from moving elsewhere. A law allowing tax incentives to companies, he noted, was approved by the state legislature, not by him. Even so, before it was passed, building in the city had virtually stopped.

Before I became the Mayor, in Morris County, New Jersey, which has only 400,000 people in it, there was more commercial space built than in all of New York City with seven and a half million people. In that year there were maybe two or three buildings—built in the whole city. So the state legislature said the city of New York can provide tax incentives financial incentives—to get people to build. I want to tell you what that meant.

Koch went on to make the argument that tax abatements eventually pay more in return than they cost, backing up his argument with a flurry of numbers and an appeal to civic pride.

As a result of tax abatement programs, we have built in this city commercial buildings that over a 20 year period . . . will pay . . . 13 *billion* dollars. And for residential buildings built, there's no question a lot of them were luxury. That's all right; they pay taxes that make it possible for the rest of us to hire cops to send into poor districts or to help us rehabilitate abandoned buildings. [There's] nothing wrong in having rich people live in the city of New York. I think it's pretty terrific myself; it helps the tax base. Now, residential taxes, all taxes considered, bring in 10 billion over a ten year period. So the total of taxes coming into the city of New York in a twenty-year period as a result of tax abatement was 23 billion dollars, and the amount that we lost... [was]... a billion 500 thousand dollars. I think that's pretty good leverage. I want to tell you, were we alone? New Jersey is doing it. Now, you can say—as I would say—that if every city and state in the union said, "We're not going to give any tax abatement: you come if you want to, and if you don't come, we don't care." then we wouldn't give it either. But that's not the real world. We have to compete. And I think we have competed quite successfully. Let's take NBC. NBC was offered all kinds of tax incentives to move to New Jersey. All kinds. The rent is cheaper; I think they were offered something for somewhere between 15 to 18 dollars a square foot. Now in New York City they're paying—I don't know exactly what they are paying—but you pay anywhere from 40 to 50 dollars a square foot. And they can move and get new studios, and we ultimately kept them here. And I'll tell you what it cost. It's no secret. It cost us in lost taxes 3 and a half million dollars a year for 30 years: roughly a hundred million dollars . . . . Is it worth it? Was it worth it?

A chorus of constituents shouted, "No."

Well, then, that's *so* foolish! If you don't think that it's worth keeping NBC here at a cost to us of three and a half million dollars less in taxes—they pay taxes, but three and a half million dollars less—than, I'm sorry. We can't have a rational discussion. Do you know what it would have meant to this city if NBC had left? And then CBS went, and then all of the other channels? You know what it means not only in jobs, in taxes, but in prestige? So when that person—I heard one voice, maybe two—said, "No, it wasn't worth it," I can't argue with you, because you're *wrong*, simply *wrong*.

The recital of these numbers came with the characteristically animated Koch delivery, his voice rising and falling with exaggerated emphasis. But a pattern for the evening was set in the combination of laughter, boos, and applause that followed his explanation. The mayor's directness ("You're *wrong*, simply *wrong*") sanctioned an equal boldness from some in the audience who increasingly challenged him as the meeting progressed. In turn, he would issue his own comments on their shortsightedness, and in this instance he actually booed them back. For half-a-minute the meeting turned into a shouting match. Several constituents made it clear that they had grown tired of long explanations and challenged Koch to give briefer answers.

"Point of order, your honor . . . ," a man pleaded from near the back wall.

"No," Koch cut him off. "Out of order. Sit down." To the next questioner he signaled, "You're next."

But another audience member asked to be heard. "Point of order, this is a town meeting, people are trying—"

Koch would have none of it. He was in danger of losing control of the meeting to the increasingly impatient group. He cut off charges that he was too long-winded and insisted that the next questioner ask a new question or sit down in favor of someone who would.

Moments like these might have traumatized another politician, but they clearly energized Koch, whose persona is an unlikely combination of prosecuting attorney and stand-up comic. Most politicians tend to reign in their impulses to express irony and disbelief. They corset their inflections in the monotones of discursive speech. But Koch liked to challenge opponents with one-liners and asides. He admired the similarly inclined Fiorello LaGuardia far more than more recent mayors, who usually relied on an aura of distant reserve. How many other American politicians boo back to their constituents? Koch knew that such insults contributed to the stereotype of New York as a place "where four fifths of life is an argument."[39] Koch was part of that *ethos* and clearly cherished it. It is easy to imagine how another quintessential New Yorker like film director Woody Allen could have invented the irreverent mayor for one of his odes to the city.

The next question came from a district politician who knew Koch and expressed concern that part of the Bellevue Hospital campus would be sold off to a developer for luxury housing. He worried that Bellevue's function as a shelter for the homeless and for AIDS patients would be minimized. Koch responded that the apartment construction, if ever approved, would be for middle and lower incomes. He also noted that a center for the homeless would be built at the same location, a statement that produced groans from the back of the room. "You don't like that either? That's O.K." Pointing to the questioner, Koch added, "He does."

He argued that all hospitals—city and private—should share the burden of care for people infected with AIDS.

There are about 1400 AIDS patients in the City of New York in hospitals. Thirty-six percent of them are in city hospitals. We only have 15 hospitals. There are about 90 or so hospitals in the city. And we have 36 percent of all of the cases; the others are in the voluntary hospitals. We only have . . . 16 percent of the beds, and 36 percent of the patients. We don't think that that makes much sense. And I want to tell you, at Bellevue they think it makes terrible sense. And do you know why? Because at Bellevue, which is a teaching hospital, they say residents want not to treat only AIDS patients; they want to treat patients with every kind of disease, because that's the way they learn. And if at any time Bellevue becomes only an AIDS hospital, you're not any longer going to be able to get residents to come and to learn there. So you want to have a reasonable mix. I want to tell you that tonight, at Bellevue, the population is probably—this is an old figure; it might have gone up a little—a hundred and forty AIDS patients in bed. In all of San Francisco they don't have that number, in all of their hospitals put together. So when you say you want to turn Bellevue into an AIDS hospital—

The questioner tried to break in.
"That's not what I said, Mr. Mayor—"
"Or you want to add an AIDS wing, I want to tell you it may be—"
"With all due respect, Mr. Mayor, that is not what I said."
"You want to add AIDS beds?" Koch asked.

" . . . Yes, but I wanted to add them in the existing sites . . . as a hospice style—"

"It's the same thing—"

"It is *not*, Mr. Mayor. As a hospice—"

"O.K.—"

" . . . style facility—"

"O.K., we won't fight," Koch interjected.

"Because as a point of fact—"

"We *won't* fight. I want this—"

"With all due respect, Mr. Mayor, Bellevue Hospital is a matter of what happens to the people in this city—"

"Yeah—"

" . . . when I last heard, 25 percent of all of the AIDS patients in the United States of America at one time or another go to Bellevue. That's a matter of their choice—"

"Well, it may be—"

" . . . It's not to turn people away—"

The questioner continued to try to make his point, but Koch had heard enough.

Lou, *please*! I *heard* you, now you got to take an answer; you may not like the answer. *You may not like it*. The first thing is, that we believe the AIDS patients should be spread among all the hospitals and, in fact, Dr. David Axelrod has authorized 500 new medical-surgical beds which will be—we believe—exclusively for AIDS patients, and he's not giving them—and we agree with him—to the Health and Hospitals Corporation. He is mandating that they go to the voluntaries [private hospitals] for AIDS patients so that *they do their share*. In addition, we want him to do even more than that. We want him to say that the AIDS population will be distributed in some fair proportion through the whole hospital system.

After an additional question about favoring developers over people already living in the city, a man coyly asked if Koch had seen a recent issue of *New York Magazine* containing an article called "The Unmaking of the Mayor, 1989." "I'd like to read one very brief direct quotation in which you were purported to say, in relations to some problems going on in the city: 'New Yorkers are great. They'll put up with anything.' " The consitutent's question was only two words: "Wanna bet?" The room broke out in laughter and applause.

"I want to tell you what I know about New Yorkers," Koch began, "notwithstanding what was intended to be, you know, a hostile comment, which you're entitled to have. . . . I go everywhere. I go to *every* community, and they're not always as friendly as this one, and this isn't exactly—you know—Joy Street. But I learn, and I think I also explain." He went on to defend the quote by noting that he meant that New Yorkers had the "good sense" to know that the hardships of near-bankruptcy would require sacrifice. The "modern miracle" of the present city with its stronger financial standing was because New Yorkers were "so smart." They were willing to put up with several years of reduced services. His lengthy response included a summary of how the city had gradually improved its ability to sell its bonds to investors.

After the mayor and various deputies listened to concerns about muggings that had occurred in portions of the district, and the need to find constructive activities for children whose families have all but abandoned them, a constituent raised the issue of high rents. One sore point with many of the city's merchants was the mayor's support for continued regulation of apartment rents but not for the leases that small businesses pay to their landlords. A young woman pursued the argument that this was an inequity.

"I'm all for free enterprise, and I think we all are," she began. "But when landlords jack up rents 100, 200, 300 percent, forcing many small shopkeepers to close their doors—not just mom and pops, but larger ones—as you're aware, I think that there is something wrong with the system." She paused amid scattered applause. "And I want to ask you why you are so opposed to a commerical—"

"I'll tell you why," Koch interjected.

" . . . O.K., commercial rent control—"

"Let her finish," someone pleaded from the back of the room.

" . . . thank you—that's regulated in some way so that it's equitable for both—"

"I will tell you why."

" . . . the shopkeeper—"

"I will tell you why."

"—and the renter."

"I will tell you why. I will tell you exactly why. I believe that we need—and I have fought to maintain—residential rent control, because I consider that to be an absolute necessity. You have to have a place to sleep—"

In response to more unwelcome interjections from others around the room, Koch added, "Please! You have to hear my answer. You may not like it, but you have to hear it."

He went on to argue that "there is no city in America that has commercial rent control" because "the cure is worse than the disease." Trying out a lengthy and unclear example about the price of goods that a bakery with rent control would have to charge, Koch again had to climb over a series of small challenges. One vocal constituent interjected, "What's that got to do with it?" and another added, "I don't understand." The mayor's response: "You're going to have to listen." Over a cascade of boos he noted that the only people who would benefit from rent control are individual storekeepers: "The community doesn't benefit."

"Do you have a followup [question]?" he asked.

"I'll made a deal with you," the young woman said. "No followup question [but] to tell you that I very respectfully disagree with you on all counts."

"Of course you do," noted the mayor.

Near the end of the meeting an older man stood up and said, "Mayor Koch, I'm sorry you didn't start the meeting by asking 'how am I doing?' I think you're doing great." A blend of groans, boos, and scattered applause followed. "And

I'm here to say . . . that when the campaign comes around, I'll be campaigning for you." Koch took the moment to ask how many would support him in the upcoming election. A few hands went up. How many thought he was *not* doing all right? More hands. The old man added, "We'll turn them around," but Koch's patience had begun to wear thin. To a loud constituent who urged him to be more responsive to the questions, he shot back, "Sir, I've taken *enough* from you, and we're not taking *any more.*" He was tired of the interruptions ("He works for us!" "Answer the questions!") and no doubt glad that only a few more minutes remained in the hour and a half meeting.

The last few comments included a short catalog of urban woes; a "tale of horror" from a grandfather whose grandson had come home from a park holding a bloody syringe in his hands; a question about why "foreigners" were given preference over "Americans" in the assignment of licenses to sell food from street carts; and a woman's expression of frustration about drug dealers selling "crack" from neighboring apartments and abandoned cars. "What you're doing now is not enough," she noted. "The question is, what are you going to do?"

"Look," Koch began, "the fact is that they're selling drugs in front of the White House. And if they can't stop the selling of drugs in front of the White House, it's very difficult for mayors to stop drugs from being sold elsewhere." The facile answer was greeted with a groundswell of boos. "I'm telling you the truth!" he retorted.

So last year 80,000 people selling drugs or possessing drugs were arrested by the Police Department. It's not adequate. It didn't stop it, and what we're doing this year is we're going to try to confiscate apartments and buildings. . . . [Now] if drugs are found in a building, . . . we can seize the building. Today we seized the one thousandth car since that program went into effect. We've taken a thousand cars away from drug pushers or drug users who were caught with drugs in their car. Now those people will think twice before they come again, and if they do, it will be in someone else's car. With respect to apartments and buildings, we hope that that will have a similar impact. That's all I can tell you.

After a brief follow-up question by the same person, the mayor announced that it was nine o'clock and ended the meeting with a crisp "Good night." There were more boos and applause as he made his way to the door. Even though he was soon gone, several disgruntled constituents tried to continue the largely one-way dialogue. "Why don't you listen?" shouted one. Another man wearing a hunter's jacket referred to the recent presidential primary, shouting, "You can't keep treating people the way you tried to treat Jesse Jackson."[40]

The following day members of the mayor's office expressed overall pleasure at the way the meeting had gone. They reasoned that Koch had defended the administration's decisions well, even in the face of many hotheads who did not want to hear considered arguments and sensible explanations. But one longtime city hall reporter reflected what many in the rest of the city's media had begun to publish about the mayor: that "the patience of New Yorkers with his often high-handed—if entertaining—performance as mayor is wearing thin."[41]

## LESSONS FOR A COMBATIVE LEADER

Even though we have only touched on a few moments in Ed Koch's public career, several key features of his rhetoric are clear enough to speculate on his kind of combative leadership. A number of key words suggest important elements of this style, among them: "prone to assertions rather than questions," "candid," "argumentative," "anxious to explain," "defensive," and "judgmental." To the extent these attributes cluster in one individual, they describe a confrontational communicator.[42] Such an advocate tends to amplify positions *not so much by their similarities with others but by their significant differences*. He is more likely to identify the defining moment of an exchange as the point at which competing asssertions surface into full view. His perception is tuned differently than the vast plurality of Americans who are more likely to define complete communication as the point at which differences begin to melt into consensus. To be sure, confronters also seek consensus, but they seem less inclined than most to minimize differences in order to achieve it. Thus, when a deputy mayor asked for a private meeting with Ed Koch to complain about another deputy's work, he probably should not have been surprised when Koch excused himself and returned a few minutes later with the accused on his arm. "Tell her what you just told me," Koch said to the complainer.[43] For the mayor, a face-to-face encounter was simply the most direct route to the resolution of differences.

Even with all the natural variations that specific individuals bring to it, the confrontational style of Ed Koch and others cited in this study invites some useful conclusions about its limits and virtues.

1. Audiences tend to give what they get. Because public discussion tends to follow in the tracks that are laid down by the parties involved, the general tone of exchanges is reciprocated. Reasonableness on one side encourages at least its facsimile on the other side. Candor begets more candor. Throughout the 1980s, for example, Ronald Reagan's benign personal style had the effect of making much of the mainstream national press virtual captives to his amiability. The "Teflon President's" popularity and apparent lack of guile made him a difficult target for political analysts and critics.[44] Over the same time, Koch established a very different standard. He was willing to pursue almost any slight or criticism. If reporters said something he deemed foolish, they were told so. If constituents offered opinions that lacked complete understanding of certain key facts, corrections of their misguided statements were willingly offered. His characterization of his administration as something like "a very large and quarrelsome Jewish family"[45] generally indicated what he expected and wanted from his years as the political leader of New York City.

2. Issues do not come to us as pure ideas. They arrive in the vessel of the advocate. We partially judge an attitude or idea by the demeanor of its advocate. This old axiom is a sobering reminder to the rhetorical street fighter that a rough and aggressive style may have the effect of eclipsing more substantive issues.

It would be an oversimplification to say that the human tendency to look for style over substance accounts for the eventual defeat of Ed Koch, but it probably contributed to it. It is revealing to consider how this bias played itself out in Koch's attacks on Jesse Jackson. By 1988 Jackson was the very model of a communicator who was able to rebuild his campaign style on an upbeat rhetoric of inclusion. As we have seen, the mayor's simultaneous decision to attack him backfired. For example, among Jackson's most successful television commercials in the campaign were those that included the enthusiastic support of white midwestern farmers who praised his efforts to win federal relief from farm foreclosures. To the television viewer, the opposing style of the two men stood in stark contrast. Jackson's multiracial and positive campaign focused in part on nondivisive issues, ranging from keeping teens in school to providing more low-cost loans to small businesses. It contrasted favorably with Koch's more personalized attacks on the leader of the Rainbow Coalition. While Jackson seemed to be reaching out to many segments and factions in the city, the mayor seemed intent on polarizing them.

3. Since television communicates as much about a persuader's *personal style* as his *ideas*, there is a strong likelihood that these two dimensions will be compressed into a simplified "rhetorical signature." Partly the genuine product of an individual's personality and partly a synthetic re-creation, these signatures become economical ways to identify familiar figures. Harry Truman's sharp tongue, Ronald Reagan's patriotic pieties, Jesse Jackson's optimism, Robert Dole's cutting wit, and Dan Quayle's blandness are—for good or ill—trademarks that have become part of their public personas. Inevitably, these features function as the rhetorical equivalents of tourist postcards: reconizable symbols that stand in for familiar landmarks. They also serve the interests of the media by creating stock characters for their daily news narratives. The presence of familiar players in recurring news dramas provides an attractive kind of continuity: a set of expectations that each new report should confirm. For example, the villain in one piece should not be the hero in the next.

But such stereotypes can exact a price. Some leaders flourish on media portrayals of their public performances, but others can be trapped by them. The identification of one invariant trait with a person's public persona can be lethal. New York governor Mario Cuomo and President George Bush are among those who have successfully reinvented their roles as their public careers and national attitudes have changed. But other figures have suffered the fate of type-cast film actors, useful only as media caricatures in other people's news dramas.

To some extent, Koch became the victim of his own rhetorical signature. What initially made him an attractive politician—his brashness and candor—

later turned into a damaging stereotype with unanticipated consequences. Throughout this long transformation, Koch maintained continued interest in communicating the details of his administrative actions. Tax figures, policy proposals, projections of agency staff levels, and the like were still a large part of his public comments. But over the years his discursive communication took a backseat to the more flamboyant facets of his rhetorical signature—especially his confrontational one-liners. This is not to say that the media attempted to sabotage the mayor. Rather, the pattern of selective coverage that first defined his combative persona and seemed to empower beleaguered New Yorkers eventually had the reverse effect. Constitutents began to perceive that he had lost his ability to differentiate between opponents and political enemies. For them his brashness had turned into a mean spiritedness. After the Jackson affair, Koch admitted that it would have been useful to try to "cultivate a bed side manner." But he knew that a marked violation of role type would not have remedied the problem of his sagging public support. After all, he observed, "you can't be what you're not."[46]

4. Part of what makes combative figures newsworthy are two strategies of verbal compression. One involves the reduction of *arguments to judgments*, allowing single evocative terms to stand in the place of more substantive discussion of an issue's merits. A second is the rhetorical reduction of *policies to people*, a strategy represented by the partial replacement of issue-centered analysis with an emphasis on the personal characteristics of advocates.

A general scarcity of media time and space creates a need for these strategies of rhetorical efficiency. There are very few successful forums in American life that nurture "long-form" exchanges of views. Television time is expensive and almost always subject to the whims of viewers in the process of consuming their leisure time. Print has far more capacity to develop ideas, but—with notable exceptions—competition for readers also pushes editors to maximize variety at the expense of depth on any one issue.[47]

These two approaches are not *just* media-driven responses, but their inherent economy makes them well suited to the short form of the television newscast or one-column news report. The Koch penchant for using one-word judgments as shorthand expressions for full arguments is legendary. Consider four simple examples: a newspaper editorial is described by the mayor as "*dopey*"; the assertion of a civil rights lawyer is "*bizarre*";[48] opponents to tax abatements are "*idiots*";[49] and the Forest Hills housing plan is "*crazy*."[50] Life would be tedious without such reductions in private discourse. As vehicles of public discussion, however, what they gain in verbal economy they relinquish in precision and understanding. For reporters with limited time and space, such terms are usually assigned primary roles in defining what are inevitably more complex positions. Stories about Koch have always been full of long paraphrases punctuated with one-word quotes. He often encouraged this pattern by capping off a well-reasoned argument with a garish but headline-grabbing word. The effect of such a sequence was often to divert attention away from other less flamboyant points, a fact of public life Koch was aware of but not willing to change. "I *can* demolish an opponent in one line," he once noted, "but that isn't the same thing as winning over the state legislature on Medicaid or pulling New York City out of bankruptcy."[51]

The same single-word examples also illustrate another trait common to much confrontational rhetoric: a frequent preference for putting a special emphasis on the role of opponents in the evolution of policy. Notice that each of the four terms that Koch used to characterize discourse about ideas—"dopey," "bizarre," "idiots," and "crazy"—are more personalistic than ideological. That is, each word more naturally serves as a summarizing judgment of a *person* than of an object or idea. Aside from the guarantee that they would make colorful quotes in news reports, their use also had the subtle effect of keeping public discussion rooted in the language of character rather than the language of policy. Terms like these carry their own partly concealed messages, begging as much for the condemnation of advocates as their proposals.

It was often Koch's strength as a newsmaker and liability as a policy advocate that he could not separate people from their ideas. In his *Playboy* interview he discussed the defeated Equal Rights Amendment (ERA), which he endorsed, noting that Congresswoman Bella Abzug, also a strong supporter, "was responsible for ERA's defeat in New York State." Koch found her to be "very pushy, counterproductive in a whole list of areas."[52] How would he describe her today? True to form, the mayor had one juicy term that would make the policy question of why the ERA lost secondary to the conflict of personalities: "Bigmouth," he responded with a chuckle.[53]

5. Finally, a word of praise for the combative impulse that was so consistently a part of Koch's career. There is something refreshing about a public figure who will risk abandoning the ritual formalities of a rhetoric of accommodation to clarify differences. Disputes that develop between individuals and factions may sometimes be unnecessary and counterproductive. They may also be fed by the outsized egos of politicians and an insatiable public appetite for news framed in the drama of conflict. Yet combative rhetoric frequently serves the vital function of defining contrasting perspectives. Most cultures would be far poorer without such leadership. What if Winston Churchill had decided that it was too much of a burden to speak against his party's ill-chosen path of accommodation with Nazi Germany?[54] Who would have preferred a more soothing Theodore Roosevelt schooled in the modern art of "management by consensus?"[55] Both of these men had varied reasons for taking on unpopular causes, not the least of which was their skillful sense of what would play well to supporters and potential allies. But neither leader would probably have been slaves to the modern presumption in favor of a "community of shared interests." Neither man would have endorsed the existence of consensus as self-evident proof that a society had solved its most pressing problems. As Elizabeth Kristol has wisely cautioned, "Pluralism requires tolerance. But a pluralistic society undermines its ability to

deal with its most serious problems when differences are denied and tolerance is transformed into a false sense of unity."[36]

The real America is far more diverse and eclectic than is usually suggested in the formal myths that are invoked in most public discourse. Combative rhetoric is not necessarily more accurate than the rhetoric of inclusion, nor does it necessarily spring from more altruistic motives. But in the form of public debates and persuasive encounters, it is absolutely essential if a society is to renew itself successfully.

## NOTES

1. Roger Rosenblatt, "A Mayor for All Seasons," *Time*, June 15, 1981, p. 28.

2. Edward I. Koch and William Rauch, *Politics* (New York: Warner, 1985), pp. 270–271.

3. Rosenblatt, A Mayor for All Seasons," p. 28.

4. See, for example, Norman Podhoretz, "Why Reagan and Koch Are the Most Popular Politicians in America," *New York Magazine*, April 6, 1981, pp. 30–32.

5. Arthur Browne, Dan Collins, and Michael Goodwin, *I, Koch* (New York: Dodd and Mead, 1985), p. 69.

6. Peter Manso, "Playboy Interview: Edward Koch," *Playboy*, April 1982, p. 76.

7. Ken Auletta, "Profiles: The Mayor—I," *The New Yorker*, September 10, 1979, p. 74.

8. Koch and Rauch, *Politics*, p. 162.

9. This is Irving Kristol's definition of a "neoconservative," quoted in Podhoretz, "Why Reagan and Koch," p. 32.

10. Quoted in Browne, Collins and Goodwin, *I, Koch*, p. 270.

11. Edward I. Koch and William Rauch, *Mayor* (New York: Warner, 1984), pp. 90–94.

12. Quoted in Andy Logan, "Around City Hall: Will You Still Need Me?" *The New Yorker*, January 2, 1989, p. 57.

13. Quoted in Auletta, "Profiles: The Mayor—I," p. 108.

14. Manso, "Playboy Interview," p. 76.

15. Ibid., p. 78.

16. Ibid., p. 98.

17. Ibid., p. 70.

18. Quoted in Browne, Collins, and Goodwin, *I, Koch*, p. 185.

19. Logan "Around City Hall: Will You Still Need Me?" p. 56.

20. "Two School Systems Compared," *New York Times*, September 25, 1989, p. B4.

21. "The Koch Years: What's Up, What's Down, and What's Different," *New York Times*, September 13, 1989, p. B4.

22. Arnold H. Lubasch, "Koch Details His Final Year as Mayor," *New York Times*, September 20, 1989, p.B3.

23. "The Koch Years," p. B4.

24. For an analysis of this problem, see Roger Starr, *The Rise and Fall of New York City* (New York: Basic Books, 1985), pp. 108–127.

25. "The Koch Years," p. B4.

26. Susan Chira, "Working Class Families Losing Middle-Class Dreams,"*New York Times*, September 3, 1989, p. B6.

27. For background analysis of these problems, see Starr, *The Rise and Fall of New York City*, pp. 204–222; and William Gorham and Nathan Glazer, *The Urban Predicament* (Washington, D.C.: Urban Institute, 1976), pp. 1–33.

28. Koch and Rauch, *Mayor*, p. 225.

29. Koch and Rauch, *Politics*, p. 158.

30. Auletta, "Profiles: The Mayor—I," pp. 114–115.

31. Quoted in Rosenblatt, "A Mayor for All Seasons," p. 27.

32. "The Koch Years," p. B4.

33. Andy Logan, "Around City Hall: Raw," *The New Yorker*, June 13, 1988, p. 109.

34. Ibid.

35. The fullest allegations of malfeasance in the Koch administration have been made by Jack Newfield and Wayne Barrett in *City for Sale: Ed Koch and the Betrayal of New York* (New York: Harper & Row, 1988). Koch's responses to these charges and to press accounts of them appear in John Cardinal O'Connor and Edward I. Koch, *His Eminence and Hizzoner* (New York: Avon, 1989), pp. 119–130.

36. "Ed Koch's New York," editorial, *New York Times*, September 17, 1989, p. 22.

37. The following partial account is taken from an audio tape transcript of the mayor's town hall meeting, May 19, 1988. The tape was provided by the Community Assistance Unit of the mayor's office, New York City.

38. Andrew Rosenthal, "Tucked Away on East Side, Two Communities Resist Project," *New York Times*, April 21, 1987, pp. B1–B2.

39. Rosenblatt, "A Mayor for All Seasons," p. 24.

40. Logan, "Around City Hall: Raw," p. 108.

41. Ibid.

42. Although broad categories are necessarily inexact, I mean to suggest that Koch is not alone in having these rhetorical tendencies. The general elements of his style are evident in a wide range of public figures, some mentioned in this book. Other American figures from politics and the media who could be identified with this style include journalist William F. Buckley, Jr., former presidential aide Patrick Buchanan, liberal theorist Michael Harrington, Senate Minority Leader Robert Dole, Mike Wallace of "60 Minutes," and former UN ambassador Jeane Kirkpatrick. Among those I would *not* identify with this style are former presidential candidates Hubert Humphrey and George McGovern, Ronald Reagan, journalist Peter Jennings, and House Majority Leader Thomas Foley.

43. Auletta, "Profiles: The Mayor—I," pp. 97–98.

44. Mark Hertsgaard, *On Bended Knee: The Press and the Reagan Presidency* (New York: Schocken, 1988), pp. 4–5.

45. Rosenblatt, "A Mayor for All Seasons," p. 27.

46. Richard Levine, " 'New' Koch Forsakes Atlanta Politicking for Europe," *New York Times*, July 19, 1988, p. B4.

47. For general background on this point, see Herbert J. Gans, *Deciding What's News* (New York: Vintage, 1980), pp. 146–181.

48. Levine, " 'New' Koch Forsakes Atlanta," p. B4.

49. David W. Dunlap, "Koch, the 'Entertainer,' Gets Mixed Review," *New York Times*, May 19, 1988, p. B4.

50. Manso, "Playboy Interview," p. 82.

51. Ibid., p. 76.

52. Ibid., p. 91.

53. Ibid.

54. See, for example, Halbert F. Gulley, "Churchill's Speech on the Munich Agreement," *Quarterly Journal of Speech*, October 1947, pp. 284–291.

55. Roosevelt was willing to spend much of his political capital in the interests of urging reform within major American institutions, including huge industries and the Republican party. See George Mowry, *Theodore Roosevelt and the Progressive Movement* (New York: Hill and Wang, 1960), pp. 3–35.

56. Elizabeth Kristol, "False Tolerance, False Unity," *New York Times*, September 25, 1989, p. A19.

# Selected Bibliography

Alinsky, Saul. *Rules for Radicals* (New York: Random House, 1971).

Alter, Jonathan, and Howard Fineman. "The Great TV Shout-Out," *Newsweek*, February 8, 1988, 20–23.

Andrews, James R., Confrontation at Columbia: A Case Study in Coercive Rhetoric," *Quarterly Journal of Speech*, February 1969, 9–16.

Arlen, Michael J. *The Camera Age: Essays in Television* (New York: Farrar, Straus, and Giroux, 1989).

Auletta, Ken. "Profiles: The Mayor—I," *The New Yorker*, September 10, 1979, 54–119.

Barnouw, Erik. *Tube of Plenty: The Evolution of American Broadcasting* (New York: Oxford, 1975).

———. *The Image Empire: A History of Broadcasting in the United States, Vol. III* (New York: Oxford, 1970).

Bitzer, Lloyd. "The Rhetorical Situation," *Philosophy and Rhetoric*, January 1968, 1–14.

Black, Edwin. *Rhetorical Criticism: A Study in Method* (Madison: University of Wisconsin, 1978).

———. "The Second Persona," *Quarterly Journal of Speech*, April 1970, 109–119.

Bode, Carl. *The American Lyceum: Town Meeting of the Mind* (New York: Oxford, 1956).

Booth, Wayne C. *Modern Dogma and the Rhetoric of Assent* (Chicago: University of Chicago, 1974).

———. *Now Don't Try to Reason with Me* (Chicago: University of Chicago, 1970).

Boyer, Peter J. *Who Killled CBS?* (New York: Random House, 1988).

———. "When One Ambush Meets Another," *New York Times* January 27, 1988, A16.

Branham, Robert J., and W. Barnett Pearce. "A Contract for Civility: Edward Kennedy's Lynchburg Address," *Quarterly Journal of Speech*, November 1987, 424–443.

Brockriede, Wayne. "Arguers as Lovers," *Philosophy and Rhetoric*, Winter 1972, 1–11.

Browne, Arthur; Dan Collins; and Michael Goodwin. *I, Koch* (New York: Dodd and Mead, 1985).

Buckley, Jr., William F. *On the Firing Line: The Public Life of Our Public Figures* (New York: Random House, 1989).

Burgess, Parke. "The Rhetoric of Moral Conflict: Two Critical Dimensions," *Quarterly Journal of Speech*, April 1970, 120–130.

Burke, Kenneth. *Permanence and Change: An Anatomy of Purpose, Second Edition* (Indianapolis: Bobbs-Merrill, 1965).

———. *A Rhetoric of Motives* (New York: Prentice-Hall, 1953).

———. "Rhetoric—Old and New," *Journal of General Education*, April 1951, 202–209.

Burns, James MacGregor. *Edward Kennedy and the Camelot Legacy* (New York: W. W. Norton, 1976).

Carpenter, Ronald. "The Historical Jeremiad as Rhetorical Genre," in *Form and Genre: Shaping Rhetorical Action*, ed. Karlyn Kohrs Cambell and Kathleen Hall Jamieson (Falls Church, Va.: Speech Communication Association, n.d.), 103–117.

Carter, Jimmy. *Keeping Faith: Memoirs of a President* (New York: Bantam, 1982).

Chester, Lewis; Godfrey Hodgson; and Bruce Page. *An American Melodrama: The Presidential Campaign of 1968* (New York: Viking, 1969).

Clark, Brian. *Whose Life Is It Anyway?* (New York: Dodd and Mead, 1978).

Cohen, Arthur R. *Attitude Change and Social Influence* (New York: Basic, 1964).

Corry, John. "A Week of Donahue Taped in Soviet Union," *New York Times*, February 12, 1987, C30.

Denton, Jr., Robert E., and Gary C. Woodard. *Political Communication in America* (New York: Praeger, 1985).

Devlin, L. Patrick. "An Analysis of Kennedy's Communication in the 1980 Campaign," *Quarterly Journal of Speech*, November 1982, 397–417.

Donahue, Phil. *Donahue: My Own Story* (New York: Simon and Schuster, 1979).

"Donahue." Program Transcript no. 02107. Multimedia Entertainment, 1987 Mimeographed copy. Taped in Moscow, February 1987.

Drew, Elizabeth. *Portrait of an Election: The 1980 Presidential Campaign* (New York: Simon and Schuster, 1981).

Duncan, Hugh Dalziel. *Communication and Social Order* (New York: Oxford, 1962).

Edelman, Murray, *The Symbolic Uses of Politics* (Urbana: University of Illinois, 1967).

Festinger, Leon. *A Theory of Cognitive Dissonance* (Stanford, Calif.: Stanford, 1957).

FitzGerald, Frances. *Cities on a Hill* (New York: Simon and Schuster, 1986).

Friendly, Fred W. *Due to Circumstances beyond Our Control* (New York: Vintage, 1967).

Gans, Herbert J. *Deciding What's News* (New York: Vintage, 1980).

Goffman, Erving. *Presentation of Self in Everyday Life* (New York: Anchor, 1959).

Gulley, Halbert F. "Churchill's Speech on the Munich Agreement," *Quarterly Journal of Speech*, October 1947, 284–291.

Harrington, Mona. *The Dream of Deliverance in American Politics* (New York: Knopf, 1986).

Heath, Jim. *Decade of Disillusionment: The Kennedy-Johnson Years* (Bloomington: Indiana University, 1975).

Hersh, Burton. *The Education of Edward Kennedy* (New York: William Morrow, 1972).

Hofstadter, Richard. *The American Political Tradition, Twenty-fifth Anniversary Edition* (New York: Knopf, 1973).

Hovland, Carl I.; Irving L. Janis; and Harold H. Kelly. *Communication and Persuasion* (New Haven: Yale University, 1953).

Iyengar, Shanto, and Donald R. Kinder. *News That Matters* (Chicago: University of Chicago, 1987).

Janis, Irving. *Victims of Groupthink* (Boston: Houghton Mifflin, 1972).

Johannesen, Richard L. *Ethics in Human Communication, Second Edition* (Prospect Heights, Ill.: Waveland, 1983).

Katz, Elihu, and P. F. Lazarfield. *Personal Influence: The Part Played by People in the Flow of Mass Communications* (Glencoe, Ill.: Free Press, 1955).

Kendrick, Alexander. *Prime Time: The Life of Edward R. Murrow* (Boston: Little, Brown, 1969).

Kennedy, Edward M. "Tolerance and Truth in America," Speech at Liberty Baptist College, October 3, 1983. Mimeographed text.

Kennedy, John F. *Profiles in Courage, Memorial Edition* (New York: Perennial Library, 1964).

Klapp, Orrin. *Symbolic Leaders: Public Dramas and Public Men* (Chicago: Aldine, 1964).

Koch, Edward I., and William Rauch. *Politics* (New York: Warner, 1985).

————. *Mayor* (New York: Warner, 1984).

Krauthammer, Charles. "The Myth of Thomas Szasz," *The New Republic*, December 22, 1979, 13–17.

Kuhn, Thomas S. *The Structure of Scientific Revolutions, Second Edition* (Chicago: University of Chicago, 1970).

Lasch, Christopher. *The Culture of Narcissism* (New York: Norton, 1978).

Lippmann, Walter. *The Public Philosophy* (Boston: Little, Brown, 1955).

Logan, Andy. "Around City Hall: Raw," *The New Yorker*, June 13, 1988, 104–111.

MacNeil, Robert. *The People Machine* (New York: Harper & Row, 1968).

Manso, Peter. "Playboy Interview: Edward Koch," *Playboy*, April 1982, 67–98.

McCombs, Maxwell. "The Agenda Setting Approach," in *Handbook of Political Communication*, ed. Dan D. Nimmo and Keith R. Sanders (Beverly Hills, Calif.: Sage, 1981), 121–140.

Meyrowitz, Joshua. *No Sense of Place* (New York: Oxford, 1985).

Minow, Newton N. "Address to the 39th Annual Convention of the National Association of Broadcasters," Washington, D.C., May 9, 1961, reprinted in Glen E. Mills, *Reason in Controversy* (Boston: Allyn and Bacon, 1964), 271–282.

Murrow, Edward R. "A Reporter Talks to His Colleagues," *The Reporter*, November 13, 1958, 32–36.

Newfield, Jack. *Robert Kennedy: A Memoir* (New York: E. P. Dutton, 1969).

Rather, Dan, and Mickey Herskowitz. *The Camera Never Blinks* (New York: Ballantine, 1978).

Report of the Chicago Study Team to the National Commission on the Causes and Prevention of Violence. *Rights in Conflict* (New York: Signet, 1968).

Richards, I. A. *The Philosophy of Rhetoric* (New York: Oxford, 1965).

Riesman, David, with Nathan Glazer and Reuel Denney. *The Lonely Crowd, Abridged Edition*, (New Haven: Yale, 1961).

Rivers, William. *The Adversaries: Politics and the Press* (Boston: Beascon, 1970).

Rosenblatt, Roger. "A Mayor for All Seasons," *Time*, June 15, 1981, 22–28.

Rudolph, Harriet. "Robert F. Kennedy's University of Capetown Address," *Central States Speech Journal*, Spring 1982, 319–332.

Scarf, Maggie. "Normality Is a Square Circle or a Four-Sided Triangle," *New York Times Magazine*, October 3, 1971, 16–17, 40–42, 44–45, 48–49.

Schlesinger, Jr., Arthur M. *Robert Kennedy and His Times, Volume II* (Boston: Houghton Mifflin, 1978).

Scott, Robert L., and Donald K. Smith, "The Rhetoric of Confrontation," *Quarterly Journal of Speech*, February 1969, 1–8.

Sedgwick, Peter. *Psycho Politics: Laing, Foucault, Goffman, Szasz, and the Future of Mass Psychiatry* (New York: Harper & Row, 1982).

Sennett, Richard. *The Fall of Public Man* (New York: Vintage, 1978).

———. *The Uses of Disorder: Personal Identity and City Life* (New York: Vintage, 1970).

Sherif, Carolyn; Muzafer Sherif; and Roger Nebergall. *Attitude and Attitude Change: The Social Judgment-Involvement Approach* (Philadelphia: W. B. Saunders, 1965).

Shipler, David K. *Russia: Broken Idols, Solemn Dreams* (New York: Times Books, 1983).

Simons, Herbert W. *Persuasion: Understanding, Practice, and Analysis, Second Edition* (New York: Random House, 1986).

———. "Prologue," in *Perspectives on Communication in Social Conflict*, ed. Gerald R. Miller and Herbert W. Simons (Englewood Cliffs, N.J.: Prentice-Hall, 1974), 1–13.

Small, William. *To Kill a Messenger: Television News and the Real World* (New York: Hastings House, 1970).

Sperber, A. M. *Murrow: His Life and Times* (New York: Freundlich, 1986).

Starr, Roger. *The Rise and Fall of New York City* (New York: Basic Books, 1985).

Stewart, James Brewer. *Wendell Phillips: Liberty's Hero* (Baton Rouge: Louisiana State University, 1986).

Szasz, Thomas. *Insanity: The Idea and Its Consequences* (New York: John Wiley, 1987).

———. *The Therapeutic State: Psychiatry in the Mirror of Current Events* (Buffalo, N.Y.: Prometheus, 1984).

———. "Back Wards to Back Streets," *TV Guide*, May 17–23, 1980, 32–36.

———. *Ideology and Insanity: Essays on the Psychiatric Dehumanization of Man* (New York: Anchor, 1970).

———. *The Ethics of Psychoanalysis: The Theory and Method of Autonomous Psychotherapy* (New York: Basic, 1965).

———. *The Myth of Mental Illness* (New York: Hoeber-Harper, 1961).

Vatz, Richard E., and Lee S. Weinberg. *Thomas Szasz: Primary Values and Major Contentions* (Buffalo, N.Y.: Prometheus, 1983).

Warner, W. Lloyd. *The Living and the Dead: The Study of the Symbolic Life of Americans* (New Haven: Yale, 1959).

Waters, Harry F. "Trash TV," *Newsweek* (November 14, 1988, 72–78).

Weaver, Richard. *The Ethics of Rhetoric* (Chicago: Henry Regnery, 1953).

Whiteside, Thomas. "Corridor of Mirrors," *Columbia Journalism Review*, Winter 1968–69, 35–54.

Windt, Jr., Theodore. "The Diatribe: Last Resort for Protest," *Quarterly Journal of Speech*, February 1972, 1–14.

Woodward, Gary C., and Robert E. Denton, Jr. *Persuasion and Influence in American Life* (Prospect Heights, Ill.: Waveland, 1988).

Yeager, Willard Hayes. "Wendell Phillips," in *A History and Criticism of American Public Address, Volume 1*, ed. William Norwood Brigance (New York: Russell and Russell, 1960), 329–362.

# Index

## ABOUT THE AUTHOR

GARY C. WOODWARD has degrees in communication and rhetorical theory from California State University at Sacramento and the University of Pittsburgh. He has taught in England as well as in the United States. He teaches and writes in the areas of politics, the mass media, and contemporary issues. He is the coauthor (with Robert E. Denton, Jr.) of *Political Communication in America* as well as of *Persuasion and Influence in American Life*. In addition, he has published articles in the area of communication and rhetorical theory. Woodward is currently an associate professor in the Department of Speech Communication and Theatre Arts at Trenton State College.

851026